# WOMEN IN
# HELLENISTIC EGYPT

# WOMEN IN HELLENISTIC EGYPT

## From Alexander to Cleopatra

## Sarah B. Pomeroy

SCHOCKEN BOOKS • NEW YORK

First published by Schocken Books 1984
10 9 8 7 6 5 4 3 2 1    84 85 86 87
Copyright © 1984 Sarah B. Pomeroy

Library of Congress Cataloging in Publication Data
Pomeroy, Sarah B.
Women in Hellenistic Egypt.
Bibliography: p.
Includes index.
1. Women—Egypt—History.    2. Greeks—Egypt—History.
3. Egypt—History—323–30 B.C. I. Title.
HQ1137.E3P65 1984    305.4'0932    84-3122

Designed by Nancy Dale Muldoon
Manufactured in the United States of America
ISBN 0–8052–3911–1

TO THE MEMORY OF MY MOTHER

# Contents

# Illustrations

# Foreword

Egypt is the very home of the goddess: for all that exists and is
produced in the world is in Egypt: wealth, wrestling grounds,
might, peace, renown, shows, philosophers, money, young men,
the domain of the *Theoi Adelphoi* ["Divine Siblings"], the king a
good one, the museum, wine, all good things you may desire,
women more in number—I swear by Kore wife of Hades—than
the sky boasts of stars, and in appearance like the goddesses
who once went to Paris to have their beauty judged.

Herodas *Mime* 1.26–35[1]

T HE Hellenistic period begins with the death of Alexander the Great, king of Macedon, and ends with the
death of Cleopatra VII, queen of Egypt.[2] The shift from
male to female monarch is but one of the profound transitions
in gender relationships that occurred in this period.

Alexander conquered Egypt and founded the city of Alexandria in 331 B.C., early in his expedition that was to bring the
Macedonians as far as India.[3] When his successors distributed
the vast territory conquered during the Macedonians' campaign,
Ptolemy I became satrap of Egypt (323 B.C.). Greeks had visited
Egypt before Alexander, and the city of Naucratis had been
founded on the Canopic mouth of the Nile as early as the Archaic period (800–500 B.C.). But under the Ptolemies, vast numbers of Greeks, both women and men, migrated to Egypt and
settled there.

The Greeks usually wrote on papyri and employed ostraca
(potsherds) for shorter messages. More papyri have been pre-

served in the sands of Egypt than anywhere else in the ancient
world, but relatively few from the city of Alexandria itself are
extant. Because of the papyri it is possible to find documentation
for the lives of ordinary women. Only among papyri appear the
personal letters, legal documents, and evidence of popular culture that have proven so useful to historians of later periods in
their studies of the private lives and *mentalité* of nonelite groups.
The documents of Ptolemaic Egypt are written in Greek and
Demotic. My training as a papyrologist has prepared me to work
with the Greek papyri, but with only those Demotic documents
that have been translated into a modern language. Therefore,
this book focuses on Greek women or Hellenized Egyptians.
Moreover, my intention was not to cover every aspect of the lives
of women in Ptolemaic Egypt, but rather to select a limited number of topics and to concentrate on those.

Written evidence from documentary papyri is complemented
by texts from the higher genres. The directions of literary creativity yield important clues to the lives and ideals of this society.
The writings of the Alexandrian literati reflect the intellectual
propensities of the elite (including the monarchs themselves),
while the literary papyri reveal the reading tastes of the schooled
living in the *chora* ("countryside"). Among both the intellectual
elite and the reading public, the popularity of works concerned
with women is striking. The pages of the great Hellenistic authors Callimachus, Theocritus, and Apollonius are replete with
women, both historical and mythical.

Furthermore, in addition to the literary sources, those of the
visual arts and archaeology—including coins, tombstones, inscriptions, and terracotta figurines—offer unique evidence for
women of all social classes. A contemporary rural life in Egypt
that in many respects echoes the past also provides valuable
testimony for the historian.

The historical data are scattered over the three centuries of
Ptolemaic rule, and here, as in other studies of the ancient world,
it has been necessary to generalize at times from few examples.
Moreover, some of the documents and artifacts were published
more than a century ago and should be reexamined in the light of
subsequent research. The most thoroughly studied archive from

Ptolemaic Egypt is that of Zenon, who worked as overseer for a high-ranking government official. However, Zenon was not married, and therefore few women, with the exception of slaves and laborers, are mentioned in his correspondence.

It is a pleasure to express my gratitude to scholars and friends who have helped me in various ways in the writing of this book. Roger S. Bagnall, Stanley M. Burstein, and Klaas Worp read and commented on the entire manuscript. JoAnn McNamara commented on the first three chapters, Alan Cameron on Chapter 2, and Naphtali Lewis on the second part of Chapter 3. I have benefitted from discussions with Willy Clarysse, Ann Hanson, Jan Quaegebeur, and Dorothy B. Thompson and from the comments of other historians, classicists, and papyrologists in the United States and abroad who heard my lectures on women in Ptolemaic Egypt. I am also indebted to Dr. Yousif Gheriani and the staff of the Graeco-Roman Museum in Alexandria, to Professors Mustafa El-Abbadi and Daoud Abdo Daoud for facilitating my research in Egypt, and to Dr. Diana Delia for sending a photograph from Cairo. Pamela Reister supplied photographs of household utensils and personal items from Caranis which are stored in the Kelsey Museum of the University of Michigan. The National Endowment for the Humanities and the Research Foundation of the City University of New York generously provided fellowships and grants which made it possible for me to study Egyptian antiquities at first hand.

# Introduction

## The Status of Greek Women in Egypt

E stablishing the status of Greek women in Egypt is a complex task, for status is a relative concept. Thus it is necessary to create the appropriate criteria for the determination of the status of all women in Classical antiquity, and then to identify the position of those of Ptolemaic Egypt among them. It is also necessary to consider variations in status according to geographical location and changes over time. For women in Ptolemaic Egypt, the most natural points of comparison are with the women of Classical Greece, women in contemporaneous Hellenistic societies, and women in the later Roman Republic.

Most of our primary information about women in the Classical period (500–323 B.C.) derives from Athens. It may well be that women were more restricted and theories about their inferiority and difference from males more eloquently framed in Athens than in other areas inhabited by Greeks. Nevertheless, since some Greek cities did imitate Athenian laws, culture, and institutions, and more attention has been paid to women in Classical Athens than to other Greek women, it is appropriate to use the Athenians as the sole point of reference for the Classical period. Because, with the exception of Ptolemaic Egypt, no single Hellenistic society offers the range of primary sources essential for the determination of women's status, it is necessary to turn at times to Hellenistic Athens or to the courts of the Seleucids or Antigonids, or elsewhere, to find a standard against which the women of Ptolemaic Egypt may be measured. Finally, because

Classical Athens was a democracy, while Ptolemaic Egypt was a monarchy with a Greek ruling class, it is sometimes useful to compare the upper-class women of Ptolemaic Egypt with those of another aristocratic society—that of Rome. It is also necessary, within each category, to compare the status of women to that of men. The distinction must be further refined by reference to the socioeconomic class of the subjects.

The status of Greek women has long been a subject of debate.[1] Scholars who have written on the subject, applying different criteria and drawing on different sorts of evidence, have reached contradictory conclusions. Earlier discussions of the status of Greek women focused on the position of women in Athens. The major criteria employed were whether husbands loved and respected their wives, or whether they treated them with disdain and contempt. These criteria are traditional. Although when they are applied alone they are woefully inadequate, they need not be dismissed. In a patriarchal society in which all respectable women are expected to marry, the attitude of husbands is certainly a factor that helps to determine women's participation in making decisions about family planning, household expenditures, choice of domicile, and so on. However, it is very difficult to find evidence for the attitude of the average Athenian husband toward his wife and to measure such an attitude.

Some earlier scholars who determined that the status of women in Athens was high adduced evidence from dramatic literature to support their judgment. Images of women ought not be ignored in favor of more conventional historical data, for it is the interrelationship between images and reality that constitutes women's condition. However, the dichotomy between image and reality in Classical Athens was vast, inasmuch as the dramatic literature was myth-based, and literature should not be taken at face value. The literature of Ptolemaic Egypt, though often formal and erudite, does at least portray real women in commonplace situations. Thus, the use of evidence from such literature is not likely to distort our assessment of women's status.

Criteria in addition to husbands' attitudes must be applied, and evidence in addition to literary masterpieces must be examined to determine women's status. The criteria I shall use to evaluate the status of women in Ptolemaic Egypt will not be applicable to women universally. Rather, they have been shaped to suit the ancient evidence as well as the secondary sources. Some general principles are, however, relevant.

Anthropologists and historians who are working to discover principles according to which women's placement in society can be evaluated have determined that where there is the greatest asymmetry between the sexes, the male sphere is most endowed with prestige and the female sphere is most devalued.[2] Such was the case in Classical Athens, where respectable women were relegated to domesticity; men engaged in politics and the arts, placed a high value on these activities, and then competed for their rewards.[3]

Aristotle gives a straightforward justification for the inequality of the sexes, even when both are citizens in a democracy. He argues that only adult males can be fully rational, and therefore capable of ruling themselves and others. The female possesses the rational principle, too, but hers is defective and not developed. It is therefore natural that the male rule the female and that he pursue activities appropriate to his capabilities. For the female, it is beneficial to be ruled by the male, and it is appropriate for her to be engaged in activities that are distinctly womanly.[4]

Aristotle, who stressed the difference between the sexes, is critical of the utopian society that Plato had outlined in his *Republic*. In the *Republic*—which is an implicit rejection of Athenian society—Plato reduces the asymmetry between the sexes: the male begets and the female bears offspring, but otherwise the capabilities of both sexes are nearly equal. The soul has no sex. Anyone—woman or man—with the proper qualifications will be admitted into the public sphere to defend and govern the commonwealth.[5]

The principal reason for the high status of women in Ptolemaic Egypt is the reduction in the polarity between the sexes. This new balance is apparent in both literature and life. While the causes of historical change are always complex and will be traced in greater detail in the following chapters, here it is sufficient to point to monarchy as the cause of change. On the highest level, queens are to be found in the traditionally male spheres of government and warfare. They appear physically in what earlier Greek societies had designated as male space—off-limits to respectable women. Among commoners, government by monarchy rather than by direct democracy meant that some men would be less involved in public life and more ready to turn to the private sphere, which was always associated with women.

The Athenian democracy was based in part on the *oikos* ("house" or "family") system. The chief function of female citizens was to produce heirs to the *oikoi* who would also be Athenian citizens. The goals of state and *oikoi* conspired to make female infanticide an acceptable practice. The sexuality of female citizens was regulated by law, lest a child who was not the offspring of a citizen be insinuated into the citizen body. In Ptolemaic Egypt, in contrast, there was no political concept of the *oikos*. A shared life, rather than reproduction, was the purpose of marriage. In Alexandria, some unmarried women had the same mores as men. They were neither chaste nor disreputable, although upper-class women were not accorded the sexual freedom of their counterparts in Roman society.

A significant portion of this book is devoted to women's participation in both the domestic and public economy. Here, too, it must be acknowledged that the status of women in Ptolemaic Egypt was higher than that of Greek women in the Classical period, although equal to that of other Hellenistic societies.

Religion had always been the one public arena in which Greek women played a role that was regarded by the whole of society as valuable and essential. This activity was enhanced in the Hellenistic period with the advent of the ruler cults, in which women participated as both goddesses and priestesses, and with the increased popularity of Mystery religions, which—being less hierarchical than Olympian cults—had always welcomed women as both worshippers and religious personnel.

Measured by the criteria mentioned above and by others that will be introduced later, the status of women in Ptolemaic Egypt was higher than that of women in Classical Greece. At the top level, some queens managed to wield more power legitimately than any Roman woman. These queens, in fact, played the same role as kings. Enjoying equal status with males in the eyes of their subjects, they eliminated gender hierarchy for a brief period in Classical antiquity.

# Table 1. Chronology

Many of the dates listed are approximate and are subject to revision in the light of new evidence. All dates are B.C.

| | |
|---|---|
| 357 | Marriage of Philip II and Olympias |
| 356 | Birth of Alexander |
| 336 | Death of Philip. Accession of Alexander |
| 331 | Founding of Alexandria |
| 324 | Marriage of Greeks to Persian women at Susa |
| 323 | Death of Alexander |
| 323–283 | Ptolemy I Soter. 317 married to Berenice I |
| 311 | *P. Elephantine* I |
| 285–246 | Ptolemy II Philadelphus. 276–270 married to Arsinoë II Philadelphus |
| 279 | Death of Berenice I |
| 274–271 | First Syrian War |
| 260–253 | Second Syrian War |
| 252 | Marriage of Antiochus II and Berenice II Phernophorus |
| 246–222 | Ptolemy III Euergetes. 247 married to Berenice II of Cyrene |
| 246–241 | Third Syrian War |
| 221–205 | Ptolemy IV Philopator. 217–205 married to Arsinoë III |
| 221 | Murder of Berenice II |
| 219–217 | Fourth Syrian War |
| 206–185 | Revolt of the Thebaid |

205      Murder of Agathoclea
204–180  Ptolemy V Epiphanes. 193 married Cleopatra I
202–200  Fifth Syrian War
196      The Rosetta Stone
180–145  Ptolemy VI Philometor. 175 married Cleopatra II
180–176  Cleopatra I regent
176      Death of Cleopatra I
145      Ptolemy VII Neos Philopator. Cleopatra II regent
170–116  Ptolemy VIII Euergetes II. 144 married
         Cleopatra II Philometor Soteira. 140 married
         Cleopatra III
170–168  Sixth Syrian War
116–80   Ptolemy IX Soter II
115      Death of Cleopatra II
114–88   Ptolemy X Alexander I
80       Cleopatra Berenice III and Ptolemy XI Alexander II
80–51    Ptolemy XII Auletes. 79 married Cleopatra V
         Tryphaena
69       Birth of Cleopatra VII
58       Cleopatra VI Tryphaena and Berenice IV
58–56    Berenice IV
52       Cleopatra VII
51–48    Cleopatra VII coruler with Ptolemy XIII Dionysus
47–44    Cleopatra VII coruler with Ptolemy XIV Philopator
47       Birth of Caesarion
30       Death of Cleopatra VII

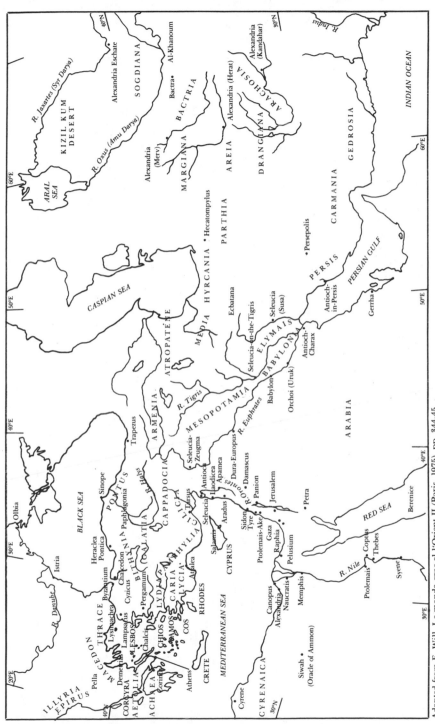

Adapted from E. Will, Le monde grec el l'Orient II (Paris, 1975), pp. 344-45.

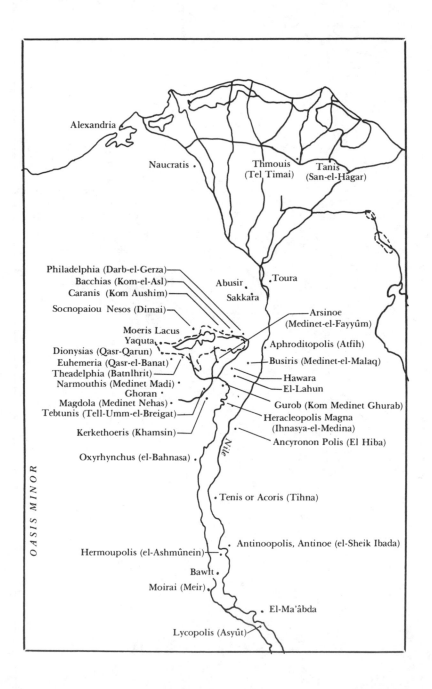

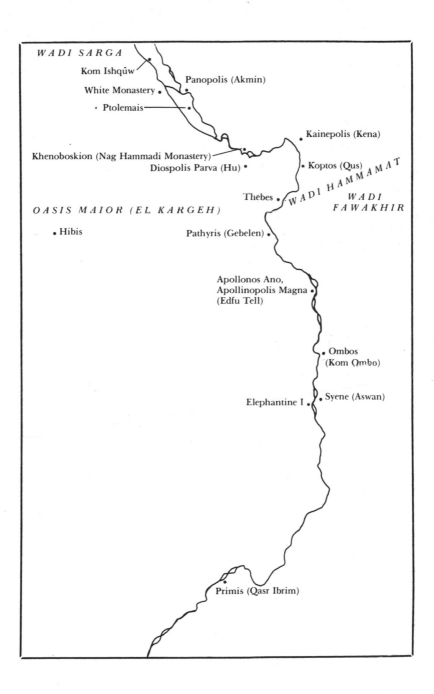

*WADI SARGA*

Kom Ishqûw

Panopolis (Akmin)

White Monastery •

• Ptolemais

Kainepolis (Kena)

Khenoboskion (Nag Hammadi Monastery)
Diospolis Parva (Hu) •

Koptos (Qus)

*WADI HAMMAMAT*

Thebes •

*WADI FAWAKHIR*

*OASIS MAIOR (EL KARGEH)*

• Hibis

Pathyris (Gebelen) •

Apollonos Ano,
Apollinopolis Magna •
(Edfu Tell)

• Ombos
(Kom Ombo)

Elephantine I •

Syene (Aswan)

Primis (Qasr Ibrim)

# WOMEN IN
# HELLENISTIC EGYPT

## Chapter 1

# Queens

I N THE Hellenistic period, Macedonians were dominant, and their queens served as new paradigms for Greek women.[1] Not only were they instrumental in the social, political, and cultural changes that transformed the Classical era into the Hellenistic, but they themselves embodied the new Hellenistic woman. In analyzing the ways in which the hegemony of the Macedonians affected women, it is instructive to look back to Macedonia before the reigns of Alexander's successors and to compare Macedonian women with Athenians.

## MACEDONIAN QUEENS

In comparison with the rest of the Greek world, especially Athens, little is known about Macedonian social history before the reign of Philip II (359–336 B.C.). It is clear, however, that the Macedonians made the same gender associations as the Athenians. From the Iron Age down to the days of Philip II, Macedonian women were buried with pottery, jewelry, and ornaments for their clothing, while weapons were associated solely with the burials of men.[2] Some Athenians enjoyed more luxury: their burials were more elaborate, so that women were interred with such items as engraved bronze mirrors and fine ceramic containers for cosmetics, and, in the Classical period, they are portrayed on their tombstones gazing into a mirror or selecting jewelry from a box. But the basic distinction between the sexes in gravegoods was the same in Macedonia as it was in Athens.[3]

3

Herodotus corroborates the evidence of the burials, which shows a strict distinction between the sexes. He reports that when Persian ambassadors were visiting the court of the Macedonian Amyntas, they sought female company. The women of the court lived in women's quarters, as did Athenian women in the same period, and did not mingle with men. Amyntas explained to the Persians, "It is our custom that men and women be separate."[4] There were no domestic slaves, even at the court. Royal women prepared food and made clothing, just as women without slaves did in Athens.[5]

During the reign of Philip II, the Macedonians radically altered their way of life. In a speech attributed to Philip's son Alexander, Arrian describes the metamorphosis under Philip:

> When Philip took you over, you were nomads and without resources, most of you wearing sheepskins, pasturing paltry herds in the mountains, and fighting for these unsuccessfully against Illyrians, Triballians, and neighboring Thracians. He gave you cloaks to wear instead of sheepskins, and brought you from the mountains down to the plains, making you worthy opponents of the neighboring barbarians so that you trusted your salvation not so much to the strength of the places you occupied as to your natural courage. He made you inhabitants of cities, and civilized you with good laws and customs.[6]

The expansion of Macedonian power not only had repercussions for native women; it introduced foreign women into the court. Satyrus, in his biography of Philip, remarked that every time the king made war he also made a marriage.[7] These marriages were emblems of Philip's alliances and conquests. He is also reputed to have chosen some wives because of their personal attractions. Philip was polygamous for reasons of state. Had he practiced serial monogamy and repudiated each wife in favor of her successor, he would have provoked international incidents. Instead, he was lavishly polygamous. Philip had at least seven wives. Several of these women were not native Macedonians (although Cleopatra, his last wife, was); rather, they were brought from non-Greek territories where they had learned to ride horses and use weapons.

A comparison between the gravegoods of one of Philip's wives (or her descendant) and those of earlier female burials underlines the difference between the two groups of women. In antiquity, the Gauls had plundered most of the tombs at Vergina, the necropolis of Macedonian royalty, but in 1977, Manolis Andronikos discovered a royal tomb that had never been opened.[8] The tomb consisted of two chambers. The larger one held a gold coffer with the radiating star of Maccdonia on its lid. In the coffer were a man's ashes and bones. The room was richly furnished with the paraphernalia of a noble warrior: a gold scepter; carefully wrought armor, including a pair of greaves; and a gold quiver. The smaller room contained a second, smaller coffer, also decorated with a Macedonian star. The remains within were more thoroughly reduced to ashes than were those in the larger coffer, indicating that the bones of the second person had been more fragile. The ashes were wrapped in a purple and gold cloth embroidered with leaves and flowers. The feminine floral motif was repeated on some of the gravegoods.[9] A gold wreath of myrtle leaves and flowers and a diadem with blue flowers were found, but—what is most remarkable for a woman—no earrings, bracelets, or mirrors. Instead, there were arrowheads, a pair of bronze greaves engraved with gold, a pectoral on which was engraved a row of four horsemen charging, and a quiver of gilded silver embossed with a scene of the capture of a city. The occupants of the tomb were clearly a nobleman and a noblewoman, but it was not possible to determine beyond a doubt which couple, specifically, they were. No writing was found to help identify them, nor were there any coins to help with the dating.

Andronikos proposed that the tomb was that of Philip II and that the woman entombed with Philip was the last of his wives, the Macedonian noblewoman, Cleopatra. Because weapons would not be appropriate for a native Macedonian, Andronikos suggested that some of the gravegoods found in the woman's chamber belonged not to her but to the man.[10]

N. G. L. Hammond concluded that the military artifacts—quiver, arrowheads, and greaves—were signs that the woman was not Cleopatra but one of Philip's warrior wives: either Meda, a princess of the Getae of Thrace, or a Scythian princess whose name is not known to us.[11] According to Stephanus of Byzantium, suttee was practiced by the Getae.[12] Herodotus ascribed the custom to both the Scythians and Thracians.[13] Among the Thracians, who were polygamous, the wives volunteered and vied with one another to be the one chosen for immolation. Hammond thought that the Scythian princess was more likely than Meda to be entombed with Philip II, since the quiver that was entombed with the queen was fashioned in the peculiarly Scythian style.[14]

There were still other possibilities, including Audata, an Illyrian princess who was probably Philip's first wife. Although she took the Greek name Eurydice when she married Philip, she does not seem to have adapted to the ways of Greek women. Rather, she succeeded in passing on distinctive Illyrian traditions to her daughter and granddaughter. These three women constitute the earliest example in Greek history of the preservation of a family tradition in the female line. We are familiar with the aphorism "like mother, like daughter." Doubtless the female personality perpetuated itself through generations in antiquity too, but we rarely have evidence for successive generations of women. Our knowledge of women is so checkered that it is difficult even to discover their names and consequently to determine whether their names alternated, as they often did in the male line. We are therefore fortunate to have some continuous information about Audata-Eurydice, her daughter Cynane, and her granddaughter Eurydice. Cynane campaigned with her father, Philip, in Illyria—her mother's place of origin—and killed an Illyrian queen in combat.[15] As a widow, she participated actively in the dynastic disputes of the Macedonians after the death of Alexander. She arranged for her daughter Eurydice to marry Philip III Arrhidaeus, even though he was feebleminded. He was a son of Philip II, and the royal blood was of paramount importance. Cynane hired a mercenary force with her own funds and eventually was killed on the battlefield.

Cynane, in turn, had taught her daughter Adea to hunt and fight. Because she harbored political ambitions, Adea took the name Eurydice. Thus she reminded the Macedonians not only of her own grandmother but of the mother of Philip II, a figure from the glorious past. Duris of Samos reports that the first war waged between women was fought by Eurydice against Olympias.[16] According to Duris, Eurydice dressed in Macedonian fashion and Olympias was costumed as a Bacchante. The colorful details of the anecdote must be disregarded, for Olympias is not known to have been so foolish as to engage in battle armed with nothing but a *thyrsus* (a wand carried by devotees of Dionysus)—if that is what the description implies. Still, the general tone of the story is consistent with what we know about the audacity of Eurydice. After her victory, Olympias had Eurydice imprisoned. Not yet twenty, she took her own life. It may, in fact, be this Eurydice whose ashes rest in the coffer in the royal tomb at Vergina.[17] In that case, the dead man is not Philip II but Philip III Arrhidaeus. As a corollary, it has also been suggested that Cynane was the occupant of a cist tomb near the royal tomb. This cist tomb was looted, but the wall paintings of female figures and of the rape of Persephone indicate that its occupant was a woman.[18]

That there were several royal women qualified to wear greaves and be buried with quiver and arrows is noteworthy. Probably the ancestors of women like these are the reality behind the legendary Amazons. Herodotus stated that the Sauromatians (or Sarmatians) were the descendents of the union of Amazons with Scythian men.[19] Excavations reveal that the Sauromatians buried women with weapons. Some female burials from the sixth to the second centuries B.C. yielded not only jewelry and mirrors, but also arrows, quivers, other weapons, and a suit of armor.[20] Although women of other nomadic tribes in the region rode in wagons, the Sauromatian women mounted horses.[21] Analyzing the literary evidence and the gravegoods, T. David goes so far as to say that, among the Sauromatians, men and women of the top social class enjoyed equality.[22] At any rate, it was never said of Philip—as it was, later, of Alexander—that he married an Amazon.[23] But he did marry some women from societies in which the sexes were not segregated and in which sex roles were defined differently from the ways in which traditional Greek societies defined them.

The Macedonians, as the speech quoted from Arrian shows, did not dwell in cities before the reign of Philip II.[24] They were pastoralists. In Greek society, rural women enjoyed more freedom of movement than urban dwellers such as the Athenians. First of all, chores such as gardening and caring for small animals made it mandatory that women go out of doors. Secondly, in less densely populated areas, there was less danger that women would come in contact with men who were strangers to them. Unfortunately, the nature of the evidence allows a comparison only between respectable Greek women of all social classes, on the one hand, and the royal women of Macedonia, on the other. However, it is evident that the Macedonians did not declare certain areas off-limits, at least to women of the court. Hence, women such as Olympias, Eurydice, and her daughter and granddaughter can be found on the battlefield. After Olympias retired from her struggle for power against Antipater, her son Alexander declared that it was just as well, for the Macedonians would never submit to being ruled by a woman.[25] The remark is more testimony to the public power of a queen such as Olympias than denial of it. The notion that a woman might be sovereign among the Macedonians in the king's absence actually crossed Alexander's mind. That a woman might enjoy any political power at all among the Athenians, for example, was too far fetched to be contemplated. It is in the nature of monarchy to supersede gender differences for dynastic interests.

According to Aristotle, the majority of martial and warlike races, if they do not openly honor attachments between males, are ruled by women.[26] Aristotle was referring to the structure of Spartan society, where the men were perpetually at war while the women did as they pleased. Aristotle died before he could take cognizance of the transformation in Macedonian society, but the principle he set forth applied, to some extent, to the Macedonians, as well as to other women whose men were at war. Thus, in the second half of the Peloponnesian War, when war was waged in the winter as well as the summer, when a large contingent of men had departed on the expedition to Sicily and numerous slaves had deserted to the Spartan outpost at Decelea, Athenian women were forced to emerge into public space and perform tasks previously reserved for men and slaves. From this period there are several instances of upper-class Athenian women—normally the most secluded group—breaching the standards of decorum by entering the agora, giving testimony quoted in court, and living with men to whom they were not married.[27] But with the recovery of Athens after the defeat, the traditional rules of conduct were revived. The Second Punic War had a similar effect on upper-class Roman women. Just after the war, women were able to organize a demonstration in the streets and demand that the government repeal a sumptuary law that they considered obnoxious. Philip's wars were intermittent, but waged at some distance from Macedonia itself. Alexander started out on his campaign with about 48,100 soldiers.[28] In Caria, he allowed only the newly married soldiers to return to their wives.[29] We can speculate that, just as Olympias tried to jump into the breach left by Alexander's departure, so other Macedonian women did assume the responsibilities of men with more success.

Macedonia expanded from a tribal nation to a world power in two generations. Another principle of women's history is applicable here: Often there are fewer constraints on women when a society is in a period of rapid transition and the attention of men is diverted than when a society is stable. The Macedonians did not have the time nor, presumably, did they see the need to create elaborate codes of behavior to suit their new situation.

We may pause to observe that the names of the women in the Macedonian court sometimes commemorated events in the history of their nation. Philip II's daughters Thessalonice and Europe were named in honor of their father's sovereignty over Thessaly and Greece. Alexander's niece Cadmeia was given her name to celebrate the king's conquest of Thebes, the city founded by Cadmus. (With comparable ambitions, in the fifth century B.C. Themistocles had named three of his five daughters Italia, Asia, and Sybaris.)[30] Boys, in contrast, were not named for the attributes or ambitions of their male relatives. Their ties to their lineage were of paramount importance: they were given traditional Macedonian names at birth.

The names of some women were changed when they were mature, either for political reasons or in commemoration of historical events. Whether the women involved changed their names voluntarily is not always clear. As we have mentioned above, the foreign-born Audata took—or was given—the Greek name Eurydice, as did her granddaughter.[31] Olympias is reported to have borne no less than four names, but some of these may have been epithets or nicknames rather than a replacement of a previous name. Her first was Polyxena, an ordinary mythological name.[32] She next took the name Myrtale. The myrtle was associated with fertility as well as with the cult of the Cabiri, to which she was devoted; therefore, it has been thought that Polyxena became Myrtale either in connection with her initiation into the Samothracian Mysteries or with her marriage. Philip gave her the name Olympias because he had won a victory at Olympia in the summer when she gave birth to Alexander. We can only speculate about whether she considered this change in name a loss of identity or rather an affirmation of his bond with her. Myrtale was a common name, whereas Olympias appears more suitable to this queen's ambitions and achievements. Her last name, Stratonice ("Victor in War"), alludes to her own victory over Eurydice. Later in Macedonian history there appears a woman named Cratesipolis ("Sovereign over a City") who conquered the city of Sicyon at the head of her late husband's mercenary forces. The use of epithets to commemorate the bearer's own victories was, of course, customary among men and indeed necessary along with other nicknames to distinguish the many rulers who bore such popular names as Alexander, Demetrius, and Antigonus.

Such are the historical forces that worked to create the women who went out to rule as queens in the kingdoms established by the successors of Alexander. As they grew up, they had witnessed or heard tales about the activities of women such as Olympias and Eurydice. Theirs was not to be the role of Greek women in other places and at other times: to be passive and protected. Instead, they would need to think for themselves in order to survive and to protect their children. These women assumed leading roles in Hellenistic history. That they were Macedonians as well as members of a ruling monarchy made an important difference to other women in the Hellenistic world.

## THE QUEEN'S ROLE

The role of the Hellenistic queen has never been defined. Grace Macurdy's *Hellenistic Queens* remains the standard reference for the details of the reigns of specific Macedonian, Seleucid, and Ptolemaic queens, but Macurdy did not attempt to forge out of the details a general statement that would characterize the role played by a queen.[33] The major part of the problem is that queenship was not a public office and therefore cannot be defined except as a private role. Private roles were flexible and depended upon individual personalities; there was no "typical" queen. Furthermore, I know of no general sociological study of queenship applicable to European women even in later historical periods.

Claire Préaux in *Le monde hellénistique* devotes one chapter of 113 pages to the role of the Hellenistic king.[34] Passages totaling one page deal with queens.[35] In this first attempt to define the role of Hellenistic queens, it is imperative to review the king's role briefly and to determine whether the queen's was similar, or whether, like the Homeric queen, she played a role complementary to the king's. A study of the inequities between the sexes in antiquity leads us to posit that, even if the roles were qualitatively the same, there might be a quantitative difference. For example, a queen may be found to dispense gifts derived from the income from a single city or by occasionally tapping royal revenues, while a king's benefactions could be larger and more frequent, since his income derived from an entire country and was totally at his disposal.

For the king, the immediate role model was Alexander; a close second was Philip II. The Hellenistic period was a time of continual strife. The most important function of the king, therefore, was to assure victory for his country. He not only served as commander in chief of his troops but was a courageous warrior himself. Hellenistic soldiers owed allegiance to a leader, rather than to a nation, and the king had to command their respect. A king enjoyed enormous wealth. A ruling Ptolemy not only owned most of the land of Egypt but derived an income from taxes, royal monopolies, and occasional windfalls in war. With this vast wealth, the king was expected to play the role of generous benefactor. Kings gave gifts to cities, temples, and individuals. Not only wealth but education enabled kings to be leading patrons of the arts. The Ptolemies endowed great cultural institutions, such as the Museum and Library in Alexandria. Poets paid them the compliment of assuming that they could discriminate between their own creations and those of less gifted artists.

The king, of course, wielded supreme political power. He was normally his father's heir apparent, and he, in turn, had the right to designate his own successor among the potential heirs produced by his various marriages. The king was supreme lawgiver and dispenser of justice. He played an economic role by regulating markets and taxes, and minted money in his own name. Moreover, the king had the power to delegate his roles by choosing others to represent him. Within the royal family, he was both king and patriarch. As such, he arranged the marriages of those who were subordinate to his authority and assigned dowries to the women.

In respect to his subjects, the king played the role of a god. By his very presence he brought fecundity, prosperity, and well-being. He was decked in the symbols of superhuman power, wearing a diadem and a royal robe. His idealized portrait appeared on the obverse of coins, where previously the faces of the immortals were portrayed.

No obvious role model presented itself to the wives of Alexander's successors. Roxane, the wife of Alexander, did not leave a lasting impression on historians—nor, one suspects, on her contemporaries.[36] Moreover, her misfortunes would surely have dissuaded any other woman from consciously imitating her. She and her son were mere victims in the dynastic struggles following the death of Alexander. The discussion of the gravegoods in Macedonian burials has shown that there were at least two distinct styles of life available to women who survived at the court: one sharing the experiences of men in battle, the other involving activities in a separate female sphere. According to Polybius, the ideal Hellenistic king was Attalus I of Pergamum.[37] He writes that Apollonis of Cyzicus, wife of Attalus, was also worthy of commemoration and praise for several reasons:

> For the fact that, being a commoner, she became queen and maintained this preeminence until the end, without recourse to the persuasive charms of a courtesan, but employing self-control, courteous dignity, and virtue, she deserves to be remembered with honor. And, in addition, having given birth to four sons, she preserved toward all of them an unsurpassable goodwill and affection until the end of her life, although she survived her husband for a substantial amount of time.[38]

Some qualities of the ideal queen appear in a decree issued by Hierapolis in honor of Apollonis sometime between around 167 and 159 B.C. In addition to the virtues cited by Polybius, the decree mentions the queen's piety toward the gods and respect for her parents.[39]

## PTOLEMAIC QUEENS

Like Philip II, the first Ptolemy enjoyed both serial and simultaneous liaisons with several women, and this pattern was followed by his successors. The distinction between wife and concubine continued to be as unclear as it had been in the days of Philip. For example, Athenaeus reports that Ptolemy married (*egamethe*) the famous courtesan Thaïs.[40] That she held the position of legitimate wife is suggested by the fact that Ptolemy gave his father's name, Lagus, to a son produced by this liaison[41] and gave their daughter in marriage to a minor king. Ptolemy made several marriages for reasons of state, but his choice of his last wife, Berenice I, was dictated by personal inclination rather than by political expediency.

Berenice I exhibited traditional female virtues. Plutarch reports that when Demetrius Poliorcetes was in Egypt he courted Berenice in particular because he observed that, among the wives of Ptolemy, she had very great power (*megiston dynamene*) and was foremost in virtue (*arete*) and wisdom (*phronesis*).[42] Virtue, wisdom, and influence among men had characterized good queens such as Penelope and Arete in the earliest Greek literature, and these traits continued to be displayed by good queens such as Berenice I and Apollonis.

Ptolemy I arranged the first marriage of his daughter Arsinoë II. As was usual for upper-class girls, she was wed at about the age of sixteen. Her sixty-year-old husband, Lysimachus, king of Thrace, had served with her father in the campaigns of Alexander. His lavish gifts to his young wife, including entire cities in the rich Black Sea region—unless they simply fulfilled a marriage contract concluded between Ptolemy I and Lysimachus— were symptomatic of the power that she wielded over her elderly husband. Arsinoë came to possess a vast amount of wealth. It is probably fair to say that, overall, the Macedonian queens controlled more wealth than any Greek women before their time, although some royal women in third-century Sparta rivaled them.[43] In some Greek states it was unusual for Greek women to own land (see Chapter 5). However, both Spartans and Macedonians did so. Some Macedonian women had the income from substantial territories at their disposal. They were given these territories as part of their dowries or, as in the case of Lysimachus and Arsinoë II, as gifts. The dowry of Lanassa (daughter of Agathocles) who married Pyrrhus included the island of Corcyra. Berenice, the daughter of Ptolemy II and Arsinoë I, had so lavish a dowry when she married Antiochus II that she was titled Phernophorus ("Dowry-bringer"). When Antiochus II repudiated his first wife, Laodice I, to marry Berenice Phernophorus, he granted territories near Babylon and Borsippa to Laodice.[44] It was especially contrary to the custom of the Ptolemies to grant land to women outright (see Chapter 5). Ptolemy II granted the revenue derived from the fish in Lake Moeris to Arsinoë II. She was to use it for unguents and personal adornment. The value of the daily catch amounted to one silver talent.[45] Some royal women held land, which, of course, was cultivated by others. Berenice daughter of either Philadelphus or Euergetes I had a vineyard at Hephaistias in the Arsinoite nome. A princess Cleopatra held land at the end of the second century B.C. at

Crocodilopolis. Part of the land was reserved for the cultivation of vegetables. An unidentified queen (probably Cleopatra VII) in 51/50 B.C. had land at Heracleopolis on which arakos (a legume) was grown. Cleopatra II owned ships that were used to transport royal grain.[46]

Macedonian queens not only enjoyed great wealth; what is more, they controlled their own resources. Whereas, according to the laws traditional in most Greek states, a woman could manage her own property only with the approval of a male guardian, there were no restraints on these Macedonian queens. Their legal code, whatever it had been, had simply not kept up with women's sudden acquisition of great wealth. There is no evidence that the Macedonian kings were bothered by women's possession of wealth; on the contrary, they were themselves the donors. This lack of concern contrasts sharply with the attitude of the Spartans and Romans in the Hellenistic period, both of whom attempted to limit the wealth held by queens and upper-class women.[47]

The queens employed their resources in many of the same ways the kings did, though mostly on a smaller scale. Gifts to gods and sanctuaries were most common. For example, Olympias had sent a *phiale* ("cup") to the goddess Hygieia in Athens.[48] Roxane sent a dedication of some bracelets and other items to Athena Polias.[49] Arsinoë II dedicated an entire building, the Arsinoeion at Samothrace, site of a Mystery cult. This structure was the largest walled round building in the Greek world up to that time.[50] After an earthquake at Rhodes, several Hellenistic rulers, including Antigonus Doson, sent donations to relieve the city. Chryseis, the wife of Antigonus, gave 100,000 measures of wheat and 3,000 lead talents in her own name.[51] The acts of Hellenistic queens in two cases differed from those of kings in that beneficiaries of queens' charities were exclusively female: in these cases, they provided dowries for the needy.[52] (In the Classical period, this obligation had often fallen on the male friends and relatives of the poor.) Phila, wife of Demetrius, at her own expense gave away poor girls in marriage.[53] Laodice III established a foundation at Iasus to provide dowries for daughters of the poor.[54] Laodice was able to employ royal revenues for her project, since the funds for the dowries were derived from the sale of grain grown on royal land.

In the Hellenistic period, money bought armies for kings and queens alike. After Lysimachus was killed, Arsinoë II was able to take over troops that remained loyal to her as the widow of Lysimachus as well as to hire her own mercenaries and engage in military struggles in her attempt to ensure a throne for her sons and herself. I will pass quickly over the details, for they are available elsewhere.[55] The episodes of her life sound like a pastiche of mythology. She was married three times. Like Phaedra, she was said to have been attracted to her first husband's young son, and eventually caused Lysimachus to murder him. Like Clytemnestra, she endured to see her children torn from her arms and killed before her eyes. The murderer was her half-brother and second husband, Ptolemy Ceraunus. (Indisputably, he was a poor choice for a husband, but that a queen might make such a decision for herself in those days of arranged marriages is in itself remarkable.) And like Hera, Arsinoë II married her own full brother, Ptolemy II.

Laws of various Greek states had permitted marriages between half-siblings, although they were uncommon, but marriage between full siblings was outlawed everywhere.[56] It is, in fact, considered incestuous in nearly every known human society. By incestuous marriage, the Ptolemies distinguished themselves from ordinary mortals. Among both Greek and Egyptian gods, brothers and sisters married without censure. Some of the most important divinities—including Zeus and Hera, and Isis and Osiris—married siblings. Moreover, the Greeks apparently believed that there had been precedents for brother–sister marriage among the Pharaohs, and the Ptolemies certainly wished themselves to be considered their successors.[57]

Brother–sister marriage became as normal as exogamy among the Ptolemies. Arsinoë II, Arsinoë III, Cleopatra II, Cleopatra Selene, Cleopatra VI Tryphaena, and Cleopatra VII were all married to their brothers. That there were no problems with the succession—and that the list ends with one of the most able of all the Ptolemies—indicates, incidentally, that incestuous marriages did not have an adverse effect on the genes of this family.

In virilocal marriage, a bride is isolated at the home of her husband and in-laws. Hellenistic history is studded with tales of wives—such as Berenice Phernophorus, daughter of Ptolemy II and Arsinoë I—who were murdered at their husband's court. Dynastic marriages were arranged to seal alliances between kings. When the alliance was dissolved, wives might find themselves hostages in a hostile land. In contrast, some of the Ptolemaic princesses who married their brothers could take advantage of an opportunity to consolidate their own power at home. In later generations of Ptolemies, sibling rivalry was common.

The first of the Ptolemaic queens to marry her own brother was Arsinoë II. Both Arsinoë II and Ptolemy II were children of Ptolemy I and Berenice I; when they were wed, they were titled, appropriately, Philadelphus ("sibling-lover").

The question that concerns us here is whether the idea for the marriage came from Ptolemy II or Arsinoë II. An answer to this question would be useful in evaluating Arsinoë's subsequent power and influence over her brother. Grace Macurdy[58] and, more recently, Gabriella Longega[59] have argued that, during the period of her reign in Egypt, Arsinoë was the leading force in the government. Stanley Burstein disputes this theory.[60] The ancient sources yield little information about Arsinoë's deeds for the five years during which she was queen in Egypt. Therefore, arguments about her power must be based on psychohistorical theory, historical inference, and the use of evidence dating from after her death. On the score of strength of personality alone, Arsinoë appears to have had the advantage. Before returning to Egypt, her life was fraught with calamity. She not only managed to survive, but to become queen of Egypt at its zenith. Ptolemy, on the other hand, simply inherited the throne. Like many an heir of a powerful father, he was a notorious pleasure-lover. Moreover, even in discussions about royalty, the human element should not be ignored. Arsinoë was eight years older than Ptolemy, and, as adults, older siblings often maintain their authority over younger ones, even if the older one is female and the younger one male. Further, she had already been married to a half-brother, while Ptolemy had no form of endogamy in his past.

The written evidence, in contrast, supports Burstein's view. It has been argued that there is no reason to believe that Arsinoë was politically astute.[61] The elimination of Agathocles, her first husband's son, and her choice of a second husband were both ill conceived. Ptolemy II, even before Arsinoë's return to Egypt, had some military victories to his credit, so his successes after marrying his sister need not be attributed to her. Four years after Arsinoë's death, in the Chremonides decree of 268/267 B.C., Ptolemy was recorded as having followed the policy of his ancestors and his sister in his zeal for the common freedom of the Greeks.[62] Grace Macurdy observed that this was the first time among the Macedonians that the political policy of a woman was recorded in a public document.[63] It has been suggested, however, that Ptolemy II was reaping political gain in attributing the policy to his dead sister. Burstein has asserted that, although Arsinoë might have at one time been favorable to the theory of Greek freedom—insofar as she supported traditional Ptolemaic policy—in this particular case the policy was actually detrimental to her ambitions for her surviving son.[64]

The argument about Arsinoë II is reducible to the common question of "the power behind the throne." What did Plutarch mean by describing Arsinoë's mother Berenice I as "having very great power"? The impulse for such power can come from either the married couple together or the wife alone. The *Odyssey* provides a good example of the former relationship. Odysseus is told that, if Queen Arete thinks well of him, then he can hope to reach his homeland. King Alcinoüs honored Arete as no other woman on earth was honored. She was honored by her children, by Alcinoüs, and by the rest of the Phaeacians, who looked on her as a god. She wielded judicial powers and resolved disputes, even among men.[65] The originator of a woman's political influence can also be the woman herself, and such influence is often surreptitious. Historians have detected such an influence among Roman matrons in the late Republic and among Roman empresses. Roman historians have relatively rich sources for their analyses. The literary sources for early Ptolemaic history, in contrast, do not permit us to make a definitive evaluation of this immeasurable component of woman's power. But an awareness that women of the past—even queens—comprise a "muted group" must inspire a historian to look behind the face value of these sources.[66] Relying on Greek sources alone, it is impossible for a modern historian to evaluate the extent of Arsinoë's influence or even to be specific about the events she affected. But when the queen is in all respects the equal of the king and reigns in her homeland, as did Arsinoë II, then it is simplistic to assign credit for all events to the king, except where an ancient source explicitly attributed them to the queen. To return to an earlier question about whether it was Arsinoë II or Ptolemy who first thought the sibling marriage would be a good idea: if the answer is Arsinoë, then, *ipso facto*, she is shown to have wielded power over her brother. If the answer is Ptolemy, then historians ought to accept the king's judgment about the advantages of ruling with his sister, for surely he knew her better than we do.

The Egyptian sources give a different picture of Arsinoë's power.[67] She was designated as a Pharaoh as "King of Upper and Lower Egypt." This title was, perhaps, conferred on her after her death. Since Ptolemy II derived no advantage from designating his sister as "king" and the practice was not continued by his immediate successors—although, in other respects, the cult of Arsinoë II was a model for the cult of later queens—the title is likely to be an indication of Arsinoë's special power. Therefore, it appears that the Greek sources consciously or otherwise suppressed this manifestation of a woman's power, for Greeks in the early period of Ptolemaic rule were not accustomed to or tolerant of a woman who played the role of king. The Egyptians, on the other hand, did not hold such a narrow view of women's proper sphere and, indeed, in the great Hatshepsut and in Taousert (Nineteenth Dynasty) had historical precedents for female Pharaohs. Jan Quaegebeur has argued that Arsinoë's title is a reflection of her influence in the government and that she truly shared the sovereignty with her brother.[68]

Most scholars using Greek sources would agree that Arsinoë
II left her mark on Hellenistic poetry. Ptolemy I engaged Philetas, a scholar and poet, as tutor to Ptolemy II.[69] Arsinoë's education was probably the same as her brother's.[70] Philetas must have
given his pupils a taste for the erudition that is characteristic of
the Alexandrian style, for the poet Theocritus, whose work was
influenced by Philetas, managed to obtain the favor of the royal
couple for a time. That he was equally adulatory of both king
and queen is some testimony to Arsinoë's influence in this realm.
As a patron of culture and religion, well able to pay the expenses
herself, Arsinoë sponsored an extravagant entertainment that
was presented for the delectation of the population of Alexandria. Theocritus describes this event in his fifteenth idyll.

Berenice II of Cyrene (see Plate 1), who married her cousin
Ptolemy III, figures in the poetry of Callimachus. She dedicated a lock of hair in the Alexandrian temple of Arsinoë Aphrodite to assure her husband's safe return from Syria. Precedents for the offering of hair existed in both Egyptian and
Greek cults. Numerous terracotta heads of women with elaborate coiffures found in Ptolemaic sites (see Plate 2) may have
been used in such cults.[71] In the conceit of Callimachus' poem,
the hair was taken aloft and became a constellation. "The Lock
of Berenice" is known through a version by Catullus.[72] An
original fragment of poetry by Callimachus published in 1976
celebrates Berenice's victories in chariot races at Nemea.[73]
Berenice's victory at Olympia was already known.[74] Of course,
the women of this period whose horses raced at Greek festivals
did not personally ride in the races. But their sponsorship of
horses reveals a personal interest in equitation rather than a
mere desire to exhibit their wealth. It is no accident that the
first women whose horses won at Olympia were two Spartans,
Cynisca and Euryleonis, and Bilistiche, a mistress of Ptolemy
II.[75] Spartan women engaged in athletics and raced in chariots
drawn by two horses.[76] The earliest testimony that they rode
horseback is a poem by Propertius.[77] Erotic poetry intimates
that Bilistiche was also a rider.[78] Berenice II was also a horse-
woman. Like her royal predecessors, she is said to have ridden
in battle, killed many enemies, and routed the rest.[79] The next

1. Figure of a queen (presumably Berenice II) holding a cornucopia. From a *oinochoe* made for the ruler cult. Probably from Alexandria. *New York. Metropolitan Museum of Art Egyptian Department 26.7.1016. Gift of Edward S. Harkness, 1926.*

2. Terracotta heads of Alexandrian women. *Alexandria. Graeco-Roman Museum 9258, 10536, 18329.*

women recorded as victors were Zeuxo, wife of Polycrates of Argos, and their three daughters.[80] They won a chariot race at the Panathenaea sometime after 197 B.C. Zeuxo, like Berenice II, came from Cyrene, a land known for horse-breeding.

Berenice is portrayed in Egyptian art as the living companion of her husband, dressed, as he is, in ceremonial attire.[81] In Demotic papyri she is titled "the female Pharaoh."[82] With power like this, there is no need to wonder why she was assassinated by her son Ptolemy IV.

In the second century B.C., when Egypt was wracked by foreign attacks and civil unrest, queens began to assume the prerogatives of kings with greater regularity than they had in the preceding century. In successive reigns, the populace increasingly accepted these powers of the queens as legitimate. Dating prescripts of Greek and Demotic papyri record this evolution, although in this turbulent period the same prescripts were not used uniformly throughout Egypt.[83] In some papyri of her regency (180–176 B.C.), the name of Cleopatra I precedes that of her son, implying that she is not merely regent for him but actually sovereign herself. The prescript is: "The Pharaohs Cleopatra [I] mother, the goddess Epiphanes ["Manifest"], and Ptolemy [VI] son of Ptolemy, the god Epiphanes." Cleopatra I even issued coins in her own name.[84] Cleopatra I was the daughter of the Seleucid Antiochus the Great. Thereafter, in Ptolemaic history, all the queens who assumed the role of "king" were native Lagids, but descendants of this Seleucid Cleopatra. Although the names of Hellenistic kings are relatively few, only in Egypt were all the males given the same name. This naming pattern was a symptom of dynastic strength and exclusivity. The female Ptolemies had borne several names, including Berenice, Arsinoë, and Cleopatra. At this point in history, the name Cleopatra began to acquire the aura associated with that of Ptolemy. Cleopatra II, daughter of Cleopatra I and Ptolemy V, was married successively to two of her brothers: to Ptolemy VI and, after his death, to Ptolemy VIII. The dating prescripts from these two reigns name her as Pharaoh: "The Pharaohs Ptolemy [VI, then VIII] and Cleopatra [II]." From the period of her struggle for power against Ptolemy VII (132/131–131/130 B.C.), there are papyri with dating protocols naming Cleopatra II alone. She titled herself Cleopatra Philometor Soteira ("Savior").[85] Cleopatra III, daughter of Cleopatra II and Ptolemy VI, usurped her mother's office and married her uncle Ptolemy VIII (140/139 B.C.).[86] She eventually ruled with both of her sons successively. In dating formulas, her name is first.[87]

Beginning in the early second century, the visual arts also reflect the increased political power of the queens. Whereas in the earlier period queens had usually been shown with the *stephane* ("crown") associated with Aphrodite and the veil worn by goddesses as well as by commoners, the Cleopatras preferred to be portrayed like kings—wearing only the *tainia* ("headband") as headdress.[88]

Cleopatra Berenice III, daughter of Ptolemy IX, reigned alone for a few months in 80 B.C., before her son Ptolemy XI Alexander II was associated with her. The queen's name precedes her son's in official documents.[89] Following the departure of Ptolemy XII Auletes to Rome in 58 B.C., Egypt was ruled by two sisters, Cleopatra VI Tryphaena and Berenice IV. They were not rulers *pro tempore*, but were recognized as sovereigns. After the death of Cleopatra VI, Berenice IV ruled alone (58/57–56/55 B.C.).[90] In order to resume the throne when he returned, Auletes was obliged to have his daughter murdered. The assassination of Berenice IV, like that of so many of her royal predecessors, is testimony to her power. Although Auletes left the throne to both Ptolemy XIII and Cleopatra VII, Cleopatra ruled alone at first (52/51 B.C.),[91] and then with her brothers successively.[92]

The ancient sources for Cleopatra VII (69–30 B.C.) are not only more abundant than those for any other Ptolemaic queen; they are more hostile.[93] Cleopatra's life intersected with those of some of the greatest Romans during the civil wars at the end of the Republic. She furnished supplies for Pompey and charmed Julius Caesar and Marc Antony, but she was defeated by her enemy Octavian (Augustus), and it was Octavian who had the last word about her.

Viewed in the context of Ptolemaic rather than Roman history, Cleopatra VII does not appear as an anomaly.[94] Like

Cleopatra II, she was married to two of her brothers in succession. She finally eliminated all her siblings and became sole ruler, thus bringing to a culmination the long process of historical change that granted a woman the undisputed right to occupy the throne of Egypt. Like her Ptolemaic and, indeed, Macedonian ancestors, Cleopatra VII rode horseback, hunted, and was at home on the battlefield. Like her father, Ptolemy XII Auletes, she attempted to come to terms with Rome.

Cleopatra's relationships with Julius Caesar and Marc Antony may have been romantic liaisons from the Roman point of view—both these men were notoriously attractive to women—but from the queen's perspective they were the equivalent of dynastic marriages. Her dowry was Egypt; through her "marriages," she expected to win dominion over the Roman world.

Because Octavian was Caesar's nephew and heir, his propaganda minimized the relationship between Caesar and Cleopatra. They met in 48 B.C. under what have often been described as romantic circumstances. Caesar regulated the tumultuous affairs of Egypt by reinstating Cleopatra on the throne and marrying her to her brother, who was then about eleven. After Caesar's departure, she bore a son, Caesarion. Ancient sources hostile to Cleopatra—emanating from Octavian, whom Caesar designated in his will as heir—as well as modern scholars have argued that Caesarion was not, despite the assertions of Cleopatra and Antony, Caesar's son.[95] The date of Caesarion's birth has been disputed. Plutarch gives conflicting testimony. From his *Life of Caesar* we learn that Caesarion was Caesar's son and that he was born in 47 B.C.[96] A Demotic text confirms this date.[97] Yet, in his *Life of Antony*, Plutarch writes that Caesarion appeared to be Caesar's son and was born after Caesar's assassination.[98] Some scholars admit that, if Caesarion was born in 47 B.C., Caesar could have been the father, but, calculating from Caesar's movements, he could not have fathered a child born in 44 B.C. This argument makes the Romans appear extremely credulous. If the dates when Caesar could have had intercourse with Cleopatra were not appropriate to the birthday of the baby, surely the Romans and Egyptians would have figured it out—even if they did believe babies were born only in the eighth or tenth, rather than the ninth, month after insemination. An argument that Caesar's history proves that he was sterile after the birth of Julia (ca. 83 B.C.) is also questionable.[99] That he had no children by Calpurnia indicates merely that she was sterile, or that this specific combination was infertile, or that his long absences worked against reproductive success. With other partners, each one may have proven fertile. Moreover, that no children were produced despite Caesar's numerous extramarital affairs can be attributed to the fact that the upper-class Roman women who were his partners had the means to limit their pregnancies;[100] further, they were often married, so any child would appear to be the offspring of the husband. Cleopatra was unlikely to be having intercourse with a younger brother in the course of her affair with Caesar. Ptolemy XIII was barely old enough to have fathered Caesarion; and he was dead, at any rate, in 47 B.C. Ptolemy XIV was assassinated in 44 B.C. at about the age of fifteen. Yet no one has proposed a candidate other than Caesar for the father, and rumor would have named one if he existed. Rumors about sexual liaisons were rife in Rome in the first century B.C., and the hated Cleopatra would not have been immune from gossip.

Cleopatra was never said to have been sexually promiscuous. From her point of view, it was a great advantage and not a scandal to bear Caesar's child. Previous male Ptolemies had practiced serial monogamy, bigamy, and adultery. Thus, in her marriages, Cleopatra was also following a male pattern. Her marriage to a brother was no deterrent to an association with Caesar. Moreover, Caesar's wife was childless, and it would have been natural for her to hope that her son would be designated Caesar's heir.

That Marc Antony was the father of Cleopatra's other three children was never questioned. Augustan propaganda exploited these children as the product of a liaison that was presented to the Romans as flagrant, obnoxious, and life-threatening. Antony was considered to have been mistaken in opposing Octavian, but he was still a Roman. The real villain was Cleopatra, who had led the virtuous Roman astray. When a declaration of war was made in 32 B.C., it was directed against Cleopatra alone.[101] Cleopatra was an anomaly among the Romans. There was no category appropriate for her. In sophisticated Roman society, some upper-class matrons dressed and behaved like Hellenistic courtesans. Courtesans, in turn, had dinner with senators. But there was one distinction between the two groups of women that could not be violated: men of the senatorial and equestrian classes married within their class. Courtesans did not supplant wives.

Cleopatra, then, coming like the courtesans from the Hellenized East, was classified with them by her enemies and called "*regina meretrix*" ("courtesan queen").[102] Unlike most courtesans, Cleopatra did not have to be concerned about her means of support. She was able to furnish luxurious settings in which to make her skillful appeals to all of Antony's senses. Reports about her cleverness and his dissipation are reminiscent of traditions about earlier queens and kings in Egypt:

> Her beauty was not altogether beyond compare, nor such as would strike those who looked at her; but her companionship was irresistible and spellbinding. Her appearance, added to the persuasiveness of her conversation and to her character—which somehow encompassed her social relationships—had something animating about it. There was sweetness, too, in the sound of her voice, and her tongue, like a many-stringed instrument, she could easily turn to whatever language she wished, so that she very seldom needed an interpreter. When she met with barbarians, she gave her answer to most of them by herself, whether they were Ethiopians, Troglodytes, Hebrews, Arabians, Syrians, Medes, or Parthians. She is said to have learned thoroughly the languages of many others, although the kings before her had failed to grasp the Egyptian language, and some had even forgotten their Macedonian dialect.[103]

Cleopatra was reputed to be an expert in the arts and accoutrements of seductive women and to have used these to bewitch Antony. For many generations, Ptolemaic queens, including Arsinoë II and Berenice II, had taken a special interest in perfumes and unguents.[104] These concoctions have affinities with drugs. In fact, Helen of Sparta[105]—who was knowledgeable about drugs (as well as about female adornment)—was reputed to have received instruction in Egypt. After Cleopatra's death, treatises on cosmetics, hair-dressing, and hair-curling were attributed to her.[106]

Cleopatra has been accused of twice betraying Antony, first by abandoning him at the fateful battle of Actium and finally by attempting to come to terms with Augustus after Antony's suicide. She probably did neither, but if she had done so, her motivation need not have been execrable. Both these actions could have been inspired by a monarch's and a mother's desire to save Egypt for her children. Everyone, even her Roman enemies, must have admired her for her suicide, inasmuch as it was elegant, theatrical, and successful. It was surely by design that Cleopatra chose to be killed by cobra's poison, for this animal was an ancient symbol of Pharaonic power.[107] When her handmaiden Charmion described Cleopatra's death perfectly as "fitting for the descendant of so many kings," she used the masculine form of the Greek word for "descendant."[108]

## QUEENS AND GODDESSES

In the symbolic realm, Ptolemaic queens were at least as powerful as kings. Both queens and kings were the objects of worship in dynastic cults introduced by the Greeks, in native Egyptian cults as the successors of the Pharaohs, and as the incarnations of various Greek and Egyptian divinities.[109] The historical sources for these cults include papyri, inscriptions, poetry, and prose literature. Complementing the written word are the manifestations in art, including temple sculpture, depictions on coins, and implements made specifically for the various cults.

The worship of selected outstanding human beings as divine was traditional among the Greeks. Founders of cities, warriors who had fought at Troy, and even outstanding athletes were worshiped as heroes in various locations in the Greek world. Cults in honor of women were rare. Iphigenia was venerated as a heroine at Brauron, a suburb of Athens. The clothing and unfinished weaving of women who had died in childbirth were dedicated to her.[110] Heroic cults were essentially chthonic in nature and were similar to cults celebrated by individual families in honor of their ancestors. The objects of veneration were usually worshiped at their tombs, for they had met with death before heroization.

Alexander asked for and received divine honors in his lifetime. Denying that his father was Philip II, who had begotten other sons and rival heirs, Alexander is said to have claimed that his mother, Olympias, had had intercourse with Zeus in the form of a snake. Olympias laughed this off, saying "Will Alexander never stop slandering me in the eyes of Hera?"[111] In Egypt, early in his expedition he was proclaimed the son of Zeus-Ammon. Alexander was identified with Heracles and Dionysus.[112] All three were sons of Zeus by mortal mothers; all were conquerors as well as benefactors. Moreover, the genealogy of the Macedonian royal line connected him with both Heracles and Dionysus. The Macedonians traced their descent from Hyllus, the son of Heracles and Deianira. Deianira was, in myth, the daughter of Oeneus. Since the Greek word for wine is *oinos,* through a strained etymology Oeneus, grandfather of Hyllus, was thought of as a wine god. The cult of Dionysus was favored by Macedonian royalty from the earliest times for which we have historical testimony. Euripides wrote his *Bacchae* at the court of King Archelaus. Plutarch tells us that Alexander's mother, Olympias, was an ardent devotee of the Dionysiac rites.[113] She is the first historical, rather than fictional, Maenad whose name is known.[114]

Ptolemy I instituted a cult in honor of Alexander, in the city which he had founded and named for himself, and where his body was entombed. During the reign of Ptolemy II, the framework of the dynastic cults was firmly established. While Ptolemy was married to Arsinoë II, the two were elevated to the status of Divine Siblings (*Theoi Adelphoi*). Next, a cult was created in honor of Arsinoë alone. Whether this occurred before or after her death has been a subject of much controversy.[115] Coins of the Ptolemies that show Arsinoë II wearing a diadem are clear evidence of her deification, for the diadem was hitherto worn only by divinities and by royalty who presented themselves as divine. Moreover, on some jugate coins showing Ptolemy II and Arsinoë II, the legend *Theoi Adelphoi* appears, but these coins have not yet been definitively dated. Dorothy Burr Thompson argues that, since it would be peculiar for Ptolemy to show himself next to a dead person, Arsinoë must have been apotheosized before her death.[116] Of course, Arsinoë when dead was no longer a mortal but a goddess, so Ptolemy may have chosen to be portrayed with this manifestation of divine grace. Thompson also suggests that literary competitions were the principal feature at the festival established in honor of Arsinoë, the Arsinoeia, in celebration of the queen as patron of the arts.[117] Thompson considers the cult so "strangely feminist" that she is tempted to assert that Arsinoë, rather than Ptolemy, was its creator. Certainly, even if it could be established beyond doubt that the cult was actually created shortly after the death of Arsinoë, she nevertheless could have formulated the plans for it.

The difference between the deification of Macedonian kings and the deification of the queens is that, for the kings, they were bound to follow the example of Alexander. There was more to gain by association with this great figure than could possibly be acquired by innovation. For the deification of women there were no binding precedents, though the cult of Berenice could be used as an example, albeit on a much smaller scale. A new concept and a new iconography had to be created for Arsinoë. This model was adopted not only for subsequent queens in Egypt, but for rulers in other realms. She herself influenced the directions of her own dynastic cult by her sponsorship of the tableau of Aphrodite and Adonis described by Theocritus.[118] In his encomium to the royal pair, Theocritus had compared Arsinoë to Hera, queen of the heavens.[119] Both Hera and Arsinoë had married their brothers. Theocritus' suggestion was not adopted. Not Hera but Aphrodite became to the Ptolemaic queens what Dionysus and Heracles were to the kings. The reasons for the choice of Aphrodite are not known to us, but some tentative explanations may be suggested.

The most practical reason for selecting Aphrodite was that she was the only major Greek goddess associated with territory under Ptolemaic control. Hera, Artemis, and Athena, for example, had special connections with Argos, Ephesus, and Athens, and these places—with intermittent exceptions in the case of Ephesus—were ruled by Ptolemy's rivals. As early as

Homer, however, Aphrodite had been known as "the Cyprian" and Cyprus was governed by the Ptolemies.

Our view of Greek goddesses is severely biased by the reports of their activities in Homeric epic and in tragedy. Epic shows Aphrodite not only as the power that inspires love, but as a lover herself, fickle and adulterous, and a protector of people—such as Helen—who behave as she does. It is certainly difficult to erase the portrait of Aphrodite that Euripides paints in *Hippolytus*—ruthless, irresponsible. This literature, which is mostly Athenian and the product of male authors, gives a one-sided view of the goddess that must be enlarged by surveying the role of Aphrodite in cult throughout the Greek world. Among the Spartans, for example, Aphrodite served as goddess of marriage—a function that was Hera's in the cults of some other Greek states and, of course, in Homeric epic.[120]

Aphrodite is the patroness of the sexually passionate wife.[121] The Greeks did not believe that it was inappropriate for respectable women to be interested in sex, since the principal function of such women was reproduction. Athenian vase paintings of the Classical period depict Erotes (Cupids), the goddess's helpers, in attendance on brides.[122] Not only does Aristophanes frequently allude to the sexual interests of married women, but Socrates in Xenophon's *Symposium* states that women enjoy intercourse (*aphrodisioi*).[123] The decision of Teiresias as to which sex enjoys intercourse more appears for the first time in Hellenistic literature; he had been both male and female and was able to declare with authority that the woman had nine times more pleasure than the man.[124] According to the *Argonautica* of the Alexandrian poet Apollonius "of Rhodes," Lemnian wives had long neglected the rites of Aphrodite. The angry goddess punished them by instilling in their husbands a passion for slave girls.[125]

In Hellenistic literature, Aphrodite's various epithets prove that, whatever else she is, she continues to be a goddess of marriage. She is called goddess of the bridal chamber (Thalamon), goddess who joins together in matrimony (Harma), and goddess of the wedding (Nymphia).[126] According to Diodorus Siculus, when Zeus was distributing prerogatives to the other gods, he entrusted to Aphrodite the youth of maidens, the years when they should marry, and the care of such matters as are still observed in connection with marriages.[127] Plutarch writes about the worship at Delphi of Aphrodite who brings together in matrimony: "In the case of lawful wives, intercourse is the beginning of friendship, a partnership, as it were, in great mysteries. There is little pleasure, but the respect and charms and mutual love and trust that develop daily from it prove the wisdom of the Delphians in calling Aphrodite the goddess who joins together."[128] Stobaeus asks, "Where could Love preside more legitimately than over the lawful intercourse of man and woman? Where could Hera? Where could Aphrodite?"[129]

Like Aphrodite—mother of two—a good queen did not need to be personally fecund, but by her grace she endowed her land with prosperity. Thus Odysseus says to Penelope:

Lady, no mortal man on the endless earth could have cause to find fault with you; your fame goes up into the wide heaven as that of some king who, as a blameless man and god-fearing, and ruling as lord over many powerful people, upholds the way of good government, and the black earth yields him barley and wheat, his trees are heavy with fruit. His sheep flocks continue to bear young, the sea gives him fish because of his good leadership, and his people prosper under him.[130]

Aphrodite was endowed with a dual nature, expressed in myth by two versions of her birth. According to one, she was born of the anthropomorphic intercourse of Zeus and a little-known goddess named Dione. This Aphrodite received the epithet "Pandemus," which should have the political meaning of "worshiped by the whole community." But this meaning was corrupted in the fourth century to signify as well "common," as in "common prostitute."[131] Pandemus is distinguished from the Aphrodite called Urania, who was born out of the genitals thrown into the foam of the sea when the sky god Uranus was castrated. The association with the sea was fostered by the fact that the Greeks connected the name of the goddess with their word for foam, *aphros*.

Alluding to her birth, Hellenistic sculpture often depicts Aphrodite bathing. The goddess is, of course, totally or partially nude.[132] The connotations of such nudity were not inevitably lewd, but could be heroic.[133] The Greeks considered that exercising in the nude distinguished them from (inferior) non-Greeks, and in the Classical period they represented only the male figure in sculpture without drapery. In the Hellenistic period, nudity endowed the female body with the idealization previously reserved for athletes and gods. At least one type of the numerous sculptures of the nude Aphrodite apparently originated in Egypt.[134] A Roman copy of this statue, the Venus of the Esquiline, shows the goddess standing nude next to a hydria ("water jar") on which her clothing rests. Associations with Egypt are suggested by the asp or uraeus twined around the hydria (see Plate 3).

The Ptolemies were able to exploit the distinction between the two Aphrodites to cleanse their cult of its associations with lawless, excessive, or commercial sex. According to an Alexandrian decree concerning sacrifices to Arsinoë Philadelphus, the male and female goat are specifically forbidden as offerings.[135] Instead, vegetable offerings are recommended. The exclusion of the goat is interesting. Goats were always considered lustful creatures and were normally sacrificed to fertility divinities such as Dionysus and Aphrodite. The interdiction of the goat in the private cult of Arsinoë Philadelphus was a means of preventing an assimilation of Arsinoë to Aphrodite in her unsuitable role of Pandemus.[136]

Aphrodite Pandemus was associated with the goat, while Aphrodite Urania was associated with the chelone. Since Aphrodite was born of the sea, the chelone with the goddess is more probably a sea turtle than a tortoise. Pausanias describes a chryselephantine statue of Aphrodite at Elis by Phidias portraying the goddess resting one foot on a turtle. The chryselephantine statue stood within her temple; a bronze statue by Scopas showing the goddess riding on a male goat was placed in the precinct outside. Pausanias reports that the latter sculpture was called Pandemus, while the Aphrodite with the turtle was called Urania.[137] Aphrodite and the turtle are connected with marriage, according to Plutarch:

Phidias made the Aphrodite of the Eleans stepping on a turtle to
be a symbol for women of staying home and keeping silence. For a
woman ought to talk either to her husband or through her
husband.[138]

In "The Distaff," Erinna employs the motif of the turtle (*chelone*). The poem deals with the youth of Erinna and her friend
Baucis, and with her friend's marriage and swift death.[139] Similarly, Artemidorus considered Aphrodite Urania to be particularly concerned with marriage and fertility:

She is especially good in regard to marriage and sexual unions and
the procreation of children. She is the cause of copulation and
progeny.[140]

As patroness of marriage, Arsinoë sponsored a festival in honor of Aphrodite and Adonis in Alexandria. Theocritus, a poet
from Syracuse, describes the first day of the festival in his fifteenth idyll. The idyll depicts two women who were born in
Syracuse and who are now living as housewives in Alexandria.
They complain about the mundane matters that married women
often grumble about: the thoughtlessness of husbands, domestic
help, how shopkeepers dupe husbands, and the price of clothing. These two join the crowds going to the palace to see the
show that Queen Arsinoë has produced in honor of Aphrodite
and Adonis. Their off-color remarks pertain to marriage. Praxinoa says, "Women know everything—even how Zeus married
Hera." And later she says, "All inside—as the man said when he
turned the key on the bride." Then the women view the pageant. A singer glorifies Aphrodite, who changed Berenice
(mother of Ptolemy and Arsinoë) into a goddess, dropping ambrosia into her breast. Aphrodite embraces Adonis, who is called
her bridegroom—certainly a more attractive partner than her
usual husband Hephaestus. The singer foretells that on the second day Adonis—who will then have died—will be immersed in
the sea and women will mourn for him. A papyrus from the
Fayum indicates that on the third day of the festival Adonis is
resurrected. The Adonis festival is often considered to be a

3. Venus of the Esquiline. Roman copy of a Greek original or Classicizing work of the first century B.C. The Egyptian derivation is suggested by the asp on the hydria. *Rome. Capitoline Museum 1141. Photo courtesy of the Deutsches Archäologisches Institut, Rome.*

meeting of Aphrodite of the Gardens with an Adonis who is a spirit of vegetation, and that would certainly describe the situation on the second and third days of the festival. But Theocritus has given the festival a domestic context and has described only the wedding night of Aphrodite and Adonis, because he is celebrating Aphrodite as goddess of marriage.

One may wonder why Arsinoë would have wanted to draw attention to marriage *per se* in the cult that she favored, since her own was highly questionable. In *Idyll* 17, Theocritus, who sought the patronage of the Ptolemies and therefore flattered them, exalts the marriage of Ptolemy and Arsinoë by comparing the two to Zeus and Hera, another brother–sister pair. He writes of them as a loving couple: "Ptolemy and his noble wife: no better wife embraces her bridegroom in their house, loving with all her heart her brother and her husband."

The sea-born Aphrodite received the epithet Euploia ("Goddess of Smooth Sailing"). Aphrodite Euploia, goddess of navigation, protected the fleet—most appropriately, for the Ptolemies explored the Red Sea and sent their fleet as far as the Indian Ocean. Alexandria became the greatest port in the eastern Mediterranean. The white marble lighthouse, built in the early third century B.C., was one of the seven wonders of the world.

Alexandrian poetry is replete with allusions connecting Arsinoë with Aphrodite.[141] In "The Deification of Arsinoë," according to ancient commentary, Callimachus stated that Arsinoë was wafted to heaven by the Dioscuri, Castor and Pollux. These divine twins protected sailors and were identified with the Cabiri. Arsinoë II took a special interest in the Mysteries of the Cabiri at Samothrace. The Dioscuri were also brothers of Helen, a favorite of Aphrodite. Theocritus described Arsinoë as "lovely as Helen." If portraits of this queen on coins and in sculpture are realistic, then the poet was not merely flattering nor idealizing his patroness[142] (see Plate 4). These portrayals are all the more intriguing inasmuch as she did not assume the throne until she was thirty-seven—an age at which most Greek women would have been considered decrepit. Theocritus also recorded that Berenice, the mother of Arsinoë II and Ptolemy II, was a favo-

4. Portrait of Arsinoë II. *Bonn. Akademisches Kunstmuseum B 284.*

5. *Oinochoe* made for the ruler cult showing Arsinoë II holding a double cornucopia. The vase is inscribed "of the Good Fortune of Arsinoë Philadelphus." Said to be from Canosa. *London. British Museum 73. 8–20.389.*

rite of Aphrodite and that the goddess welcomed the queen to her divine entourage, saving her from death. A fragmentary cult hymn celebrates Arsinoë as the foam-born Aphrodite.[143] After her death, Ptolemy II continued to lavish funds in celebration of his sister-wife as divine (see Plate 5). An extravagant design for her temple at Alexandria called for constructing a roof of a magnetic substance so that an iron statue of Arsinoë would appear to be suspended in midair. Thus, like a goddess, the queen would have no earthly moorings. The project was interrupted by the deaths of the architect and of Ptolemy himself.[144]

The best-known temple erected for the ruler cult out of private funds was built for Arsinoë-Aphrodite-Zephyritis by Callicrates, admiral of the royal Ptolemaic navy. The temple stood on a promontory between the city of Alexandria and the Canopic mouth of the Nile, overlooking the Mediterranean. It was in this temple that Berenice II dedicated a lock of hair which disappeared and was discovered in the sky as a comet by the astronomer Conon (see p. 20). Posidippus wrote two dedicatory epigrams for the temple itself, and Callimachus commemorated the offering of a seashell in it.[145]

In Western tradition, Shakespeare's description of Cleopatra VII as Aphrodite and Marc Antony as Dionysus has been the best-known feature of the ruler cult. Shakespeare's source was Plutarch's narrative of their first meeting:

> Though she received many letters of summons both from Antony himself and from his friends, she so looked down upon and laughed at the man that she sailed up the river Cydnus in a barge with gilded stern, its sails spread purple, its rowers urging it on with silver oars to the sound of the flute with pipes and lutes. She herself reclined beneath a canopy spangled with gold, adorned like Aphrodite in a painting, while boys like Erotes in paintings stood on either side and fanned her. Her most beautiful maids were dressed like sea nymphs and graces, some steering at the rudder, some working at the ropes. Marvelous perfumes from numerous censers diffused themselves along the shore . . . while the word went through all the multitude that Aphrodite had come to revel with Dionysus.[146]

Ptolemaic queens were identified with many other goddesses, both Greek and Egyptian. Foremost among them was Isis.[147] Isis was an ancient Egyptian divinity, but the Isis of the Ptolemies was a new Hellenistic creation who herself assumed the attributes of other goddesses. Sailors and merchants carried the cult from Alexandria to Greek and eventually to Roman settlements around the Mediterranean. Like Aphrodite, Isis protected those who travel by sea. Her appeal to men was also as a mother goddess. She had none of the ferocity of earlier mother goddesses, but rather was consistently tender, compassionate, and merciful. She took a personal interest in each of her devotees, thus providing permanent solace to the deracinated cosmopolites of the vast Hellenistic world. Isis was extremely popular among women. Though a goddess, she had shared the experiences of mortal women. She was both wife and mother. She had endured the loss of her brother and husband Osiris, and like a mortal woman she had mourned for him. In her many aretalogies, she presents herself as a goddess of women, patroness of married life, protector of childbirth and infants, and inventor of spinning and weaving and of marriage contracts. She is the reason that children love their parents.

Women are conspicuous among those who held official positions in the various cults of Isis, although it cannot be demonstrated that they were more numerous than men or held the highest positions. They are also responsible for a very high proportion of dedications to this goddess in the Greco-Roman world.[148] Although nowhere and at no time do they outnumber men, insofar as women generally draw on narrower financial resources than men do, the extent to which they do make dedications to Isis is noteworthy.

We may ask whether the gender and personality of a divinity reflect the status of women in a society. Classical Athens provides an excellent contrast to Hellenistic Egypt. The supreme divinity was Athena. Biologically female, she denied her mother and referred only to her birth from the head of her father Zeus. She remained a virgin and, sexually unthreatening, was accepted as a compatriot of men. As befits the supreme divinity of the Athenians, Athena was patroness of wisdom and crafts, but she was also a martial goddess. There could be no greater contrast to masculine Athena than the feminine divinities of Ptolemaic cult. The earliest Ptolemaic kings favored Heracles. Even this hero had once served a woman, Queen Omphale. The majority of the kings were assimilated to Dionysus, the most feminine of all the great gods.[149] And there was no goddess more representative of the female than Aphrodite or her Egyptian counterpart Isis. According to Diodorus Siculus, because of Isis the Egyptian queen had greater power and honor than the king. Among commoners, the wife ruled the husband, the husbands agreeing in the marriage contract that in all matters they would obey their wives.[150] Doubtless Diodorus, following the example of Herodotus, exaggerated the difference between Greece and Egypt. Moreover, the symbolic power of a queen can be but one small aspect of the status of women in a given society. Nevertheless, as we shall see, Ptolemaic queens not only maintained the direction of the Hellenistic period, with its increased opportunities and freedom for women, but themselves set the fashion for other upper-class women in Alexandrian society.

Chapter 2

Alexandrian
Women

THE Ptolemies were of Macedonian stock, but their city of Alexandria attracted immigrants from a variety of backgrounds. In this cosmopolitan population, the Greeks constituted a privileged class through which the Ptolemies ruled the Egyptians. Greek societies were always hierarchical, but the political changes in the Hellenistic period altered the emphasis in the stratification. In the earliest Greek societies, as known through epic, the principal distinction was between aristocrats and commoners. Thus, the hero Odysseus rebukes a common soldier, Thersites, for daring to speak up to his social superiors, whereas he treats his wife Penelope as his equal.[1]

In contrast, in the Classical democratic polis all male citizens were equal, but within the family—which was the basic unit of the polis—the husband ruled the wife and children. Tragedy and comedy, which were the popular literary forms in the Classical polis, reveal the strains that the polarization of the sexes within the family created. Aeschylus, Sophocles, Euripides, and Aristophanes all chose to depict heroines who defied their husbands, and in tragedy even went so far as to destroy them. Although most of these heroines were upper-class, their closest intimates were female slaves and commoners. The theme of hostility between the female and the male served as a model for many other sorts of antitheses.[2] Macedonian society, like Homeric, was heroic and aristocratic. In Greek families in Alexan-

41

dria, the man was still the head of the house, but the primary stratification was between the ruling class and the native population. The literature of the Greeks in Alexandria often emphasizes intimacy rather than hostility between the sexes. Of course, this comment must be tempered by the observation that Athenian drama was created for the masses, while Alexandrian literature was largely written for aristocratic patrons.

## WOMEN OF THE PTOLEMAIC NOBILITY

The wives and daughters of high-ranking officials in the service of the Ptolemies belonged, *ipso facto*, to the Alexandrian upper class. Numerous dedications in honor of these women have been found on Cyprus.[3] Cyprus was the most important and longest-lasting possession of the Ptolemies outside Egypt itself.[4] Though not so cosmopolitan as Rhodes or Delos, it was an important locus of Ptolemaic propaganda. Strategoi of Cyprus were always among the highest-ranking administrators in the service of the Ptolemies, and in the second century B.C. they were the most exalted Ptolemaic officials outside Egypt.[5] Statues of these officials were erected by various individuals, groups, and organizations who wished to honor or curry favor with them. The reason for the honor is stated in the inscription on the pedestal, e.g., "because of his loyalty to the Ptolemies." In Mediterranean society a man is usually morally, if not always legally, responsible for his wife and children, for better or for worse. Honor paid to a man's family accrues as well to the man himself. Thus, there are also numerous Hellenistic statues in Cyprus in honor of the wives, sons, and daughters of the high-ranking administrators. The administrators, of course, had actually resided on the island. However, that dedications were made in honor of their families is not evidence that the families accompanied them. Indeed, in the second century B.C., statues of Roman women were being erected in Roman provinces, although Roman governors were not legally permitted to bring their wives with them to their posts.[6] Cyprus had a long and vital tradition of portrait sculpture, and it is possible that the statues of the Alexandrian nobility were created on the island.[7] But it is also possible that they were sculpted in Alexandria and then shipped to Cyprus, so it cannot be assumed that the women whose statues were erected in Cyprus ever gave up their luxurious life in Alexandria, even temporarily.

At least eight inscriptions from statue bases in Cyprus concern members of the family of Polycrates and Zeuxo.[8] Their statues had been arranged in a group near the temple of Aphrodite in Old Paphos. They were typical, but highly successful, members of the Ptolemaic nobility. Polycrates enjoyed an outstanding career as a military commander and as governor of Cyprus. He amassed a large fortune for himself on the island and in the years following his return to Alexandria.[9] His chariot won a victory at the Panathenaea, and, as has been mentioned (see p. 23), the female members of his family were also victorious in horse-racing. It has been suggested that Polycrates actually won all the victories himself but, being a fond husband and father, distributed the credit among his female relatives.[10] However, considering that all the other women who are known to have owned teams of horses were independently wealthy, it is reasonable to assume that Polycrates shared his wealth with his family and that each of them chose how to spend his or her portion. In addition, Zeuxo, like other upper-class women, had her own funds in the form of a dowry from her natal family. Coming from Cyrene, she was certainly likely to have an interest in horses, and her name, which corresponds to the masculine Zeuxippus ("Yoker of Horses"), is prophetic of this special interest.[11] Like the queens, but on a proportionately smaller scale, aristocratic women such as Zeuxo and her daughters must have had their own funds to spend as they wished—on horses or dedications or on whatever took their fancy.

Women dedicated a large number of statues in Cyprus. Some did so as a group; a thiasus of *aposkeuai* (soliders' families) is mentioned on an inscription from Chytroi.[12] Most of the dedications by women were made to other members of their family, both male and female. Women are also honored by dedications. Of course, in Cyprus, as elsewhere in the Greek world,[13] men outnumbered women as both dedicators and dedicatees, because women had less money to spend and had fewer accomplishments deemed worthy of commemoration. Wives and daughters of important men were frequently honored. In addition, parents honored their children, and children their parents. Among the honorific inscriptions from Old Paphos published by T. B. Mitford in 1961, the most common made by family members to or by women are those by mothers to sons and parents to daughters. There are four examples of each of these. There is, in addition, one example of a mother alone honoring her son and her daughter.[14] There are no examples of a mother alone honoring a daughter alone or vice versa. This omission may have been due not to any familial hostility, but rather to the fact that a married daughter was considered part of her husband's family. Indeed, one woman does make a dedication to her father-in-law. It is also likely that the daughters who are honored by both their parents are not married. The only dedication made by a woman in honor of another woman is that in honor of Zeuxo by Stratonice, an Alexandrian, daughter of Nicias.[15] Unfortunately, nothing is known about either Stratonice or Nicias. Moreover, since the reasons for the dedications at Paphos are inscribed only when the dedicatee is a man, and even then only when he is not a friend or a relative of the dedicator, it is impossible to know the reasons for Stratonice's dedication. Since it dates from the period of Polycrates' strategeia, it is not in celebration of the victory of Zeuxo at the Panathenaea, which is known to us.

Zeuxo and Polycrates had three daughters and two sons. By the standard of Classical Athens, this family was large; by comparison with other Hellenistic families, it was enormous. Particularly ostentatious—in a period when Posidippus wrote, "Everyone, even a poor man, raises a son; everyone, even a rich man, exposes a daughter"[16]—is the large number of daughters.[17]

It is unusual to find more than two daughters in Greek families, or to find a sex ratio that favors daughters over sons. Raising a number of daughters was indicative of great wealth and pride, on the same scale as owning horses that were victorious at pan-Hellenic festivals. Owning such horses at Athens was evidence that a man belonged to the liturgical class.[18] The Athenian Callias, who won three victories in chariot-racing—two of these in a single year—raised three daughters.[19] Themistocles had five.[20] Adimantus, who commanded the Corinthian fleet at Salamis, had three.[21] Later in the second century, there are other families with a remarkable number of daughters in the Ptolemaic aristocracy and in an upper-class family near Thebes. Demetria, who held eponymous priesthoods from 187 to 184 B.C., had two sisters.[22] Theodorus, strategus of Cyprus, and his wife Olympias had at least three, and probably four, daughters and one son.[23] Agathoclea, who will be discussed below, had at least two sisters. Dryton, a cavalry officer, raised five daughters.[24] One son and one daughter of Polycrates and Zeuxo were named for their parents; none were named for their grandfathers, Ariston and Mnasiadas. There may have been additional offspring who had been named for their grandparents in the normal Greek fashion and who did not survive.

A declining birthrate often coincides with an improvement in women's status. But when it is coupled with female infanticide, as was the case in parts of the Greek world in the Hellenistic period, the two factors for assessing women's status are contradictory. However, since the members of the Ptolemaic nobility were wealthy enough to rear large families and obviously did not eliminate their female offspring, it appears that the status of women in such families was high in comparison to that of other Greek women.

Unsurprisingly, the women of the Ptolemaic nobility seem to have married their equals. For example, Myrsine was the wife of Pelops, the first attested strategus of Cyprus; their fathers may have known each other at Samos, where Myrsine's father was honored and where Pelops' father held a military command during the reign of Ptolemy II.[25] The husband of Artemo, sister of Theodorus, strategus of Cyprus, was important enough to have been eliminated by Ptolemy Euergetes in the bloodbath of 144 B.C.[26]

## CITIZENSHIP

Laws governing the citizenship at Alexandria tended to encourage the rearing of daughters, their marriage to their peers, and the maintenance of a caste of ethnically unmixed Greeks. In Alexandria, Ptolemy I had bestowed a legal code after consultation with Peripatetic philosophers at his court.[27] The code was the result of their study of various legal systems in the Greek world. Citizenship in Greek cities could be inherited from either parent, but, according to Aristotle, the normal prerequisite was descent from both a mother and father who were citizens.[28] The latter type of citizenship law prevailed in Greek cities as disparate as Sparta and Athens.

A restrictive citizenship law has the effect of limiting the number of citizens. It is characteristic of a polis whose citizenship is considered to have legal, economic, and emotional value. A state that is attractive to foreigners and is becoming cosmopolitan would be more likely to define its citizenship strictly and reserve it for natives of double-citizen parentage. A restrictive citizenship law is also protective of native-born women: it gives them an advantage in the marriage market, since only their children can be full citizens.[29] Such a law is particularly appropriate to an elite group whose men come into contact with foreign women, or other women in their country who are not members of the elite. In the Hellenistic period—a time favorable to migration and exogamous marriage—a number of cities employed restrictive citizenship laws based on the Athenian model instituted in the days of Pericles (451/450 B.C.).[30] Whether descent through both the maternal and paternal line for the inheritance of citizen status at Alexandria was invariably necessary is unclear. This ambiguity is a result of the paucity of primary evidence from the Ptolemaic period for women's citizenship,[31] the possibility of change under Roman domination, and the problems raised by the topic of Alexandrian citizenship in general.

Some women at Alexandria, as well as in the other Greek cities in Egypt, bore the status designation *aste* ("citizen"). Although women as citizens did not enjoy political rights in a modern sense, they did have civic status. According to Aristotle's definitions, citizenship does not entail only the right to rule, hold political offices, and administer justice, but it also can include upholding the laws made by those in power and submission to being ruled.[32] Greek women, as citizens, belonged to the latter category.

Women were not enrolled in tribes, or demes, at Alexandria.[33] In contrast, possession of the demotic, or deme name, was the supreme guarantee of citizenship for men in Alexandria.[34] Scholars agree that the women who were designated as *astai* ("citizens") received this title through their relationship to a demesman (a full citizen).[35] Thus it is generally agreed that the wives and daughters of demesmen were called *astai*. The question that concerns us here is whether this term also designated the mother of a citizen. P. M. Fraser cautiously writes, "The normal practice would be for citizenship to be restricted to persons of Greek parentage, of whom the father at least was a citizen."[36] In contrast, M. A. H. El-Abbadi postulates that the Alexandrian citizenship was based on the Athenian model: Double-citizen parentage was required.[37]

Reliable evidence for Alexandrian citizenship dates from the Roman period only. Two privileged statuses in Roman Egypt were restricted to those whose parents on both sides had the requisite lineage. To be enrolled as an ephebe at Alexandria, it was necessary for a boy to have a father who was a demesman and a mother who was an *aste*.[38] The ephebate as an institution was well established in the Ptolemaic period. It would be strange if membership in the ephebate were governed by a restrictive law, while citizenship itself was not. Metropolitan status—a Roman innovation which granted certain privileges and immunities from taxes—likewise had to be proven through the maternal and paternal line.[39] Thus, El-Abbadi's hypothesis that Alexandrian citizenship required matrilineal and patrilineal descent from citizens seems more acceptable than Fraser's equivocal statement. It would certainly have been more profitable for the Romans to reduce the number of privileged citizens in Alexandria. Yet they are not known to have introduced a double-parent requirement in any conquered territory. It is far more likely that the restrictive law had already existed in the Ptolemaic period and that women who were citizens were the most attractive brides for men who were citizens.

## MEMORABLE EVENTS

Inscriptions and papyri mentioning upper-class women give their identities and status, but there is little additional information about their individual lives. They probably conformed to a pattern expressed on an expensive funerary monument from another Greek city in North Africa.[40] Six metopes of a unique biographical tomb from Cyrene narrate important events in a woman's life. Estimates of the date of the tomb range from 370 B.C. to the early period of Egyptian domination of Cyrene under Ptolemy I. The painting has faded, and it is not always possible to understand exactly what the artist intended to depict. Each of the metopes shows two figures. All the figures are female, with the exception of one male figure in the final scene, who must be Charon, the ferryman of the dead. The first metope shows two seated figures in an attitude of sadness. Both are well dressed and wearing jewelry. Perhaps the scene is a portrayal of the deceased woman and a sister mourning the death of a parent. On the second metope, a woman is kneeling before a standing woman who holds a rod. The theme is education. Certainly schooling was available to girls in the fourth century. If the standing woman is imparting secular knowledge to her student—assuming that they are not mother and daughter—then the tomb is one of two of the earliest pieces of evidence of formal teaching by a female teacher. The other piece of evidence is the tradition that Sappho taught (*paideuousa*) aristocratic women, who came to her not only from her native land, but from Ionia. This story can be traced back to the middle of the third century, to Callias of Mytilene, a contemporary of Aristophanes of Byzantium.[41] Female schoolteachers are otherwise unknown in the Greek world before the early Roman Empire.[42] Considering Greek attitudes, it appears likely that girls would be given female tutors. It is also possible that the standing woman is giving instructions about the proper behavior in some religious ceremony and using the rod as a pointer. The third metope depicts the woman spinning on a distaff as she walks, followed by a slave carrying a small chest. This scene is clearly one of a marriage procession. The distaff connotes women's domesticity. The chest alludes to the dowry. Yet, despite the wealth indicated by the dowry and by the tomb itself, the woman was not lazy, for she spins even while she walks! The fourth metope shows one figure in repose while a standing woman experiences emotional stress, perhaps in mourning. This simultaneous expression of a variety of emotions brings to mind the pictorial cycle at the Villa of the Mysteries in Pompeii. Perhaps the metope depicts an initiation ceremony in which a novice feels terror, while the initiate has already found peace. In the fifth metope, one woman is on a swing while another stands behind her. The two may simply be playing, or, more likely, the swing may allude to the worship of Dionysus.[43] On the last metope, Charon helps the dead woman into his boat. The biographical tomb shows that the events in a woman's life that were thought worthy of commemoration on her tomb were her initiations into various cults, marriage, and death. She experienced most of the decisive events in her life in the company of other women.

Women of the Ptolemaic aristocracy, like Greek women elsewhere and at all times, participated actively in religion. Female relatives of Polycrates attended the celebration of the Thesmophoria in 203 B.C. when the events described by Polybius occurred.[44] It is to be assumed that, like the Athenian Thesmophoria, the festival at Alexandria was open to women of Greek origin, but Polybius reports a particular event involving the upper class only. Participation in the festival was limited to respectable women.[45] However, no one would have dared to question the qualifications of Oenanthe.

Oenanthe, an older woman of Samian origin who had been the mistress of Ptolemy III, was present at the Thesmophoria.[46] She was the mother of Agathocles and Agathoclea and had at least two other daughters. Who the fathers of her children were is questionable. At any rate, it was not alleged that Ptolemy had sired them. Her son has been identified with Agathocles, son of Agathocles, a priest of Alexander in 216/215 B.C.[47] Agathoclea has been identified with the daughter of Diognetus who served as priestess in 213/212 B.C.[48] If Agathocles and Agathoclea were brother and sister, rather than more distant relatives, at least one of these identifications cannot reflect a credible filiation. Barring an unlikely coincidence, the only way that the brother and sister could have borne virtually the same name was if they had the same father (an Agathocles) or if they were named for one of their mother's ascendants.[49] If Oenanthe was a *hetaira*, she may not have known who the fathers of her children were, or it may have been professionally detrimental for her and of little profit to press paternity charges. Like most unwed mothers, she may have named her children for her own family. In fact, Polybius refers to Agathocles merely as Oenanthe's son. The priest Agathocles and priestess Agathoclea—if they are not the same as Oenanthe's children—could have been named for these two. Polybius reports that Aristomenes, "prime minister" of Ptolemy V, named his daughter after Agathocles, and he may not have been the only one to do so.[50] A final possibility is that Agathoclea was indeed the daughter of Diognetus but that both she and her brother were named for her mother's family. Agathocles may have simply adopted a fictive "Agathocles" as his patronymic for the sake of appearances.

Oenanthe had been the mistress of Ptolemy III, and her son had been the king's boy lover (*eromenos*).[51] Agathoclea, in turn, became the mistress of Ptolemy IV. She must have borne a child, for she was able to serve as wet nurse to Ptolemy V.[52] The activities of Agathoclea and Agathocles were not confined to the bedroom, but, as the naming of at least one unrelated child for them indicates, they wielded political power. They were instrumental in the murders of Ptolemy IV and his wife and sister Arsinoë III (see Plate 6).

A rebellion against the authority exercised by Agathocles was at hand when Oenanthe, depressed and distressed, offered prayers at the Thesmophoria. Some of the noble women, including Polycrates' relatives, unaware of the reason for Oenanthe's distress, attempted to comfort her. She charged them with hypocrisy, rejected their advances, and cursed them. The women, rebuffed, left Oenanthe alone. Their rage increased the fervor of the rebellion.

Agathocles and his group had at one time angered the populace by taking Danaë, the mother-in-law of one of their rivals, and dragging her through the streets without a veil.[53] Although the fashion was changing at this time, an older woman such as Danaë probably regarded the veil as an item of clothing that no respectable woman would appear in public without.[54] Oenanthe as an old woman had to suffer more humiliation than Danaë, for she was led naked on horseback through the city before her death. Agathoclea and her sisters were also stripped. They and their relatives met a death that culminated in dismemberment.[55]

There can be no doubt that Greek woman participated in this butchery. Simultaneously, some of the young girls who had been raised with Arsinoë III took up clubs and stones and slew one of the queen's murderers and his son. They stripped his wife, dragged her to the street, and killed her too.[56] The daughters of Zeuxo and Polycrates may well have been among these girls. The Ptolemaic princes and princesses were brought up with a cohort of upper-class children to serve as their companions, and Polycrates was certainly important enough for his daughters to have been granted this privilege. Stories about the boyhood friends of Alexander the Great who retained their loyalty to him when he was king are familiar. The companions of Arsinoë too did not forget their queen. The official title of these "foster siblings" was *suntrophoi*.[57] Polybius uses this word to refer to the young girls who avenged Arsinoë.[58]

## MISTRESSES OF THE PTOLEMIES

The modern reader, familiar with the rigid intellectual distinction and physical segregation that the Athenians maintained between respectable women and others, may be surprised at the friendliness shown by the aristocratic ladies toward Oenanthe and by the fact that Agathoclea and her mother enjoyed the run of the palace. Though they were courtesans, these women were not restricted to men's symposia.

We have observed this flexibility about women as early as the reign of Philip II (see Chapter 1). Satyrus remarks that Philip, intending to claim Thessaly as his property, begot children by two women of this country.[59] He does not report that Philip

6. Figure of Arsinoë III from a *oinochoe* made for the ruler cult. The raised right arm might have been holding a scepter or a sword. From lower Egypt, third century B.C. *Baltimore. Walters Art Gallery 48.309.*

actually married them. Philinna bore him Philip Arrhidaeus. Sources describe Philinna as a common entertainer of undistinguished background.[60] Yet her son Arrhidaeus was not relegated to the status of an illegitimate child. Rumor has it that he was so much a threat to Alexander as heir apparent that Olympias saw to it that the boy became feeble-minded. Moreover, after the death of Alexander, a faction of Macedonians proclaimed Arrhidaeus as king.

Scattered references in Ptolemaic history show that mistresses bore children who were not snubbed and who sometimes held not insignificant political posts. Demetrius received Leontiscus, son of Ptolemy I and Thaïs, as an ally.[61] (As we have mentioned in Chapter 1, another of Ptolemy's sons by Thaïs was given the family name Lagus.) Ptolemy Apion, son of Ptolemy VIII and his Jewish mistress (Eirene or Ithaca), became king of Cyrene.[62]

More is known about the courtesans of the reign of Ptolemy II than about those of any other Ptolemaic king. Varied historical sources include the records of Olympic victors mentioning the triumphs of Bilistiche,[63] an encyclopedic list in Athenaeus' *Deipnosophistae*,[64] and the polished works of Alexandrian poets. Plutarch, advocate of conjugal affection, refers disapprovingly to Ptolemy's girlfriends.[65] Women such as these strengthen the theme running through Ptolemaic history that the kings of Egypt, from Ptolemy II to Marc Antony, were addicted to pleasure and easily dominated by women.

Bilistiche was the most famous and most favored of Ptolemy's mistresses. Athenaeus also names Didyme,[66] Stratonice,[67] Myrtion,[68] Mnesis,[69] Cleino,[70] and Agathoclea.[71] Agathoclea may be a mistake arising out of confusion with the mistress of Ptolemy IV, but the list is still quite long. In addition, Ptolemy II is associated with two female entertainers, Aglaïs[72] and Glauce.[73] Of the eighteen *hetairai* and entertainers listed in the *Prosopographia Ptolemaica*, half are attributed to the reign of Ptolemy II.[74]

The precise years during which each of Ptolemy's mistresses enjoyed her ascendancy cannot be fixed, but there is no reason to assume that their activities commenced only with the death of Arsinoë II.[75] Sexual monogamy should not be attributed to a Macedonian king. Nevertheless, Bilistiche apparently gained a valuable asset from the king when he was newly widowed, inasmuch as her colts won their first Olympic victory just two years after Arsinoë's death.[76] She must have continued to be financially secure in old age, for two fragmentary papyri show that she made two loans in Oxyrhynchus in 239/238 B.C.[77] In her ownership of racehorses, Bilistiche joined the company of royalty, for the only women whose horses had won previously were of the Spartan royal house, while the next woman to be victorious was a Ptolemaic queen, Berenice III.[78] Agathoclea was also prosperous, for she was a shipowner. The only other identifiable women who owned ships on which royal grain was carried were members of the highest court circles. They include a queen (Cleopatra II), Philotera (canephore ["basket-bearer"] in 172/171 B.C.), and Berenice (canephore in the last third of the third century B.C.).[79] That courtesans were well paid is to be expected. What is more surprising is that Ptolemy II endowed two of his favorites with a spiritual and religious power qualitatively similar to, though quantitatively less than, the power he bestowed on his wife and sister. If, in granting such honors to his mistresses, Ptolemy revealed that he thought them trivial, then there is room to doubt his sincerity when, in an earlier period, he bestowed similar honors on Arsinoë.

Ptolemy II had statues of his cupbearer Cleino erected in many quarters of Alexandria. She personified the goddess Philadelphia (Sibling Love) and carried a rhyton, or cornucopia—a symbol of fertility which was an attribute of the queen as well.[80] He also inaugurated the worship of Bilistiche on a grand scale. Temples and shrines were dedicated in honor of Aphrodite-Bilistiche.[81] Ptolemy was not the first Macedonian to venerate a courtesan as Aphrodite.[82] In the fourth century, Harpalus, a comrade of Alexander the Great, had actually erected a temple and an altar to a *hetaira*, Pythionice. Athenaeus declares that, in establishing the worship of Aphrodite-Pythionice, Harpalus displayed his contempt for the gods.[83] Plutarch, similarly, voices his disgust that Bilistiche, "a barbarian woman bought in the marketplace," should have been apotheosized.[84] Other ancient sources assign an Argive or Macedonian origin to Bilistiche.[85] In recent times, in affirmation of Plutarch's remark, a Phoenician origin has been suggested, for Bilistiche's name was unusual among Greeks.[86] Although the rest of Ptolemy's mistresses bore Greek names, at least one of them was not of Greek origin: Didyme was an Ethiopian.[87] Asclepiades writes of her, "If she is black, what of it? So are coals. But when we warm them, they gleam like budding roses."[88]

## PRIESTESSES

Bilistiche, Agathoclea, and Hermione (daughter or grand-daughter of Polycrates and Zeuxo) were all appointed to epony-mous priesthoods.[89] The inclusion of women among epony-mous officials did not originate with the Ptolemies. In Argos, for example, the priestesses of Hera were eponymous, filling the same role as the ephors in Sparta and the archons in Athens. In Ptolemaic Egypt, women are not the only eponymous officials, but they are listed in dating protocols after the Ptolemies and the priest of Alexander. For example, the Rosetta Stone begins:

> In the reign of the young one [Ptolemy V] . . . , the priest of Alex-
> ander and the Savior Gods and the Brother-and-Sister Gods and
> the Benefactor Gods and the Father-Loving Gods and the God
> Manifest [and] Gracious [Ptolemy V] being Aetus son of Aetus, the
> athlophore of Berenice Euergetes being Pyrrha daughter of Phili-
> nus, the canephore of Arsinoë Philadelphus being Area daughter
> of Diogenes, the priestess of Arsinoë Philopator being Eirene
> daughter of Ptolemy, on the fourth of the month Xandicus, the
> eighteenth of the Egyptians' [month] Mecheir: decree.[90]

Because of their appearance in the dating protocols, the names of many women with their patronymics are extant. Al-though papyrologists are still discovering eponymous priestesses or redefining the dates of known ones, gaps remain in the lists. At times the scribes, through laziness or ignorance, lapse into an empty formula, writing, for example, "when whoever was the athlophore ['prize-bearer'?] was athlophore and when whoever was the canephore ['basket-bearer'] was canephore." When a document is damaged and only a few letters of the name survive, it can often be supplied by applying a rule named in honor of the papyrologist Sir Harold Idris Bell.[91] According to Bell's Law, the same woman usually served as athlophore one year and as canephore the next.

The names can often be reconstituted if a few letters and the total word length are known, since most of them are ordinary Greek names. However, a few Egyptian names do appear in Greek texts; the earliest of these were built on the stem "Isis." In 138/137 B.C. there is one Thermouthis,[92] and even earlier, the hybrid Isidora[93]—a Greek name formed on the name of an Egyptian goddess. Thaubarium[94] appears as priestess in 107/106 B.C., but she was certainly a Greek, for her brother was Helenus, governor of Cyprus. It has also been proposed that Simariste bears an Illyrian name.[95] But these women were exceptional. The most common names of the eponymous priestesses were Berenice and Arsinoë. These dynastic names were so popular, in fact, that they even appear among the purely Egyptian names in the sacerdotal milieu at Memphis.[96] In general, so little is known of naming patterns for Greek women that the most one can safely say is that sometimes the names can be restored because they run in certain families. The naming of Agathocles and Agathoclea has already been discussed. Polycrates and Zeuxo had a daughter called Hermione (and another Zeuxo), and their son Polycrates also named a daughter Hermione. Artemo appears at least twice in the lines of Seleucus and his son Theodorus, both governors of Cyprus. A Stratonice and a Berenice were sisters, as were perhaps a Cratea and a Polycratea. A few women bore their father's name in feminine form: e.g., Aristomache daughter of Aristomachus, Athenodora daughter of Athenodorus, Nicostrate daughter of Nicostratus, Theodoris daughter of Theodorus, Nymphaïs daughter of Nymphaion, and three examples of Ptolemaïs daughter of Ptolemaeus. Those parents who named a daughter for her father must have felt, consciously or otherwise, that a female child was in some way able to perpetuate her father's lineage. Perhaps observing that the female Ptolemies were not excluded from the succession to the throne led them to realize that their own daughters could be viewed as retaining ties to their natal families.

The qualifications for serving as an eponymous priest are not known, but some guidelines may be deduced. That they were ethnic Greeks should not be surmised from their names alone, but other factors make this conclusion more than likely. Not all the women came from the most illustrious families.[97] Due to lack of information, the social class of some eponymous priests cannot be determined at all, but since there was no financial remuneration for the holders of eponymous priesthoods, their families must have been able at least to provide clothing appropriate to their office. Many of the women were daughters of the highest-ranking men, including strategoi of Cyprus and other officials, and bearers of aulic (honorific) titles. The same families appear again and again in the lists. Three daughters of Theodorus, strategus of Cyprus, were appointed to eponymous priesthoods in one year. There are several other examples of sisters and cousins serving within a short interval.[98]

The priestesses were not appointed at the acme of their father's career, but rather after several years had elapsed. How old they were cannot be precisely determined, since the only datable event in the lives of most of the priestesses is their tenure of the sacred offices. From the observation that a daughter's appointment was a facet of her father's honor, we may suppose that the daughter was young and not yet married. If she had been married, she would have been considered part of her husband's family, and the honor to her father would have been more remote.

The canephoroi who walked in the Panathenaic procession in Athens had to be young virgins of unblemished reputation.[99] Sexually experienced women were not explicitly taboo in Alexandria, but most of the canephoroi presumably were virgins. The norm was breached—as it later was at the Thesmophoria—by royal mistresses. Bilistiche was chosen as canephore for 251/250 B.C., when she must have been at least thirty years old. Agathoclea was canephore in 213/212 B.C. Since she owned a ship in 215 B.C.,[100] she must have been old enough to be Philopator's mistress when she was canephore.

The priestess of Arsinoë Philopator held office for life and was not obliged to be a virgin. The Eirene who was named on the Rosetta Stone is the first woman attested in this office.[101] She was the daughter of Ptolemaeus, a strategus of Cyprus, and her son erected a statue in her honor on the island. Evidence confirms her tenure for 199/198–171/170 B.C., but she probably held the office from its inception in 203 B.C. Among the priestesses of Arsinoë Philopator are good examples of long-lived women. Another Artemo, daughter of Seleucus and sister of Theodorus, held this priesthood from 141/140 to 116/115 B.C.[102]

To be the canephore of Arsinoë Philadelphus was a demanding job for a young woman.[103] In Alexandria, there was only one canephore, and she led a grand procession, followed by *prytaneis* (city officials), ephebes (youths), and wand-bearers.[104] The Alexandrian populace lined the streets in celebration.

The canephore, as her name indicates, carried a basket; the basket was gold and contained offerings or implements needed for ceremonies. Greek women usually carried baskets on their heads. The daughters of the Ptolemaic nobility must have needed to practice before serving as canephore, for surely they had rarely had to bear burdens on their heads—leaving such labor to slaves.

In 211/210 B.C., Ptolemy Philopator inaugurated a special cult in honor of his mother, Berenice II. A new eponymous priesthood was created; the holder of the office was titled athlophore. The word means "prize-bearer" and may refer to Berenice's victories in the chariot races. What the athlophore actually did, in addition to lending her name to the year, is not known. She took precedence over the canephore in dating protocols. As we have noted above, the same woman usually served as athlophore and canephore in successive years.

In addition to the priestess of Arsinoë Philopator, the canephore of Arsinoë Philadelphus, and the athlophore of Berenice II, there were other sacred offices designated for women.[105] The importance of these positions varied through time. Moreover, there were other cults open to women. The Thesmophoria was reserved for women, and the cult of Adonis was extremely popular among them.[106] Of course, women were enthusiastic participants in the great variety of religious activities available in Ptolemaic Egypt.[107] The occasional appearance of Egyptian names in the lists of eponymous priests merely hints at the appeal that the indigenous religion held even for members of the Ptolemaic nobility.[108] Two principles that pertained to Greek women in other places and at other times were true as well of Alexandrian women: First, religion was the only state-supported activity that reserved an official place for women. Second, religion was an area of particular interest to women.

## EDUCATION

Religious festivals in Alexandria must have required that some women, at least, be literate, for female choirs had to be able to read words and musical notation.[109] The upper-class girls who were raised with Ptolemaic princesses must have been educated along with them by royal tutors (see p. 51). The tradition of educating the female members of the Macedonian ruling houses can be traced as far back as Eurydice, mother of Philip II. Of her own volition she learned to read and write when she was already the mother of mature sons. Olympias may have been literate, too, for she and Alexander exchanged letters, although they probably employed secretaries in any case. The royal women in the early generations of the courts of the successors were not merely literate but became active patronesses of erudite literature. Arsinoë II was patroness of Theocritus for a time; Berenice II of Callimachus; and Phila, wife of Antigonus, played a similar role toward Aratus.

If the education of princesses provided the occasion for the education of the daughters of the nobility who were raised with them, the question is whether educated women can be found at successively lower levels of Alexandrian society. There is no direct evidence for elementary education for either boys or girls in Ptolemaic Alexandria. Schools did exist elsewhere in the Hellenistic world; some of these were endowed and provided a free education for children of both sexes. Otherwise, education was private. The wealthy, like royalty, would obtain private tutors—often slaves—who instructed children at home. At the next economic level, parents would bring their children to schoolmasters who taught a number of children for a fee. Because of the ab-

sence of relevant papyri, there are no contracts or letters between schoolmasters and parents from Ptolemaic Alexandria
(but there is abundant documentation from Roman Egypt).[110]
Some girls certainly could read. Terracotta figurines from Ptolemaic sites in Alexandria portray girls and young women looking
at diptychs in their lap (Plate 7).[111] The cloaks worn by some of
the girls suggest that they received their schooling outside the
home. Terracottas were not manufactured for a wealthy elite.
They were mass-produced in molds and priced accordingly.
The historian must assume that the activities portrayed on terracottas record the realities of everyday life of people comfortable
enough to afford more than the bare necessities.

Terracottas also depict girls and young women dancing and
playing musical instruments (Plate 8). Music and dancing were
two facets of *mousikē* (the musical arts). According to Aristotle,
the subjects in the basic curriculum were reading and writing,
gymnastics, the musical arts, and—some add as the fourth—
painting.[112] The curriculum of boys and girls was the same, except that respectable girls did not practice gymnastics. Instead,
they received their physical exercise by dancing. Musical accomplishments could enhance the reputation of a respectable
woman. On the grave stela of Nico, an Alexandrian citizen,
daughter of Timon, the dead woman is seated in a mournful
pose (Plate 13). A small girl offers her a lyre.[113]

Some of the women went beyond the rudiments of elementary
education to attain a high level of achievement in the liberal arts.
The only evidence that women painted in Alexandria is that
there were two professional artists.[114] One was Helena, daughter
of the artist Timon of Egypt.[115] She lived at the end of the
fourth century B.C. and painted a scene of the battle of Issus that
was brought to Rome and displayed in the Forum of Peace in the
days of Vespasian. Her painting may have served as the original
of the extant "Alexander mosaic" from Pompeii. Another professional artist who may have lived in Alexandria was Anaxandra,[116] daughter of the artist Nealces. The achievements of
these women painters must be attributed more to the fact that
they were both daughters of painters than to any opportunity
they may have had to study painting at school.

Female scholars and philosophers worked in Alexandria. As
was true for the artists, these women often chose to work in the
same area as their fathers. Agallis was the daughter of Agallias,
who was himself a pupil of Aristophanes of Byzantium.[117] She
came from Corcyra, the island that was thought to be the Phaeacia
of the *Odyssey*. Agallis patriotically declared that her country-
woman Nausicaa had invented ball-playing, doubtless because
she was the first person in literature to be portrayed playing with
a ball. Hestiaea was a grammarian who wrote a treatise on
whether the Trojan War had been fought around the city named
Ilium in her own day.[118] The achievements of Agallis and Hestiaea may seem trivial, but they are typical of the pedestrian brand
of Alexandrian scholarship, whose practitioners were mostly
men. The work of Diophila may have been more inspiring. The
scholia on Callimachus may be interpreted as stating that the poet
consulted a poem on astronomy by Diophila for his writing of the
*Aetia*.[119] Since serious Greek writing on astronomy did not pre-
cede Eudoxus (ca. 390–340 B.C.), Diophila's poem must be dated
at the earliest to the late fourth or early third century.

The writing of Agallis, Hestiaea, and Diophila has not survived, but approximately fifty lines on musical theory written by
Ptolemaïs are extant.[120] Ptolemaïs came from Cyrene to Alexandria around 250 B.C. Although in a dispute between the Neopythagoreans and Peripatetics she supported the doctrines of
the latter, because of her subject matter scholars have considered her a Neopythagorean.

The largest number of women philosophers in the Hellenistic
period appear among the Neopythagoreans, and some of the
Neopythagorean pseudepigrapha are attributed to women.[121]
These works constitute the only extant body of Greek prose
literature attributed to women in the pre-Christian era; for this
reason they deserve attention here. Conjectures about their
dates range from the fourth century B.C. to the second century
A.D.[122] Some of these were written in Alexandria, and others in
Southern Italy. According to the most recent editor of these
texts, works originating in the East tended to be written in the
Ionic dialect, while those from the West used Doric.[123] Literature circulated between the two settlements, for letters of Me-

7. Terracotta figurines showing girls reading. The cloak suggests schooling outside the home. *Alexandria. Graeco-Roman Museum.*

8. Elegant woman with a lyre. Terracotta. *Alexandria. Graeco-Roman Museum.*

lissa and Theano were discovered paraphrased from the Doric version in a recently published papyrus (*P. Haunienses* II 13).

Some scholars have doubted that the authors of the Neopythagorean treatises were actually women, and suggested that men who adopted the names of earlier female disciples and relatives of Pythagoras as pseudonyms wrote them. The arguments against female authorship consists of two parts: (1) the names of the women authors are pseudonyms, and (2) the treatises were written by men using the pseudonyms.[124]

Some of the authors have unexceptional names such as Melissa and Phintys. Such names occur elsewhere in the Greek world and have no particular significance in a philosophical context. There would have been no point in forging works under a name like this unless such a name were found among Pythagoras' female disciples. Other authors are named for Theano (wife of Pythagoras), Myia and Arignote (his daughters), and Perictione (Plato's mother). Several of the male authors as well—for example, Archytas, Cleinias, Megillus, Milon, and Lysis—bear names that appear in earlier Pythagorean and Platonic traditions.

It is likely that the names are authentic, for, as a declaration of principle, Neopythagoreans would give their daughters names that occurred in the Pythagorean tradition. The names of children often reflected (and still do) their parents' religious persuasions or intellectual interests.[125] Naming children for their ancestors is a statement of familial solidarity; by naming their offspring after earlier Pythagoreans, the Neopythagoreans strengthened their bonds with their spiritual forebears. Moreover, disciples sometimes marry the daughters of their teachers. Thus Aristotle's will directed that his daughter marry Nicanor or Theophrastus; later, among the Neoplatonists, Theagenes, benefactor of Marinus, married Asclepigenia daughter of Archiadas.[126] Couples such as these expressed their spiritual affiliation and their blood filiation simultaneously in choosing names for their children.

There were precedents for the activities of the Neopythagorean women. Iamblichus named 17 women among the 235 disciples of Pythagoras whom he lists,[127] and Philochorus, who died in the 260s and may therefore have known some Neopythagorean women, wrote a volume on Pythagorean women.[128] Among the original Pythagoreans, women participated on equal terms with men.[129] This phenomenon was unique in the Greek world of the sixth and fifth centuries B.C. That the philosopher himself was responsible for this innovation or at least thoroughly approved is indicated by the fact that the women mentioned by name included his wife and daughters. According to Diogenes Laertius, Theano wrote a few things.[130] This part of the story is not necessarily true, although it need not be totally rejected.[131] In the Classical period, there were some literate women. Richard Bentley apparently did not believe this report about women's participation at all: in a discussion of the authenticity of a Neopythagorean treatise ascribed to Perictione, he wrote, "[The forgers of treatises simply] thought it a point of decorum, to make even the female kindred of philosophers copy after the men."[132] The *Speeches of Pythagoras*, which have been dated to the late fifth or early fourth century, are an early source for the tradition about women's participation in Pythagorean society. The speeches are addressed to both men and women, and include discussion of appropriate behavior for women.[133] Although the tradition about women's participation, like others concerning the life of Pythagoras, is not preserved by a contemporary author, there is no need to assume that it is entirely a biographical fiction. The original Pythagoreans lived together in close-knit communities, abiding by a strict discipline extending to dietary matters, wearing apparel, and the proper seasons for sexual intercourse. Under such circumstances, it would have been mandatory that both sexes understand the doctrines.

Both among the original Pythagoreans and among the Neopythagoreans, such women must have read philosophy or sat in on classes or lectures or informal discussions. Indeed, the statement of Lysistrata that she was instructed by listening to her father and other older men in her family is perfectly credible and pertinent here.[134]

It is not surprising that female philosophers in antiquity often were related to philosophers. Arete of Cyrene was the daughter of Socrates' companion Aristippus. Her son Aristippus, who was nicknamed "Mother's Disciple," was the founder of the Cyrenaic school.[135] In the case of Hipparchia, her brother Metrocles was the catalyst. Crates the Cynic visited Metrocles, who had been a Peripatetic, and inspired him to become his follower. Hipparchia was captivated as well.[136] Magnilla, a philosopher who was both a daughter and a wife of philosophers, is named in an inscription from Apollonia in Mysia.[137] Phila of Macedonia, though not a full-fledged philosopher herself, apparently was attracted to philosophy through the influence of her son Antigonus Gonatas. Antigonus was himself a philosopher and entertained other philosophers at his court. A painting from Boscoreale after a Greek original of the middle of the third century B.C. depicts Phila and Antigonus listening to a philosopher who may be the Cynic Menedemus of Eretria. Phila is in the foreground, gazing up at the philosopher, showing much more interest than Antigonus.[138] One of the most famous female philosophers, Hypatia, was the head of the Neoplatonic school at Alexandria in the late fourth and early fifth centuries A.D. Her father, Theon, had been in charge of the school before her. Thus the Neopythagorean authors, especially those bearing philosophically significant names—like other creative women working in philosophy, scholarship, and art—simply followed their male relatives' careers.

Women participated in some of the other Hellenistic philosophical groups, including Epicureanism and Cynicism and, earlier in the fourth century, Platonism.[139] Moreover, for the period just after the one being discussed here, there is ample evidence for women's involvement in philosophical and religious groups, particularly in the eastern part of the Roman Empire.[140] Some scholars have attributed some of the early anonymous Christian literature to female authors.[141]

In the case of Neopythagoreans, we are dealing not with anonymous literature but with a substantial amount of writing with female bylines. Learned Neopythagorean women were lampooned in at least three New Comedies.[142] Cratinus the Younger wrote that it was the custom of these pedants, if they came upon a stranger, to examine him on doctrines and to confuse and confound him with antitheses, definitions, and equations, crammed with digressions and magnitudes.[143] Considering that the other Alexandrian women—including Ptolemaïs, Hestiaea, Agallis, and perhaps Diophila—were capable of writing on subjects more difficult than those discussed in the Neopythagorean moral treatises, there is no reason to believe that the education of women would have not rendered them adequate to the task of writing the pseudepigrapha. In fact, if some contemporary women did not write prose treatises, and if the very notion that women could write such works were considered outlandish, there would have been no point in circulating such treatises under women's names.

Hypercritical scholarship suggests that, because women were the subject of these treatises, they were published under women's names to win them credibility among their readers.[144] Thus, two Greek sex manuals were purportedly written by women, but their female authorship was doubted even in antiquity.[145] Similar arguments have been proposed denying that the female poet Erinna wrote "The Distaff." Because the extant fragments of the poem deal with girlhood and mention dolls, a mother, and young wives, it has been asserted that the man who wrote the poem cleverly adopted a female pseudonym to lend the flavor of authenticity.[146] I have argued elsewhere that Erinna is, in fact, the author.[147] Nevertheless, assuming that such an argument has validity, it is necessary to examine the Neopythagorean writings attributed to women from this point of view. A large portion of the work attributed to women does deal with the proper conduct of women, but not all of it does. For example, although both of them wrote about women, Perictione also wrote on wisdom and Theano wrote on the theory of numbers and the immortality of the soul. Furthermore, male writers also spoke of women. Callicratidas described marriage as a harmony of opposites. Works on women's obligations in religion, marriage, general conduct, and avoidance of luxury were attributed to Pythagoras himself.

Thus, adhering closely to Pythagorean doctrine, the Neopythagorean treatises by women and about women discuss the proper behavior of women, recommending, for the most part, purity, control of one's appetites, and tolerance of a husband's vices. The authors are notably preoccupied with the temptations of adultery. Excessive use of makeup, fine clothing, and frequent bathing are viewed as preludes to seduction. Many of the ideas in these treatises were traditional in Greek thought. Precedents can be found in the most misogynistic of earlier authors, Hesiod and Semonides. Yet these attitudes need not persuade us that the Neopythagorean treatises were written by men. It would be unreasonable to expect the Neopythagorean women to write like modern feminists. Orthodox writings by women were much more likely to gain publication and circulation than radical works.

The Neopythagorean Perictione bore the name of Plato's mother. This name was an obvious one for a Neopythagorean to give to a daughter, since Plato had had links with Pythagoreanism and, like Pythagoras, had had female pupils.[148] According to Perictione, the ideal woman was harmonious:

> We must deem the harmonious woman to be one who is well endowed with wisdom and temperance. For her soul must be very wise indeed when it comes to virtue so that she will be just and courageous [lit. "manly"], while being sensible and beautified with self-sufficiency, despising empty opinion. For from these qualities fair deeds accrue to a woman for herself as well as for her husband, children, and home: and perchance even to a city, if in fact, such a woman were to govern cities or peoples, as we see in the case of a legitimate monarchy. Surely, by controlling her desire and passion, a woman becomes devout and harmonious, resulting in her not becoming a prey to impious love affairs. Rather, she will be full of love for her husband and children and her entire household. For all those women who have a desire for extramarital relations [lit. "alien beds"] themselves become enemies of all the freedmen and domestics in the house. Such a woman contrives both falsehood and deceits for her husband and tells lies against everyone to him as well, so that she alone seems to excel in good will and in mastery over the household, though she revels in idleness. For from all these activities comes the ruination that jointly afflicts the woman as well as her husband. And so let these precepts be pronounced before the women of today.
>
> With regard to the sustenance and natural requirements of the body, it must be provided with a proper measure of clothing, bathing, anointing, hair-setting, and all those items of gold and pre-

cious stones that are used for adornment. For women who eat and drink all sorts of extravagant dishes and dress themselves sumptuously, wearing things that women are given to wearing, are decked out for seduction into all manner of vice, not only the bed but also the commission of other wrongful deeds. And so, a woman must merely satisfy her hunger and thirst, and if she is of the poorer class, her chill, if she has a cloak made of goatskin. To be consumers of goods from far-off lands or of items that cost a great amount of money or are highly esteemed is manifestly no small vice. And to wear dresses that are excessively styled and elaborately dyed with purple or some other color is a foolish indulgence in extravagance. For the body desires merely not to be cold or, for the sake of appearances, naked; but it needs nothing else. Men's opinion runs ignorantly after inanities and oddities. So that a woman will neither cover herself with gold or the stone of India or of any other place, nor will she braid her hair with artful device; nor will she anoint herself with Arabian perfume; nor will she put white makeup on her face or rouge her cheeks or darken her brows and lashes or artfully dye her graying hair; nor will she bathe frequently. For by pursuing these things a woman seeks to make a spectacle of female incontinence. The beauty that comes from wisdom and not from these things brings pleasure to women who are well born.

Let a woman not think that noble birth and wealth and coming from a great city and having the esteem and love of illustrious and royal men are necessities. For if a woman is well off, she has nothing to complain about, if not, it doesn't do to yearn. A clever woman is not prevented from living without these benefits. Even if whatever falls to her lot be great and marvelous, let not the soul strive for them, but let it walk far away from them. For they do more harm than good when someone drags a woman into trouble. Treachery, malice, and spite are associated with them, so that a woman so endowed could never be serene. A woman must reverence the gods if she hopes for happiness, obeying the ancestral laws and institutions. And I name after these [the gods], her parents, whom she must honor and reverence. For parents are in all respects equivalent to gods and they act in the interest of their grandchildren.

A woman must live for her husband according to law and in actuality, thinking no private thoughts of her own, but taking care of her marriage and guarding it. For everything depends on this.

A woman must bear all that her husband bears, whether he be
unlucky or sin out of ignorance, whether he be sick or drunk or
sleep with other women. For this latter fault is peculiar to men, but
never to women. Rather it brings vengeance upon her. Therefore,
a woman must preserve the law and not emulate men. And she
must endure her husband's temper, stinginess, complaining, jeal-
ousy, abuse, and anything else peculiar to his nature. And she will
deal with all of his characteristics in such a way as is congenial to
him by being discreet. For a woman who is affectionate to her
husband and treats him in an agreeable way is a harmonious
woman and one who loves her whole household and makes everyone in it well disposed. But when a woman has no love in her, she
has no desire to look upon her home or children or slaves or their
security whatsoever, but yearns for them to go to perdition just as
an enemy would; and she prays for her husband to die as she
would a foe, hating everybody who pleases him, just so she can
sleep with other men. Thus, I think a woman is harmonious if she
is full of sagacity and temperance. For she will not only help her
husband but also her children, relatives, slaves, and her whole
household, in which reside all her possessions and her dear kin and
friends. She will conduct their home with simplicity, speaking and
hearing fair words and holding views on their common mode of
living that are compatible, while acting in concert with those relatives and friends whom her husband extols. And if her husband
thinks something is sweet, she will think so too; or if he thinks
something bitter, she will agree with him. Otherwise she will be out
of tune with her whole universe.[149]

In a harmonious person, reason and the passions are in total
balance and attunement—like the stretched strings of a lyre. In
keeping with the musical metaphor, *sophrosyne* has been translated as "temperance," but it also connotes chastity and self-
restraint. *Sophrosyne* was the preeminent virtue of Greek women;
it is mentioned more frequently than any other quality on
women's tombstones.[150] The Neopythagoreans did not restrict
*sophrosyne* to women, but considered it especially appropriate for
married people.[151]

The first three beneficiaries of a woman's virtue (husband,
children, and home) are traditional in Greek thought. The
one good type of woman listed in Semonides' *Diatribe Against*

*Women* causes her husband's "property to grow and increase, and she grows old with a husband whom she loves and who loves her, the mother of a handsome and reputable family."[152] That a woman can win acclaim by governing is a more unusual idea, doubtless inspired by Hellenistic queens and perhaps by contemporary and earlier barbarian monarchs of the East. It should be observed, in contrast, that Phintys, a member of the western group of Neopythagoreans earlier in the Hellenistic period, declared that women should not take part in government.[153]

The Hellenistic period was a time of renascence for women poets. Although poets of any sex are never numerous, the Hellenistic period was reminiscent of the Archaic in that women poets were not anomalous. Those of the Hellenistic period include Nossis, Anyte, Moero, Philaenis, and Hedyle, and perhaps Erinna, Melinno, and Corinna. Traveling women poets and musicians are also known, for the most part through inscriptions that record their victories.[154] However, none of these illustrious poets or musicians was born in or visited Alexandria, although some of their work did influence the male poets who wrote there in the third century B.C. On the other hand, Alexandria was a center of scholarship, and the only women scholars and prose writers of the Hellenistic period worked there.

We should beware of assuming that the majority of women in Alexandria were artists or intellectuals. This generalization would not apply to men either. Most women, no doubt, were like the housewives portrayed by Theocritus in *Idyll* 15, concerned with children, husband, cooking, clothing, prices, other women friends, domestic slaves, and having a little innocent fun when the opportunity presented itself in the guise of religion. Luxury of the sort that the Neopythagorean Perictione railed against must have also brought pleasure to the Alexandrian women who could afford it.

The education and achievements of women in Ptolemaic Alexandria were fairly typical of those of Greek women elsewhere in the same period. Inscriptions and terracotta figurines testify to the spread of elementary education for girls in many areas inhabited by Greeks. Like their counterparts elsewhere, many of the Alexandrian women who attained special distinction in the liberal arts followed in their father's footsteps. Where the woman's lineage and family connection are indicated, it is usually by patronymic and place of birth. Although this pattern of naming does not necessarily exclude a husband, it appears that the influence of fathers on their daughters in choosing careers was far more substantial than that of husbands on wives. In the Hellenistic period, the fathers of women artists provided their daughters with the professional skills they might use to support themselves even in lieu of marriage. In fact, one famous woman artist from Cyzicus who worked at Rome is known to have been highly successful financially and to have remained unmarried.[155] The woman scholars, in contrast, pursued knowledge for its own sake. Although some male scholars were granted financial support by the Ptolemies, female scholars were not similarly favored. We may observe that the accomplishments of Hestiaea and Diophila mentioned in the ancient sources were limited to the publication of one work apiece. If what appear to be extremely modest publication records are not simply artifacts of the vagaries of textual transmission, the reason may be that these scholars had just enough time to write one work while they were young women still living at home with their fathers, but that their creativity was finally curtailed by the duties of marriage and motherhood.

## WOMEN IN ALEXANDRIAN LITERATURE

Many themes of epitaphs composed in Alexandria for women were traditional in the Greco-Roman world.[156] There are examples of lamentation for the young bride who died before bearing children,[157] for the woman whose death was due to childbirth,[158] and for the woman who is mourned by husband and children.[159] The vicissitudes of life in the Hellenistic period added new themes. Epitaphs express regret that the deceased woman died far from her native land and blood relatives. Although surely a relative or a neighbor or friend paid for the tombstone and commissioned a poet to write an epitaph, or saw to it that the will of the deceased woman to this effect was carried

out, the sense that the woman was isolated in Egypt is under-
lined. Bio, for example, emigrated to Egypt at a fairly advanced
age:

> Five daughters and five sons did Bio bear to Didymon,
> but she reaped no joy from any one of them.
> Virtuous, favored with offspring, when she died, Bio was buried
> not by her children but by strange hands.[160]

The remains of a woman who had left Athens to work at the
court in Alexandria were brought back home by her mother.
Her epitaph was found in Sunium, in Attica:

> An Athenian mother once raised her daughter
> to be a lady-in-waiting in foreign halls.
> She hastened for her daughter's sake and came to the palace of the king
> who had put her in charge of his abundant property
> Nevertheless, she did not bring her home alive.
> But at least she has a grave in Athens, instead of Libyan sand.[161]

Hellenistic epigrams supply a great deal of information on
women of the demimonde. Although the epigrams may not be
biographical in the strict sense, and the women named may have
been fictional, it seems reasonable to assume that the situations
and personalities described in the poems had real-life counterparts. Like Bio and the Athenian daughter who worked in Alexandria, the women encountered in epigrams were often immigrants without family in Egypt. As seems to have been the case
with Simaetha (in Theocritus' *Idyll* 2), some may have originally
come to Egypt with male relatives. However, when their relatives
died or went away on military service, they were left alone. In
the older Greek cities, such girls would become the wards of
more distant male relatives or of a magistrate such as the archon
basileus at Athens. In Alexandria, they were on their own, free
of both male control and protection. Like Gorgo and Praxinoa
(in Theocritus' *Idyll* 15), who preferred each other's company
because they were both Syracusans, unattached women sought
the company of others from their native land. Women immi-

grants from Samos paid Callimachus to write the epigram of
their friend Crethis:

> *The daughters of the Samians often seek Crethis,*
> *so full of stories, so skilled in pretty games,*
> *their sweetest coworker in wool, always chattering.*
> *But here she sleeps the sleep due to every woman.*[162]

Several women probably contributed small amounts to pay the
poet's fee, for the salary of a female woolworker was not generous. In one of his epigrams, Asclepiades mentions a woman who
worked as a seller of perfume.[163] Like unattached women without much money in large cities at other times and in other
places, some of these women drifted into relationships with
men, who invited them to parties and had sexual intercourse
with some of them. The epigrammatists write of these women,
sometimes describing the postures in which they enjoyed intercourse. Whether they should be called *hetairai* depends on the
viewpoint of the person doing the labeling.

The Athenians of the Classical period knew of three categories of women. In the speech "Against Neaera," an orator classified these women from the male point of view: mistresses
(*hetairai*) for the sake of pleasure, concubines (*pallakai*) for daily
service to the body, and wives (*gynaikes*) to bear legitimate children and to be the faithful guardians of the household.[164] The
*hetairai*, in this context, must include all women who were paid
for their sexual favors—ranging from high-priced courtesans
such as Aspasia and Thaïs to prostitutes in waterfront brothels.
A concubine was a woman with whom a man had a long-term
liaison, sometimes with legal implications that make the status
of a concubine closer to that of a wife than of a prostitute. For
the Athenians, as for others in periods when sexuality was
strictly regulated, any woman except a concubine who chose to
have sexual intercourse with a man who was not her husband
was either a *hetaira* or a prostitute. Respectable women could
not even speak to men who were not their relatives except at a
religious festival. To be sure, such a standard remained in
force among some groups in Alexandria. Gorgo and Praxinoa

were Syracusans, and Dorian women had always enjoyed more freedom than Ionians such as the Athenians. The women in Theocritus' *Idyll* 15 walk through the streets of the city escorted by their slaves. They are in a situation where they can speak to strange men only because they are at a festival. Simaetha, in Theocritus' *Idyll* 2, lived in her own house and was left with an old nurse as a chaperone. Nurses are notoriously poor chaperones, since they are most interested in the happiness of their young charges, and, being slaves, they have no power to oppose them. Thus Simaetha was smitten by a young man at a religious festival, and her nurse permitted her lover to visit her at home.

Brief and painful love affairs appear as well in the Alexandrian epigrams. Like Theocritus, the epigrammatist Asclepiades wrote a lament for a women rejected by a lover. Although the couple still frequent the same society, he does not even pay light-hearted attention to her.[165] However, the unattached women in the Alexandrian epigrams seem to belong to a lower stratum of society than Simaetha. They are too poor to have a slave as chaperone. They have no need to preserve their virginity, for without kinsmen to supply a dowry, they will never find a husband. There can be no doubt that some of the women became streetwalkers. Alexandria was a cosmopolitan city and there was plenty of prostitution. Procurers and prostitutes appear in the work of Machon and Herodas, and many are found as well in the epigrams. However, scholars in the recent past—a period of sexual liberation in comparison to Classical Athens— have tended to a less censorious view of some of the women in Alexandrian epigrams.[166] They have argued that those for whom financial remuneration was not foremost should not be labeled prostitutes or *hetairai*. In fact, that two of the poet Asclepiades' friends preferred a lesbian relationship proves that they, at least, were not primarily in quest of lucre. Although the poets themselves addressed erotic epigrams to boys, Asclepiades wrote about the lesbians with indignation:

> *The Samians Bitto and Nannion will not enter the precinct of Aphrodite according to the rules of the goddess herself.*

*But they desert to other things which are not seemly.*
*O Cyprian, hate these fugitives from your ways of love.*[167]

Asclepiades invented the erotic epigram. The genesis of this genre in the third century B.C. has been examined in the context of literary history.[168] The appearance of the love interest in Hellenistic literature may also be attributed to human emotions and historical phenomena. The love epigram as a purely selfish declaration of interest in another person is certainly consistent with other manifestations of individualism in the Hellenistic period. In the Classical period, in tragedy, romantic love was viewed as antisocial. The love of Phaedra for Hippolytus, of Medea for Jason, of Heracles for Iole, and of Haemon for Antigone, for example, conflicted with obligations toward kin and state, and finally destroyed entire families and cities. In the milieu of the Alexandrian poets, in contrast, there were fewer attachments to kin group and state. Romantic liaisons between individuals flourished in their stead. For the demimonde, romantic love created the social bonds that in other societies of Greeks were generated by such patterns of human interaction as the exchange of women in marriage or adherence to the same political faction.[169]

The epigrammatist Hedylus lived in Alexandria during the reign of Ptolemy Philadelphus. Both his mother (Hedyle) and his grandmother (Moschine) had been poets.[170] According to an epigram of Hedylus, a beauty contest for women was held at Alexandria, probably during a festival of Priapus:

> *The halter and the purple chiton and the Laconian dresses*
> *and gold piping for the chiton*
> *were all awarded to Niconoë,*
> *for the girl was an ambrosial blossom of the Erotes and Graces.*
> *Therefore to Priapus who judged the beauty contest*
> *she dedicated a fawnskin and this golden jug.*[171]

Modern readers should not be inevitably offended, as they might be by a "Miss America" contest. An awareness of women's beauty permeates Greek thought from the earliest times and appears in authors—such as Sappho, Alcman, and Homer—who have the greatest sense of women's worth.[172] It was also traditional to evaluate the particular features of women, rating them, for example, according to the appearance of ankles, stature, or hair. The judging of women, part by part, reached the ultimate absurdity in a story told about the selection of a model for a painting of Helen. Zeuxis, the fourth-century painter, did not believe he could find perfection in one body. Consequently, he selected five beautiful women and copied the best parts of each.[173]

There were several antecedents for beauty contests among Greek women. The competition among Athena, Hera, and Aphrodite that was judged by Paris provided a mythical precedent. The historical competitions among mortals were conducted in the context of religious celebrations. Annual beauty contests were held at Lesbos in a religious sanctuary, and there were competitions as well in Tenedos.[174] At Elis, the winners performed special sacred services. In Arcadia, beauty contests were held at the festival of Demeter of Eleusis. The winners got to wear golden garments. This contest was founded in the Archaic period and was still held in Athenaeus' time.[175] There is no reason to make any assumptions about the respectability of women who participated in a beauty contest conducted at a festival in honor of Priapus. The obvious attribute of Priapus was a huge phallus, but in Alexandria his power as a fertility god had been generalized so that he was regarded as a bringer of wealth.[176] Terracotta figurines give us an idea of the standard of female beauty in Alexandria (see Plate 8). The women appear tall, slender, and elegant, with graceful long necks and blond hair. They are often attired in rich clothing such as Niconoë won in the beauty contest.

The employment of the woman's viewpoint is a remarkable and novel feature of some Alexandrian literature. The reasons for any cultural change are always complex, and the study of Alexandrian literature can be approached in many ways. The following brief discussion will be limited to the presentation of some images of women in Alexandrian literature and to the influence of women in the creation of this literature. It should not be construed as a general statement pertaining to the entire range of literature produced in Alexandria.

Ptolemaic queens played a substantial role as patronesses of culture. Authors' perceptions regarding the preferences of royalty certainly influenced the literature they created. Theocritus' "Adoniazusae" (*Idyll* 15) was written for a festival sponsored by a woman, Arsinoë II, in honor of her mother, Berenice I. Aphrodite, the presiding divinity, was female, and her lover, Adonis, was the object of a cult that was especially popular among women. The chief entertainer was female and she was identified by a matronymic. The festivity was described by two women, Gorgo and Praxinoa, and they commented on features of the morning's activity that were of interest to women.[177] To them, a horse was little more than a horse, but they were impressed by the tapestry. The song too draws attention to items of interest to women: fruit trees, gardens, perfume, confections, luxurious domestic funishings, and a young and gentle bridegroom.

Theocritus also gives the woman's viewpoint in his second idyll. Before she encountered Delphis, Simaetha was totally involved in the company of women. These women finally persuaded her to attend the festival at which she met Delphis, and lent her clothing so that she could wear something new for the occasion. The tryst of Simaetha and her lover was similar to that of Aphrodite and Adonis in that it occurred in the privacy of her own home. There can be no greater contrast between Theocritus' placement of amorous couples in comfortable private settings and the group sex scenes portrayed in the art and literature of Classical Athens.[178]

In *Idyll* 2, Theocritus provides a psychological portrait of the jilted woman, strictly from the woman's point of view. Euripides, it is true, had been aware of the male bias of Greek literature. The female chorus of his tragedy *Medea* had declared:

> Streams of holy rivers run backward, and universal custom is overturned. Men have deceitful thoughts; no longer are their oaths steadfast. My reputation shall change, my manner of life have good report. Esteem shall come to the female sex. No longer will malicious rumor fasten upon women. The Muses of ancient poets

will cease to sing of my unfaithfulness. Apollo, god of song, did not grant us the divine power of the lyre. Otherwise I would have sung an answer to the male sex.[179]

Euripides was a maverick among Athenian authors. Even so, despite his frequently sympathetic portrayals of women, he presents heroines such as Medea, whose passions and suffering lead her to kill the innocent, even to murder her own children. In the *Argonautica*, Apollonius "of Rhodes," who worked in Alexandria in the third century B.C., presents a less savage Medea. For example, Medea's brother pursued the couple when they fled from Colchis with the golden fleece. According to one mythical tradition, Medea killed her brother and dismembered him. However, in Apollonius' epic, Jason performed this gory deed. Apollonius' Medea is like Theocritus' Simaetha in that both are more ardent lovers than their male partners. It is traditional in Athenian New Comedy for a young man to catch sight of a girl at a festival and to rape her. In a reversal of this story pattern, Simaetha and Medea (with divine prompting) fell in love and took the initiative. Both Simaetha and Medea were women suffering from intense physical desire for a man. There is no condemnation of these women for their feelings. En route, Medea and Jason encountered Circe. She, too, is kinder than the Circe of earlier literature and does not transform men into swine. Apollonius concludes his epic before the calamitous events in Medea's life that Euripides chose to dramatize.

Apollonius' predecessor, Callimachus, had radically transformed the epic. No longer was the protagonist a male adventurer viewing females in relationship to his own needs. Heroines were no longer simply those women who managed to endure the havoc created by men. Instead, in *Hecale,* Callimachus invented a new type of protagonist.[180] Hecale was an old woman of humble background. Because of her generosity to Theseus when he was in quest of the bull of Marathon, he awarded her heroic honors. The focus of the poem is on her goodness rather than on his conquest.

Finally, there are several epigrams in defense of women whom earlier literature had maligned. Although these women may have been fictional, the epigrammatists treat them as historical personages. The Archaic poet Archilochus had written of his courtship and seduction of the daughters of Lycambes.[181] When Lycambes rejected him as a suitor, the poet made public the sexual experiences of the girls. In an epigram of Dioscurides, the daughters of Lycambes point out that if they had truly been wanton, then Archilochus would never have wanted to make them the mothers of his legitimate children.[182] Dioscurides also wrote a paradoxical epigram in defense of Philaenis. Philaenis of Samos was said to have been the author of an erotic handbook. In Dioscurides' poem she announces, "I am not the woman who wrote these works offensive to women. . . . I was modest."[183]

An enlightened interest in women can be traced not only in poetry and the novel but also in the scientific writings of Alexandria. Herophilus, who worked at Alexandria in the first half of the third century B.C., is responsible for great advances in gynecology.[184] In an earlier period, the Hippocratics had also been interested in women, and a larger proportion of the Hippocratic corpus is devoted to obstetrics and gynecology than to any other field of medicine. But the doctors of the Classical period were influenced by contemporary mores and often recommended marriage, heterosexual intercourse, and motherhood as panaceas. Moreover, the Hippocratics were woefully ignorant of the female anatomy and believed that the womb could migrate throughout the body cavity and cause such complications as hysterical suffocation. Herophilus, in contrast, understood the female anatomy, for he dissected human subjects. The Ptolemies were said to have supplied him with prisoners for the purpose of vivisection. Among prisoners of war, there would have been an adequate supply of women as well as men, although some of Herophilus' descriptions of the female pelvic anatomy indicate that he examined female animals as well.[185] He was the first to describe the ovaries, and possibly the Fallopian tubes. While previous physicians employed euphemisms such as *aidoia* ("the shameful parts") to describe the female genitalia, Herophilus was the first to put Greek words for the female anatomy into a medical context. He also wrote a treatise *On Midwifery*. Herophilus is cited by Soranus and Galen, often as the authority in passages where a woman's general well-being is given precedence over her reproductive potential.

For example, Soranus quotes Herophilus as saying that virginity is not harmful.[186] Other doctors were much concerned to regulate menstruation, not only for women's health but because they saw it as essential to childbearing, but Herophilus asserted that in some women menstruation is harmful.[187] The Hippocratics saw women (like old men and children) as exceptions to the rules that govern men's health, while Herophilus stated that women had no special conditions or diseases that set them apart from men.[188] Indeed, he viewed male and female genitalia as made of the same parts, and analogous to each other. Thus medical writing reflected both the separate spheres of the sexes in the Classical period, and the reduced sexual polarity in the Hellenistic.

In analyzing the emergence of the woman's perspective as one of the trends in Alexandrian literature, it is tempting to seek the influence of an educated female audience able to read and appreciate literature tailored to their concerns. The preferences of women readers certainly influenced the literary form of the modern novel.[189] However, we can do no more than speculate that other women inspired poets and influenced their choice of themes, as Arsinoë II did for Theocritus. We are on firmer ground when we draw attention to certain trends in the Hellenistic age that moved some facets of the dominant culture into the direction of realms that may be characterized as feminine.

With the advent of monarchical government, the focus of some men's lives shifted away from the public to the private realm with which women had always been associated. Although municipal life continued to flourish, and men vied for political offices, clearly their powers were fewer under monarchy than they had been when the Greeks lived in independent city-states. There was little room for love of country when armies were recruited among mercenaries who sold their services to the highest bidder. There was no need for heroism among mercenaries. In this mobile society, when few people had hordes of relatives, there was no need to wage vendettas in behalf of kinsmen. Other feelings, usually associated with women, replaced the attachments felt in smaller and more stable societies. Literature most naturally portrays women such as Simaetha and Medea at the mercy of romantic love, for women have always been less inhibited about displaying their

9. Amiable Hellenistic sphinx. Terracotta. *Alexandria. Graeco-Roman Museum.*

---

feelings. But it should not be assumed that only women harbored such emotions. Indeed, the work of the epigrammatists shows that men are active players in the game of love. Women have always experienced the feelings of outsiders, of not belonging, for they must make a fundamental shift in allegiance when they are transferred from their father's home to their husband's. In a sense, all women who were members of a traditional family lived in a miniature monarchy, as subjects of a father or husband. The experience of rootlessness, the feeling of alienation, the lack of political power, and the interest in the personal and the private which in an earlier age were characteristic of women were generalized and shared by men in Ptolemaic Egypt. The reflection of this reality imparted a feminine tone to some works of Alexandrian literature.

Chapter 3

ᛜᛜᛜᛜᛜᛜᛜᛜᛜᛜᛜᛜᛜᛜᛜᛜᛜᛜᛜᛜᛜᛜᛜᛜᛜᛜᛜᛜᛜᛜᛜᛜᛜᛜᛜᛜᛜ

# Some Married Women in the Papyri

MARRIAGE contracts[1] written on sheets of papyrus that happen to have been preserved in Egypt are the richest source of information about the ideal relationship between wives and husbands who were neither members of the royal courts nor characters in fiction. Almost all the evidence that will be adduced for the study of marriage derives from areas of Egypt beyond Alexandria, for few Ptolemaic papyri from the city are preserved. Thus, for this study, evidence of a different type from that used in the preceding chapters will be employed. Moreover, for the most part, the women whose marriages will be discussed were not the sophisticated denizens of a cosmopolitan city, but rather lived in the smaller Greek cities of Ptolemaïs and Naucratis, or in medium-sized Greek settlements scattered through Egypt, or in Greco-Egyptian communities. Some of them were fairly well-to-do, though none of them could have afforded to own racehorses as did extremely wealthy women in Alexandria. Often old-fashioned Greek customs which were not evident in the great cosmopolis of Alexandria flourished in the smaller Greek communities. Sex roles were more clearly defined and men and women were expected to function in separate spheres.

The historian must be aware that the condition of women varied according to geographical location and changed through the three centuries of Ptolemaic rule. However, the papyri that

83

may be employed for a study of marriage derive from a variety of geographical areas and time periods. Moreover, there are only about one hundred marriage contracts extant; these date from 311–310 B.C. to the sixth century A.D., and some of them are quite fragmentary.[2] Neither state nor religion had any influence on marriage contracts; consequently, no standard format was used all over Egypt, nor was precisely the same form followed by everyone in a limited geographical locality at approximately the same time. Each contract has its own stipulations and individual details that make it unique. Yet there are more similarities than differences, and, insofar as the various contracts stipulate the same rules of conduct for the wives and husbands, respectively, they reveal the ideal relationship between women and men in the society as a whole. While not denying the diversity of marriage in Ptolemaic Egypt, in this chapter we will pay special attention to those features that are typical of marriage in both Greek society and Mediterranean society at large.

The marriage contracts extant from the Ptolemaic period are written in either Demotic or Greek. In this chapter, Greek documents will be discussed and the participating parties referred to as Greeks, although it should not be assumed that everyone who uses the Greek language in Ptolemaic Egypt is totally, or even partially, of Greek lineage. However, native Egyptians who chose to use the language and laws of the Greek ruling class were likely to be assimilating other Greek values as well. Therefore, it is reasonable to view the Greek marriage contracts primarily in a context of Greek mores. The Demotic contracts and the social history of Egyptian and Greco-Egyptian families in the Egyptian countryside have been the subject of continuing study by specialists, most notably P. W. Pestman.[3] Legal historians have devoted a great deal of attention to the form, language, and content of the Greek marriage contracts. Because of the ethnic diversity of Ptolemaic Egypt, many scholars have attempted to distinguish the Greek and non-Greek characteristics of the contracts, and have identified precedents in the legal formulas of Greek states, but Orsolina Montevecchi has both catalogued the documents and written the finest general historical analyses.[4]

The purpose of each contract is to establish a legally binding agreement between the spouses. It is surprising that in some of our modern affluent communities, such as those in the United States of America, where few hesitate to engage in lawsuits on the slimmest of pretexts, brides and grooms do not usually write legally binding contracts tailored to their individual needs. Perhaps that is because it is felt that spouses coming from a common background share the same view of the mutual rights and obli gations of a married couple, whereas a written contract would be prophetic of marital discord. In contrast, the Greeks who drew up the marriage contracts did not assume that the relationship between the spouses would take care of itself. Parents did not count on the goodwill of sons-in-law, but, before they entrusted their daughters and dowries to husbands, they attempted to assure their safety. The uncertainties of life in the Hellenistic period made these contracts more essential than ever before. The migration of Greeks in this period differed from the earlier colonization in the Dark Age beginning in the eighth century B.C.; the earlier colonies were usually populated by Greeks from a single mother city. Even then, although the colonists came from a common background and had used the same laws, they often established their own new law codes for which they obtained the approval of Apollo at Delphi. In contrast, in a Hellenistic settlement of colonists from a wide variety of areas in the Greek world, not only was there no uniform law code, but there were multiple versions of the informal social contract. Thus it was essential to set forth the relationship between a bride and groom—especially when they hailed from different parts of the Greek world. For an understanding of the diversity of family arrangements among Greeks, one can simply try to imagine a marriage between a Spartan and an Athenian, where the conflict between the Dorian and Ionian ways of life would have been severe. Such a marriage was theoretically possible in cosmopolitan Ptolemaic Egypt.[5] Brother–sister marriage[6] certainly offered one way of avoiding some areas of conflict, although this was not its purpose. Because mercenaries from a given geographical area were often recruited as a group and migrated together, and because of the tendency (which we have noted in the preceding chapter) for migrants of the same ethnic background to flock together, it was possible that—at least during the early period of Ptolemaic rule—there would not be great disparity between the backgrounds of the spouses. In any event, marriage contracts between spouses who were not familiar with one another served to reduce misunderstanding.

The earliest Hellenistic marriage contract extant is dated to 311/310 B.C. and comes from Elephantine, where a Greek garrison was stationed up the Nile, far from Alexandria:

*P. Elephantine* 1 = *Chrest. Mitt.* I 283 = *Select Papyri* I 1

In the seventh year of the reign of Alexander, son of Alexander, the fourteenth year of Ptolemy's administration as satrap, in the month of Dius.

Contract of marriage of Heraclides of Temnos and Demetria.

Heraclides takes as his lawful wife Demetria of Cos from her father Leptines of Cos and her mother Philotis. He is free; she is free. She brings with her to the marriage clothing and ornaments valued at 1,000 drachmas. Heraclides shall supply to Demetria
5   all that is suitable for a freeborn wife. We shall live together in whatever place seems best to Leptines and Heraclides, deciding together.

If Demetria is caught in fraudulent machinations to the dishonor of her husband Heraclides, she shall forfeit all that she has brought with her. But Heraclides shall prove whatever he charges against Demetria before three men whom they both approve. It shall not be lawful for Heraclides to bring home another woman for himself in such a way as to inflict contumely on Demetria, nor to beget children by another woman, nor to indulge in fraudulent
10  machinations against Demetria on any pretext. If Heraclides is caught doing any of these things, and Demetria proves it before three men whom they both approve, let Heraclides return to Demetria the dowry of 1,000 drachmas which she brought, and forfeit 1,000 drachmas of the silver coinage of [Ptolemy bearing a portrait head of] Alexander. Demetria, and those representing Demetria, shall have the right to exact payment from Heraclides and from his property on both land and sea, as if after a legal action.

This contract shall be decisive in every respect, wherever Hera-
15  clides may produce it against Demetria, or Demetria and those

helping Demetria to exact payment may produce it against Heraclides, as though the agreement had been made in that place.

Heraclides and Demetria shall each have the right to keep a
copy of the contract in their own custody, and to produce it
against one another.

Witnesses:
Cleon of Gela, Anticrates of Temnos, Lysis of Temnos, Dionysius of Temnos, Aristomachus of Cyrene, Aristodicus of Cos.

Several marriage contracts from the fertile area of the Fayum
all stipulate exactly the same obligations for the spouses, making
it clear that a legal form had evolved in which the chief variables
were the date, the identity of the spouses, and the composition
of the dowry. The first of these, *P. Tebtunis* IV 974, of the early
second century B.C., is fragmentary. The second, *P. Giessen* I 2,
dated to 173 B.C., is from Crocodilopolis. This bride has a more
pretentious dowry than the others: she not only has 95 copper
talents (i.e., about 1,140 silver drachmas), but she brings with
her a slave with a nursing infant. The contract that uses the same
legal formulas as those just mentioned, but which is in the best
state of preservation, is *P. Tebtunis* I 104 from Cerceosiris. The
papyrus had been reused to wrap a crocodile mummy that was
discovered in the necropolis at Tebtunis. The date of the contract is 92 B.C.:

### *P. Tebtunis* I 104

5     In the twenty-second year of the reign of Ptolemy also called
Alexander, the god Philometor, the priesthood of the priest of
Alexander and the other priests as listed in Alexandria, the elev-
enth of the month Xandicus which is the eleventh of the month
Mecheir at Cerceosiris in the district of Polemon in the Arsinoite
nome.

Philiscus, son of Apollonius, Persian of the Epigone,* ac-
10 knowledges to Apollonia (also known as Cellauthis), daughter of

* At this period, "Persian of the Epigone" and "Macedonian of the Epigone"
(line 37) are pseudo-ethnics and do not mean that Philiscus is of Persian descent
or that the witnesses are of Macedonian descent.[7]

Heraclides, Persian, with her brother Apollonius as guardian, that he has received from her 2 talents and 4,000 drachmas in copper coinage as her dowry agreed to by him. Apollonia is to remain with Philiscus, obeying him as a wife should her husband, owning their property in common. Philiscus is to provide everything nec-

15 essary both clothing and whatever else is appropriate for a wedded wife, whether he is at home or away, according to the standard of their common resources.

It shall not be lawful for Philiscus to bring home for himself another wife in addition to Apollonia nor to maintain a female

20 concubine nor a little boyfriend nor to beget children by another woman while Apollonia is alive, nor to dwell in another house over which Apollonia has no rights, nor to throw her out, nor insult her or treat her badly, nor to alienate any of their common

25 property to defraud Apollonia. If he is shown to be doing any of these things, or not to be providing her with necessities and clothing and other things as written, Philiscus is to pay the dowry of 2 talents and 4,000 drachmas of copper in full to Apollonia, immediately.

In the same way it shall not be lawful for Apollonia to be absent for a night or a day from the house of Philiscus without the knowledge of Philiscus, nor to have intercourse with another man

30 nor to ruin the common household nor to dishonor Philiscus in whatever brings dishonor to a husband.

And if Apollonia of her own free will wishes to separate from Philiscus, Philiscus is to return the dowry unaltered within ten days from the day the demand is made. If he does not return it, as written, he is to forfeit one and a half times the amount of the dowry to her immediately.

Witnesses:

Dionysius, son of Patron

Dionysius, son of Hermaïscus

Theon, son of Ptolemy

35 Didymus, son of Ptolemy

Dionysius, son of Dionysius

Heraclius, son of Diocles (all six Macedonians of the Epigone)

Guardian of the contract: Dionysius

Signed: I, Philiscus, son of Apollonius, Persian of the Epigone, acknowledge that I have the dowry of 2 talents and 4,000 drachmas of copper as written above, and I have deposited the contract, which is valid, with Dionysius. Dionysius, son of Hermaïscus, the aforesaid, wrote for him [Philiscus] since he is illiterate.

A fragmentary papyrus from the second century B.C. records a marriage contract with the same stipulations as *P. Tebtunis* I 104, translated above, but it has an additional section dealing with the disposition of the dowry in the event of the death of the spouses:

### *P. Geneva* I 21.15–21

If one of them experiences something mortal and dies, the property that is left shall belong to the survivor and to the children that they will have in common. But if they do not have children in common, or if they are born and they pass away before they grow up, and both the spouses survive, then after the death of either one of them—if Arsinoë should die first, Menecrates is to return the entire dowry to Olympias her mother, if she is alive, if she is not, then to Arsinoë's closest relatives.

## WHO MAKES THE CONTRACTS

According to Greek law, a woman could not sign a contract of any consequence, not even a document as personal as a marriage contract.[8] Contracts were made between men. In marriage contracts, women were objects to be exchanged between men.[9] A man, the *kyrios,* or guardian, gives the bride to the groom, and, in the language of the marriage contracts, the groom "takes" (*lambanei*) her. There was no minimum age for marriage, and a girl would generally marry in her teens—before she knew enough about the world to protect herself and her dowry. As is the case in *P. Elephantine* 1, the father usually acted as *kyrios* and gave his daughter in marriage, but in this period, when the duration of life was often short, a girl's father might be dead and she could be given in marriage by a brother. This is the situation of Apollonia in Cerceosiris, in *P. Tebtunis* I 104. The Hellenistic time was a period when people moved about a great deal. Not every girl had a male relative close at hand, but some fatherless and brotherless brides did have a mother. In *P. Tebtunis* III 815, fragment 4, of 228 B.C., a groom acknowledges that he has received a dowry from the mother of his bride-to-be. Since even mature women, acting according to Greek law, needed male guardians for legal transactions, the mother acted with a male guardian. Inasmuch as such a contract would usually be made between men, the mother and daughter must have been totally bereft of available male relatives. Some other man would have had to sign the contract. Even if a woman's guardian was not related to her, he probably was not a total stranger. His appointment had to be approved by the state, and he was expected to act in her interests.[10]

*P. Elephantine* 1 is unique in that the bride's mother and father share the responsibility for giving the bride in marriage. Yet the mother has no say in deciding where the married couple will live. The customs that this family brought with them from Cos to Egypt are responsible for the naming of the mother in the contract. Cult inscriptions from this island list citizens by both patronymic and matronymic (which was unusual among Greeks).[11] Although the relevant inscriptions are later than the Elephantine marriage contract, the purpose is the same: the establishment of pure Coan descent.

In addition, however, the mother's participation in giving away the bride is evidence of the expanding legal capacity of Greek women in the Hellenistic period.[12] *P. Tebtunis* III 815, mentioned above, shows a mother giving away her daughter. Similarly, in a will of 225 B.C. (*P. Petrie* III 19c. 25–26), a testator directs his wife to give his daughters in marriage, supplying each one with a dowry. *P. Giessen* I 2 (173 B.C.) supplies the only Hellenistic evidence for a woman giving herself in marriage, although her father is still alive and acts as her guardian.[13] The bride is a Macedonian, appropriately enough named Olympias, marrying Antaius, an Athenian.

The first contract, coming from the earliest period of Greek settlement in Hellenistic Egypt, was made between two parties of Greek descent. This particular marriage contract was found stored in an urn in duplicate copies written on one sheet of papyrus. The inner one was still sealed with sealing wax depicting Heracles (Heraclides' eponym), the head of a woman, and a winged Eros. In the copy that is usually published, the husband's ethnic was omitted because of an error of the scribe.[14] The other copy—that translated above—identified him (line 2) as coming from Temnos. Heraclides was vouched for by other immigrants from Temnos, three of whom served as witnesses for the marriage contract (and none of whom has a patronymic). Neither Leptines nor Heraclides has a military title, although they may be soldiers.[15]

A copy of the marriage contract is usually turned over to one of the witnesses for safekeeping; this procedure is followed in *P. Tebtunis* I 104. However, the Elephantine contract stipulates that each party is to keep a copy of the document so as to be able to produce it against one another no matter where they are. This arrangement must have been adapted to the early Hellenistic period, when the new immigrants anticipated further migration. Both *P. Elephantine* 1 and the second papyrus in the collection, *P. Elephantine* 2 (285/284 B.C.), impart a similar feeling of married couples who may go off together away from their blood relatives. In this latter document, the husband and the wife, who are both from Temnos, bequeath everything they have to one another.

## DOWRY

The dowries in all the Greek contracts consist of movables, in contrast to dowries in most other areas inhabited by Greeks for many generations, where the daughter may take as dowry her share of her father's land (see p. 156). In a practical sense, movables were more desirable in the early Hellenistic period, when there were countless options for migration. That there is a choice of domicile for the married couple is obvious from the provision in *P. Elephantine* 1, lines 5–6, stating that the bride's father must be consulted in such a move. The primary protection a married woman had against a husband's abuse was the continuing surveillance by her own family.[16] The phrase "those representing Demetria" in lines 11–12 provides, in effect, for substitute kin to aid the married woman who has been separated from her natal family. Such a move would scarcely have been available in the preceding period of Greek history, or for contemporary Greeks on the mainland.

Demetria's parents get away with giving her a dowry that is actually nothing more than a trousseau, for it is constituted solely of personal property and had nothing that Heraclides could have controlled. Moreover, the value of Demetria's property is fixed at 1,000 drachmas, a round number that does not indicate an appraised value of the goods, but instead must represent the amount of the dowry agreed upon after many discussions by those making the contract.[17] Not only does Heraclides allow a generous valuation to be placed on Demetria's personal property—although the clothing will surely depreciate over time—but he undertakes to pay her 1,000 drachmas in hard cash if he is the one who breaks the contract. For a groom to agree to a contract that favors the bride's side as much as this one suggests that there must have been very few Greek brides available.

The dowry constitutes a daughter's portion of the parents' property; the daughter receives a share at marriage, whereas the son must wait for his father's death or voluntary retirement. Mothers alone often supplied dowries for their daughters. It is unlikely that, on the occasion of their daugher's marriage, Demetria's parents went out to buy the women's clothing and personal ornaments that comprised her dowry: if they had had cash, they would have given it to her as part of her dowry. Demetria's mother, Philotis, is named just before the contents of the dowry. Most likely Philotis had contributed the dowry from her own personal property. Mothers all over the world still bestow jewelry and other prized personal possessions upon their daughters at the occasion of marriage. If the distribution of a mother's personal property were not made at the time of a daughter's marriage and before her move to her new home (which in the Hellenistic period could be far away), this property would become part of the family's possessions which are eventually inherited by the sons. The wives of the sons would adorn themselves with their mother-in-law's possessions. A mother may prefer to have her own daughter wear her clothing and jewelry, and keep them as a tangible reminder of their days together.

In *P. Tebtunis* III 815, fragment 4 (228 B.C.), a mother provided a dowry of 700 copper drachmas for her daughter. No father or male relative is mentioned, but the document is incomplete. The dowry usually passes vertically down through the generations of a family. According to a provision in *P. Freiburg* III 29 and 30 (179/178 B.C.), if the bride dies childless, her dowry will be returned to her nearest kin, designated by a collective noun in the masculine plural. In contrast, the fragmentary ending of *P. Geneva* I 21, indicating that a dowry will revert to the bride's mother if the bride dies childless, suggests that—like Philotis or the mother in *P. Tebtunis* III 815, fragment 4—the mother had contributed it from her own property.

## THE HUSBAND'S OBLIGATIONS

The bride's father or guardian is concerned about her welfare too, and all the contracts stipulate the obligations of the husband to maintain the wife. The husband is viewed as the provider. He undertakes to give his wife what is suitable for a woman of her status, even in a document such as *P. Tebtunis* I 104, where it is stated that she has brought a dowry, that she is coruler of the house, and that their possessions are held in common.

Of the three necessities of life —food, clothing, and shelter— only clothing is specified,[18] doubtless because, of the three, it is the greatest source of marital discord. Shelter could not be an issue for debate, since the presumption is that the husband has a roof over his head; he does undertake not to evict her.[19] Food need not be mentioned, since no society sanctions the starving of a wife by a husband and the wife is in charge of the kitchen. Clothing is the only discretionary item, for a mean or frugal husband might point out that the dresses a wife had brought with her as a trousseau, though they are no longer stylish and do not suit a mature woman, are nevertheless wearable.

Ancient clothing was draped rather than cut to fit the body, so it was impossible to outgrow it. The material was so well made that it could last several generations. Therefore, it might be difficult for a wife to convince her husband that she needed a new dress. To impute to women an interest in clothing is not anachronistic. Theocritus' *Idyll* 2.74 shows a Simaetha who borrows a stole in order to go to a show, and, in *Idyll* 15.69–71, Praxinoa upbraids a man in the crowd because he steps on the hem of her cloak. Greek housewives in Ptolemaic Egypt, unlike their predecessors in, for example, Classical Athens, did not make their clothing from start to finish at home. Textile weaving was a major industry in Egypt and women did not need to weave their own.

Praxinoa confessed that she bought the fabric for her dress for more than 2 minas (more than 200 drachmas) and then fashioned the dress from it. Admittedly Alexandria was the center of high fashion, and a bride in the Fayum did not expect to adorn herself like Praxinoa; nevertheless, she had to have the assurance that her husband would supply her with enough money so that she could dress according to the local standard. Otherwise, he must return her dowry.

## DIVORCE

In the Fayum, the wife also has the right to leave the husband voluntarily, whether or not he has transgressed the provisions of the contract. Both men and women enjoy equality in terminating marriages. The wife needs neither the approval of a magistrate—such as the archon at Athens—nor the assistance of male relatives. Of course, in this mobile society a woman seeking a divorce might not be in touch with a male relative, but she does not need even the authority of a guardian to divorce her husband and demand the return of her dowry. The woman receives only her dowry; although a contract such as *P. Tebtunis* I 104 may stipulate that the couple's possessions are to be held in common, the communality of property is in effect only for the duration of the marriage.

The Fayum contracts do not specify any penalty for the wife who transgresses the provisions of the contract. The dowry—which was, after all, a daughter's portion of her patrimony—may have been an inalienable possession, at this time and in this place, and under no circumstances could she be forced to forfeit it. Despite a larger body of evidence, the same question arises concerning the fate of the dowry of the adulteress in Classical Athens.

The marriage contract from Elephantine differs from the later Fayum contracts at several key points. The Elephantine contract provides neither for the wife to separate from her husband voluntarily nor for any sort of no-fault divorce. Although the contract is shorter than those from the Fayum, approximately one-third of the text is devoted to the grounds, procedure, and penalties for divorce. A notional fund is established, consisting of the wife's dowry and a sum equal to the value of the dowry contributed by the husband. This provision is unique among Greek marriage contracts. It has elements of a game of chance that seem appropriate to the ambiance at Elephantine—a frontier settlement whose population expanded rapidly due to an influx of soldiers and other immigrants.[20] The contract stipulates that, if three arbitrators agree that one party has broken the contract, the entire fund is to become the property of the wronged party. Thus, if wronged, Demetria stands to double her capital, while the wife in the Fayum is guaranteed only the return of her dowry. If Demetria transgresses, she loses her dowry, while we do not know the disposition of the dowry of the adulterous wife in the Fayum. However, it must be kept in mind that, although Demetria must approve the choice of the three arbitrators, they are men, not women, and there is room for a range of opinion on what constitutes "fraudulent machinations" and "dishonor." Since her dowry consisted only of jewelry and clothing, the condemned Demetria would suffer a fate similar to that of the errant wife in Athens, where the penalty for adultery included a prohibition against wearing ornaments.[21]

## HONOR AND SHAME

The contracts offer a microcosm of the principles regulating acceptable behavior for married women and men, and make it clear that we are dealing with a society that is different in many respects from any earlier Greek society and that differs as well from the contemporary society of the Macedonian courts.

The monogyny clause is absolutely essential in view of the

polygynous practices of Macedonian kings. Thus, the contracts have carefully detailed stipulations obliging the husband to refrain from marrying another woman and from having any relationship that might be construed as marriage, and which would consequently threaten the wife's position as legitimate wife and mother of legitimate children. The husband is not to keep a mistress, nor to do any of the things that would be the consequence of having a mistress—live in another house or beget children who are not the wife's children. Surely, legitimate children were expected to be the natural result of formal marriage, but they are rarely mentioned in a marriage contract, except, as in *P. Geneva* I 21, in the stipulation on inheritance. Perhaps the birth of children was a foregone conclusion. Only legalistic, waspish Athenians in a state that supported the perpetuation of *oikoi* ("families") would spell out such an objective of marriage with the formula "I give you my daughter for the production of legitimate children."[22]

The husband was not expected to be sexually monogamous, certainly not when he was away from home. No ancient moral code, formal or informal, required that—but he could not have truthfully made the statement that an Athenian orator propounded in the third quarter of the fourth century in the speech "Against Neaera":

> We keep mistresses for our enjoyment, concubines to serve our person each day, but we have wives for the bearing of legitimate offspring and to be faithful guardians of the household.[23]

The husbands in the marriage contracts are permitted to indulge only in the most casual and inexpensive extramarital associations and must always make the interests of their family their primary concern. Keeping a concubine or a boy lover would be a drain on the financial resources of the family, and, in the Fayum documents, these resources are explicitly declared to be held in common. The comparison between the code of the Athenians and the code of the Greeks in Egypt is not between what the wealthy do, on the one hand, and what the poor do, on the other. In "Against Neaera," the Athenian orator was addressing an Athenian jury comprised of men who were no better off than Heraclides or Philiscus, and the men who had "kept" the woman Neaera as their mistress, although they apparently were financially secure, had frugally shared her and her support with others. No Athenian would have to return his wife's dowry because he also kept a concubine or a mistress or a boy lover. It appears, then, that the sexual freedoms of the Greek husband in Egypt were more restricted than those of his counterpart in Classical Athens.

The husband can travel freely. A husband who was a soldier might be compelled to travel, but freedom of movement is foreseen for all the husbands, including those in the Fayum, since they undertake to maintain their wives whether or not they are themselves at home, as in *P. Tebtunis* I 104.17. The travel of the wife is severely restricted. As we see from lines 27–28 of this document, without obtaining her husband's permission, the wife can go out of the house, but only as far as she can go in less than the course of an entire day.[24] Thus, she can fetch the water, check on wandering children and livestock, and visit neighbors and relatives who live close by. But she cannot stay away overnight without her husband's permission. This stipulation has both a practical purpose and a sexual basis. A household could more easily tolerate the absence of a husband than of a wife. Who would feed the husband, the children, and the chickens in the yard? Who would fetch the water? These domestic tasks are traditionally done by women, and it would be humiliating for any husband to perform them himself or even to direct a slave to perform them. This sexual division of labor was traditional.[25] Athenian drama shows us a king, Admetus, lamenting that with the death of his wife Alcestis the floors are unswept, and a husband telling his wife that in her absence the household is falling to ruin and the baby (who is in the arms of a slave) is hungry and dirty.[26] The plots of New Comedy also dramatize what is obvious about the prohibition against staying out all night: rapes were likely to occur in the dark. Moreover, when husbands were away from home, they indulged in extramarital sexual activities and, doubtless, they suspected that wives would do the same.

The idea of sexual fidelity is made explicit in the Fayum con-

tracts in the wife's agreement to avoid sexual contact with
another man, as well as neither to destroy the household nor to
dishonor her husband. In *P. Elephantine* 1.6, the "fraudulent
machinations" must be a modest allusion to the first two items,
and the wife explicitly agrees as well, not to dishonor her husband. Although it might appear that the only dishonor would
arise from adultery, the three ideas—sexual fidelity, preservation of the household, and maintenance of the husband's
honor—are closely entwined, and that is why they are listed
individually but in unbroken sequence in the Fayum contracts.
A wife can bring dishonor on a husband by any of a number of
possible assaults on his masculinity that can turn him into a
laughingstock in the community. For example, a wife who lets
her children run about in filthy rags, a wife who herself boldly
parades about the marketplace in immodest attire, or a wife who
scolds her husband in public—making it evident that he is not
the authority in the family—would be a wife who brings both
dishonor upon her husband and shame to herself.

But there is an essential connection between the sexual purity
of a wife and not destroying the household or bringing dishonor
upon a husband.[27] Any blemish on a woman's character—
including any failure to carry out her housewifely duties—was
believed to have sexual laxity as its foundation; radiant children,
a clean house, and a full larder were the emblems of a woman's
honor. This idea was traditional among the Greeks. The Archaic
poet Semonides had made the relationship between the sloven
and the slut explicit in his diatribe in which he compares women
to the earth and the water and to various species of livestock. Of
the ten possible types, the only good wife is like a busy bee. She
carefully tends her husband and her family, and not only does
not destroy her household but causes her husband's property to
grow. This is the wife who is so chaste that she does not like even
to listen to women when they talk about sex.[28]

## SOLDIERS' WIVES

Among women whose lives were most severely affected by the
historical change from Classical to Hellenistic were the wives

of soldiers.[29] Throughout the fifth century, a soldier was normally a citizen who defended his polis in times of need. He rarely campaigned at a great distance from home, nor did he stay in the field for more than a season. Thus, military obligations did not radically disturb family life. When, owing to the Spartan occupation of Decelea in 413 B.C.,[30] Athenians had to wage war all year long, the absence of men put a strain on family life. Aristophanes' *Lysistrata* gives a reflection in comedy of the loneliness of women and the disruption of Athenian society during the latter half of the Peloponnesian War. The heroine Lysistrata reflects on the hardships endured by women at that time and asserts that war is to be the business of women.[31]

Decelea was only a deme (district) in Attica. The wars of the fourth century took Greek soldiers to more distant lands on campaigns that lasted years. Greek mercenaries who served under Cyrus the Younger took along some dancing girls, and those who served under Pelopidas were accompanied by their wives and children.[32] The troops of Darius III brought women with them, a practice that contrasted with the policy of the Macedonians.[33] Philip II had not permitted women to accompany his troops, although he did make an exception for his daughter Cynane. She was not a supernumerary, but fought on horseback and killed an Illyrian queen (see p. 6).

The more important men in Alexander's army were permitted the luxury of female company.[34] It is interesting to note that the three categories of women mentioned in the speech against Neaera—courtesans, concubines, and wives—had their counterparts among the women in Alexander's expedition. Some generals brought their wives, and Ptolemy was accompanied by the *hetaira* Thaïs. Alexander also was considerate of his newly married soldiers, for he sent them back home when they reached Caria.[35] Despite his efforts, noncombatants continued to be drawn into the expedition, requiring an elaborate support system. Since these women were not formally married to soldiers, they should be labeled concubines. Using what appears to be a highly original form of triage, at one point in the expedition, when supplies were scarce, Alexander ordered that the women and children be sheltered in a dry riverbed during the flood season.[36] When Alexander had proceeded a great distance from home,[37] he permitted his troops to marry. Justin remarks that he did this so that they would assuage their desire to return home, regard the camp itself as their home, and enjoy the pleasant charm of women as a respite from their labors.[38]

Although Menander's comedy *The Samian Woman* portrays a mercenary returning to Athens from time to time to live with his mistress, historical sources present a picture more consistent with Justin's statements. The typical Hellenistic soldier was a professional granting allegiance and service to a commander for a price. Without conflicting loyalties to country, kinsmen, or political party, his family and personal possessions assumed paramount importance. Considering the army itself as his home, the mercenary lived like a nomad, bringing his family and all his material property along with him wherever he went. The soldiers' possessions, both animate and inanimate, were called collectively "those in the baggage" (*hoi en te aposkeue*). When forced to make a choice, a mercenary gave priority to the defense of his "baggage" rather than obedience to his general. If his "baggage" had been captured by the opposition, a mercenary did not hesitate to disobey his commander or even to desert to the other side.[39] Ptolemy I solved the problem presented by the soldiers' families by keeping them in Egypt. When Demetrius defeated Ptolemy's general Menelaus at Salamis in 306 B.C., he freed two thousand captives and distributed them among the units of his own army. However, Menelaus' troops deserted Demetrius and returned to their former commander, since their families had been left in Egypt.[40]

As part of their effort to attract and keep an army, and to recruit soldiers from the sons of soldiers, the Ptolemies granted parcels of land—cleruchies—to their soldiers. It was to their advantage that the soldiers' families regard Egypt as their home, rather than accompany their husbands on campaigns outside the country. The families are no longer called *hoi en te aposkeue;* the term was abbreviated to *aposkeue* ("baggage").[41] The word *aposkeue* itself sometimes narrowed its meaning from "family" to "wife" and continued to be used even when wives had ceased to travel. The women used it of themselves. From Chytroi in Cyprus there is an inscription recording a dedication by a thiasus of *aposkeuai* (a religious guild of soldiers' families).[42] In a letter from Alexandria of 126 B.C. which a wife wrote to her husband complaining that she was being unjustly subjected to legal proceedings as the result of an altercation in the market over a mattress, she tells him that she asserted that she was *aposkeue* (a soldier's wife), since, as such, she was accorded special immunities.[43] Certain legal privileges of a soldier's wife were connected to her husband's absence. Ptolemy I compelled soldiers on duty to be separated from their families, but he granted them protection in compensation. The civil code of Alexandria distinguished between methods to be adopted in legal cases against families (*hoi en te aposkeue*) when the soldiers were absent and those to be used when they were at home.[44]

*P. Halle* 1.124–46 – *Select Papyri* II 201
(middle of the third century B.C.)

No one is to bring into court a case against those who have been sent on service by the king, either against them or against their sureties, nor may the collector of debts or his subordinates arrest them. In the same way, if any persons bring cases against the families [*hoi en te aposkeue*] or the sureties [of these absentees] concerning charges that arose when those who left them behind were still at home, these cases may not be brought into court, unless it happens that, although they are members of the family, they have themselves obtained legal satisfaction from others concerning matters of complaint that occurred at the same time. If the case is against such persons, it is to be brought into court.

If any persons claim to belong to the class of members of the family, the judges will make a decision about this, and if they are recognized to belong to this class, and if the charges concern matters that manifestly occurred when those who left them behind were still at home and they have not obtained legal satisfaction from others, as noted above, the cases shall be adjourned until those who left them behind shall return. . . .

All cases in which the members of the family are accused by others of having wronged them after the departure of those who

left them behind, or in which the members of the family accuse
others, alleging they have been wronged by them after they had
been left, shall be judged before the designated court.

Philon of Byzantium, who lived in Alexandria and Rhodes in
the late third century B.C. and wrote on poliorcetics, mentioned
widows and children in the context of a passage on obtaining the
loyalty of mercenaries:

> If there are any wounded among the foreigners, they must be
> treated attentively. . . . If any of them die . . . and if they leave their
> children or wives behind, these must be looked after carefully.
> This is the best way to make them well disposed to the generals and
> citizens, so that they confront danger bravely.[45]

We do not know of any precedents in earlier Greek legal systems for the provisions for soldiers' wives. Because Philip II and
Alexander had prevented wives from accompanying husbands
on campaigns, these women were left at home in Macedonia. In
the Egypt of Ptolemy I, the soldier's wife was alone in a new
country, without friends or kin to defend her. The first marriage contract from Ptolemaic Egypt, *P. Elephantine* 1, takes cognizance of this vulnerability of the wife without recourse to
family (see pp. 91–92).

A wife left alone by a soldier-husband certainly required legal
protection. In the last half of the second century B.C., Egypt was
reeling from the invasions of Antiochus IV, civil unrest, the de-
valuation of currency, and a host of other ills. These disturbances
had led to the abandonment of cultivated plots. The government
was not only faced with a crisis in agriculture, but was deprived of
the income arising from the various taxes on land and crops. The
Greeks, unlike the Romans, did not believe women should be
exempt from compulsory physical labor. Local officials began to
compel those least able to resist to cultivate the abandoned plots.
Those pressed into service included artisans, fishermen, and the
wives of soldiers on active service in Alexandria. The soldiers
protested that, while they were serving the king, their families
should not be compelled to cultivate land. At this time Ptolemy VI

added to the privileges of soldiers' wives by exempting them from compulsory cultivation of land.[46] Unlike the legislation of Ptolemy I, which may have pertained only to Alexandrians, the provision of Ptolemy VI embraced all soldiers' wives.[47]

*UPZ* I 110 = *P. Paris* 63, col. 7.198–207

Herodes, the dioecetes, to the local officials:
The soldiers in the city [Alexandria] have once again petitioned us asserting that land is being assigned for cultivation to their families.

You appear not to have taken the slightest account of those who were excluded in accordance with regulations that were previously issued to you concerning those who must be compelled to cultivate land and those who must not at all be disturbed. Otherwise, you would not have so totally misunderstood as to harass the families of those garrisoned in the city.

## APOLLONIA (ALSO CALLED SENMONTHIS), WIFE OF DRYTON: WOMAN OF TWO CULTURES

Apollonia, also called Senmonthis, lived in Pathyris, thirty kilometers south of Thebes.[19] Her father, a descendant of a long line of soldiers, was himself a soldier. The names of four generations of Apollonia's male ancestors in the paternal line are known (see p. 104). Both an Egyptian and a Greek name are extant for all except her great-great-grandfather and some of her collaterals, who are known to us only through their Egyptian names. This nomenclature indicates that her family had lived in Egypt for at least a century, and perhaps longer. If their ethnic designation "Cyrenean" is a true ethnic rather than an example of a fictitious denomination of the sort that was bestowed on Egyptians upon entering the army, then Apollonia's ancestors had migrated to Egypt from nearby Cyrene at a time when Cyrene was under Ptolemaic control. Like other inhabitants of Egypt, they retained their ethnic designation generation after generation.

When a garrison was established at Pathyris around 150 B.C., Apollonia married a cavalry officer named Dryton.[49] (Soldiers

TABLE 2  Genealogy of Apollonia and Dryton

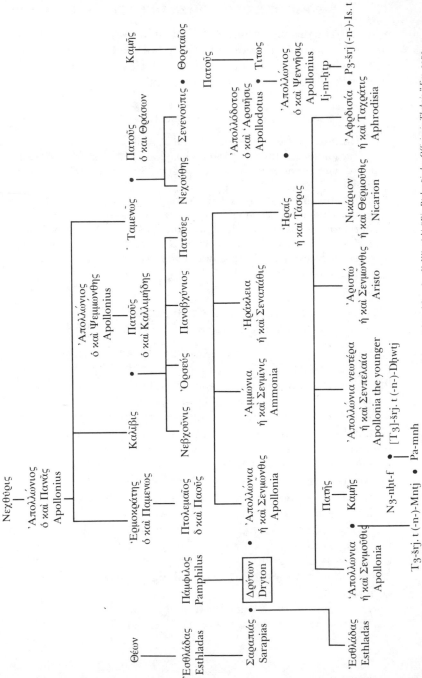

Source: Adapted from Jan K. Winnicki, "Ein Ptolemäischer Offizier in Thebais," Eos, 1972.

were attractive as husbands, for they constituted a privileged class.) He immediately wrote a short will (*P. Bad.* II 5), now fragmentary, in which he named Apollonia and his son by a former marriage as his beneficiaries. By 146 B.C., he had written a much more elaborate will (*P. Grenf.* I 12 + *P. Heid.* inv. 1285 [ψ *SB* I 4637]) naming his son, Apollonia, and their future children as beneficiaries.

## LAST WILL OF DRYTON

*P. Grenfell* I 21 ψ *Select Papyri* I 83 (126 B.C.)

In the forty-fourth year, Pauni 9, at Pathyris before Asclepiades, the agoranomos. Dryton, son of Pamphilus a Cretan, of the diadochi, of the reserve force, a hipparch over men, being healthy and of sound mind and sensible, has made the following will.

May I be in good health and master of my property, but if I suffer something mortal, I bequeath and give my property, including land and movables, and livestock and whatever else I may have acquired. The horse on which I campaign and all my armor [I bequeath] to Esthladas, my son by Sarapias my former wife, the daughter of Esthladas son of Theon, a citizen, according to the
5   laws and the will that was made through the public archives at Diospolis Parva before Dionysius the agoranomos in the sixth year of the reign of Philometor. This will includes in its provisions the designation of his guardian . . . who is a kinsman. And [to Esthladas], of the four household slaves, those whose names are Myrsine and her child. The remaining two females, whose names are Eirene and Ampelion, I leave to Apollonia and her sisters, being five, as well as the vineyard site belonging to me at Pathyris, and the wells in it made of baked brick, and the other apparatus and the wagon with the harness, and the dovecote, and the other half-completed one, and the yard of which the boundaries are, on the south, waste grounds of the said Esthladas, on the north, a vaulted
10   dwelling of Apollonia the younger, on the east, waste ground of Petras . . . son of Esthladas, on the west, waste ground of Esthladas up to the door facing west. The remaining rooms and utensils [e.g., a grain mill, oil press, stands for water jars, and sheds] and . . . the waste ground designated for a dovecote down below the door of Esthladas and to the west of the vaulted dwelling I give to Apollonia and Aristo and Aphrodisia and Nicarion and Apol-

lonia the younger, being five daughters from me and my present wife Apollonia also called Senmonthis in accordance with the laws, and also two female slaves, and the cow in equal shares for their households according to the division I have made.

And Esthladas is to give, from the waste land granted to him opposite his door facing west, four square cubits for the site of an
15 oven. Of the remaining buildings and waste ground in Diospolis Magna in the Ammonion and in the Potters' Quarter, let Esthladas have half, and Apollonia and her sisters half, and of all my other property in grain and money and movables half.

Esthladas and Apollonia and her sisters in common shall pay the expenses for the building of the designated dovecote until they finish it.

And to my wife Apollonia also called Senmonthis, if she stays at home and is irreproachable, they shall give every month for four years for the maintenance of herself and her two daughters $2\frac{1}{2}$ artabs of wheat, $\frac{1}{12}$ of croton [for oil], and 200 copper drachmas. And after four years they are to give the same amounts from their common funds to the two younger daughters for eleven years. They shall give to Tachratis [the Egyptian name of Aphrodisia]
20 for a dowry 12 copper talents from the common funds. Whatever property Senmonthis may have evidently acquired for herself while married to Dryton, she is to continue to own. And those who proceed against her concerning these . . . Year 44, Pauni 9.

Dryton holds the record for the number of wills written by one person in Ptolemaic Egypt.[50] He wrote no fewer than four, the last three of which are extant, albeit mutilated. Perhaps his record should not be attributed to a compulsive nature, but rather to luck of preservation and a lifespan of approximately eighty years.

Dryton was older than his wife. He was born early in the second century and was in his late forties when he married Apollonia.[51] Apollonia's date of birth is not known. However, her age at marriage may be estimated. She had five living offspring in 126 B.C. Their range in age shows that she probably bore these children at two- or three-year intervals—a natural spacing which could result from the contraceptive effect of nursing. Dryton's will from 126 B.C. (*P. Grenf.* I 21) mentions all the daughters. The eldest daughter is referred to by name. Since no provision is made for her dowry, she must already be married.

The dowry of the second or third daughter, Tachratis, is stipulated. Finally, the maintenance of the two youngest daughters is provided for eleven years. If the youngest are five and six years old, then their father must have expected them to be married by the time they were sixteen or seventeen, although he made no provision for their dowries. In Classical Athens, and among the Roman upper classes, the average age of marriage for girls was fourteen, but in Greco-Roman Egypt it was usually sixteen to eighteen.[52] Thus, taking minimum and approximate figures, Apollonia's daughters ranged in age from five to eighteen. In other words, by 126 B.C., she had been married twenty-two years, at least eighteen of which she had spent rearing children. This figure means that she must have married Dryton when she was, at most, twenty-five years old. Most likely she was much younger, possibly in her late teens—the age postulated for the marriage of her youngest daughters. By any reckoning, Dryton was old enough to be Apollonia's father.

The bride and groom were disparate not only in age but in social background. Apollonia's family is attested in Pathyris in 161 B.C. (*P. Giss.* II 36.17–18; *P. Stras. dem.* W.G. 16.8; *P. Berl. dem.* 15710).[53] They had not been citizens of one of the Greek cities in Egypt before moving to Pathyris, for no one in her family bears the title "citizen" (*astos*).

Dryton, too, had been active in the Thebaid in the 160's, but, in contrast to members of Apollonia's family, he was a citizen of the Greek city of Ptolemaïs. In 174 B.C., when he was a young man, as a member of a consortium, he had borrowed 100 (?) artabs of wheat from a twenty-two-year-old man (*P. Grenf.* I 10). The text of the loan describes him as fair-skinned, with bristling hair and hook nose, having a long face with a scar on the right brow. The loan was recorded on the obverse of a piece of papyrus. The verso was later used for copying a bit of literature. This work, which the editor titled "An Alexandrian Erotic Fragment," is highly stylized and rhetorical, replete with references to the power of Eros and the pain and madness suffered by the lover.[54] The genre of the work is the paraclausithyron, the lament sung by the rejected lover outside the door of the beloved. But the "Alexandrian Erotic Fragment" is somewhat original:

the rejected lover is female. Accompanied by an attendant, she wanders through the city crying:

> *I am about to go mad. Passion grips me.*
> *And I burn, being abandoned. . . .*
> *Sir, do not leave me locked out.*
> *Receive me. I am happy and anxious to be your slave.*

This sort of literature is perfectly suitable to a young man and provides an insight into Dryton's taste and intellectual aspirations. It also indicates that he was familiar with at least a literary representation of the demimonde of the Greek cities in Egypt and their games of seduction and abandonment.

Dryton had been married before he wed Apollonia. His former wife, Sarapias, came from a background similar to his own. From their names and the ethnic used by Dryton and his son, it has been deduced that Dryton came from Crete, an island that supplied the Hellenistic world with large numbers of soldiers. Greeks in Greek cities in Egypt tended to socialize with other Greeks who had ethnic roots in their own part of the world.[55] Thus, like Dryton, Sarapias was presumably of Cretan lineage and was a citizen (*aste; P. Grenf.* I 21.4) of Ptolemaïs. Sarapias had given birth to a son around 158 B.C. He was given a Cretan name, Esthladas, after his maternal grandfather.[56] Dryton and Sarapias must have been married at least by 159 B.C. If he was born around 195 B.C., he was about thirty-six or younger when he married her. (Most Greek men married at about thirty.) Dryton's first marriage was broken either by the death of Sarapias or by divorce. According to Greek law, children belonged to their father. Thus, Esthladas remained with his father. He was about ten years old when Dryton married Apollonia. His stepmother was probably in her late teens at the time.

### The Nuances of Names

In Pathyris, Dryton continued to style himself in the Greek way "son of Pamphilus, Cretan, of the deme Philoteiris," followed by a list of his military titles. He slowly but reluctantly learned to use his wife's Egyptian name.

In the first and second wills written during their marriage, he called her by her Greek name only (*P. Bad.* II 5; *P. Grenf.* I 12 + *P. Heid.* inv. 1285 [ψ *SB* I 4637]). In three loans, when Dryton acts as his wife's *kyrios*, she is identified by her Greek name (*P. Grenf.* I 18–20), although her sister and brother-in-law, who are borrowers, are each identified by a double name (*P. Grenf.* I 18). In the third will, he twice calls her by her double name (*P. Grenf.* I 21.12, 17) and once by her Egyptian name alone (*P. Grenf.* I 21.20). Dryton may have been compelled to use his wife's Egyptian name in order to distinguish her from two of his daughters, who were also named Apollonia.[57] Since these were the eldest and youngest daughters, and the eldest may well have been married when the youngest was born, sharing a name may not have caused daily confusion. The eldest daughter, Apollonia, in turn named her daughter Apollonia, so that there were four women in three generations of the same family bearing this name at the same time. Like the Romans, who used one name for all the daughters in a family (the feminine form of the father's *nomen*), they alleviated the problem by adding a second name (a cognomen or nickname). Thus the youngest daughter named Apollonia is called Neotera, "the younger."

Apollonia bears the same Egyptian name as her daughter Aristo. The sharing of the Egyptian name would have posed little problem for Dryton, for he preferred to use his daughters' Greek names. In fact, he refers to only one of them, Tachratis, by her Egyptian name (*P. Grenf.* I 21.19). Like other slave owners, Dryton called his three slaves whose names are known by Greek names (Myrsine, Eirene, and Ampelion), though they were not necessarily of Greek origin.[58]

Apparently Dryton took little interest in his daughters, and he left it to his wife to find names for them. Certainly he had nothing to do with bestowing their Egyptian names. Female names beginning with Sen ("daughter") are common, and this prefix appears in the names of Apollonia and two of her sisters, as well as in the names of three of her daughters.[59] Apollonia's Egyptian name, Senmonthis, means "daughter of Month"; her sisters Senminis and Senapathis are daughters of Min and Apachte (cognomen of Horus), respectively, while Tasris perhaps connotes "she of the necropolis of Hermopolis." The theophoric tradition continues strongly in the Egyptian names of Apollonia's daughters: Senmouthis is "daughter of Mut"; Tachratis is "the girl"; Senmonthis, like her mother, is "daughter of Month"; Thermouthis is (the goddess) Thermouthis; and Senpelaia is "the daughter of the herdsman" (cognomen of Anubis). All the names except Tasris are very common in Demotic and, with the exception of Tasris, are attested throughout Egypt. Senmonthis, Senminis, and Senmouthis point to upper Egypt.[60] Apollonia also selected the majority, if not all, of her daughters' Greek names, for the references to the god Apollo appear among her ascendants. In patriarchal societies, fathers often leave the naming of girls to mothers, for girls' names have less public significance and, after they are married, can reflect their father's lineage only very remotely. Thus, even among the eponymous priests mentioned on Greek papyri, Egyptian names—including Thermouthis, Thaubarium, and hybrids built on the stem Isis— appear earlier and more frequently among the women (see p. 56). S. D. Goitein, in a study of Jews and Moslems in medieval Cairo, has shown that mothers commonly gave names to daughters.[61] These names alluded to power in male spheres, military prowess, and dominion over men. Goitein suggests that mothers selected such names in order to compensate themselves and their daughters for their lack of such power. Thus Apollonia, wife of Dryton, named one of her daughters Nicarion ("Little Victory"). The name of another daughter, Aristo ("Best"), suggests that although she is female, and not the firstborn, she is not second best. Aphrodisia is simply a theophoric name alluding to Aphrodite. The connotations of beauty in such a name are quite common in girls' names.

### Affections and Property

In comparison to his feelings for his son, Dryton's concern for his wife and her children diminished over the years. In his first extant will, Apollonia is named before Esthladas (P. Bad. II 5). In his other wills (P. Grenf. I 12 + SB I 4637, P. Grenf. I 21), his son takes precedence. This ranking was natural, for among the patrilineal Greeks, Esthladas, as Dryton's son, would be expected to perpetuate his father's lineage, although it is not clear whether he actually married.[62] Dryton also seems to have had a particular emotional attachment to his firstborn child. Although he makes provisions for all his children, his son clearly meant more to him than all his womenfolk put together. In his last testament, in line 7, he first refers to his five daughters as "Apollonia and her sisters, being five"; in line 12, he gives all their Greek names; and, in line 15, they are again "Apollonia and her sisters." Then, in line 19, he refers to his second daughter by her Egyptian name. Evidently his first two daughters had made an impression on him, but the last three were redundant.

Five daughters would be a cause for acute embarrassment to almost any Greek man. Dryton's discomfort at the proliferation of his female offspring is perceptible in his reluctance to call them each by name and to treat them as individuals. As a soldier, Dryton must have been accustomed to the company of men and the whole spectrum of masculine activities. Apollonia herself had come from a family of four daughters and no sons, and bore five daughters. Among the families I have come across in the study of Greek history, only that of Themistocles also has five daughters.

Exposure of infants was an option that Greeks chose from time to time, especially in the case of unwanted daughters, and Dryton certainly must have known about it, even if he evidently did not practice it. One of the most decisive pieces of evidence for female exposure in the Hellenistic period derives from lists of new citizens in Miletus, inscribed mostly in the last quarter of the second century B.C. The majority of the new citizens whose ethnics are known come from Crete, Dryton's fatherland. Among these families, sons outnumber daughters in a ratio of nearly four to one. It is also interesting to note that the only evidence for exposure in Ptolemaic Egypt—a sacred law prescribing a certain number of days of purification after abortion, childbirth, and child exposure—was found in Dryton's city, Ptolemaïs (see p. 136).

Dryton was a professional soldier, and was paid for his services.[63] Because he did not hold a cleruchy (land allotted to military colonists), he bought land. He owned private property, including land, grain, money, livestock, and slaves, which he could bequeath as he pleased. Dryton divided his property in favor of his son. According to each of his wills, Esthladas would inherit his father's horse and armor. Since he was already a soldier by the time the last will was written, he must have owned his own equipment. In any event, Esthladas would know how to dispose of his father's paraphernalia if he did not wish to keep it. He also shared his father's holdings in land, grain, and money.

Dryton's daughters received the other share. Esthladas and the daughters as a group each received two slaves. His provisions for his children fall within the normal range of Greek wills of the Ptolemaic period. These wills show a variety of divisions of property among children, including partible inheritance in equal shares among children of both sexes, primogeniture, or the favoring of sons.[64] Daughters are never favored. Thus, in naming his firstborn and only son as the major beneficiary, Dryton was doing nothing unusual.

Dryton did not free his slaves by testament, for that would have reduced the value of his estate. Yet his arrangements for them show some mercy. Myrsine, a slave with one child, could well have been valuable as a concubine, too. Dryton kept Myrsine together with her child and bequeathed them to Esthladas.

The meanness of Dryton's provisions for his wife is unprecedented. The beneficiaries most often named in wills are: (1) children, and (2) wives. Sometimes the wife is not mentioned at all, and it is assumed either that she has died or that the couple no longer lived together.[65] Sometimes, in order to avoid taxes, the wife does not inherit the husband's property, but it is stipulated that she will continue to be able to live with her children who are the heirs.[66] What Dryton has done is to mention—but leave nothing to—the woman who had been his wife for some twenty-two years. His heirs are to give her a cash income in addition to wheat and croton (for a common type of oil), but only if she lives at home and looks after her two young daughters. This income will cease after four years, unless the intent of the will be construed beyond what is written: Apollonia may be omitted in the second clause because she would be the one who would take care of the two youngest daughters and would need to be supported to do so. However, even in this case, her support would cease when theirs did. Moreover, she is to receive her income only if she is "irreproachable" (*anegkletos*). The heirs—her stepson and daughters—are to be her judges. This last provision is somewhat reminiscent of a clause in the earliest Greek marriage contract from Ptolemaic Egypt, *P. Elephantine* 1, in which a jury of three is to decide whether a wife has brought dishonor and shame to her husband.

Dryton may have felt justified in cutting off his wife from his estate, because she did have some means of her own, and, although she was raising her daughters at the time, her financial transactions were concentrated in the nine years preceding the writing of the final will. Almost as an afterthought, in the last clause of the will, he stipulated that Senmonthis (i.e., Apollonia) was to keep whatever property she apparently had come to possess while living with him. Apollonia had also inherited some property. In 135 B.C., she and her three sisters engaged in litigation concerning 35 arouras of sacred land that had been left to them by their father.[67] A holding of 8¾ arouras each was a large one for an individual woman. Since Dryton's will does not mention their house specifically, the couple may well have been living in a house belonging to Apollonia.

Unlike her husband and stepson, Apollonia was a lender, never—as far as the extant documents indicate—a borrower. The archive includes a few papyri recording Apollonia's financial transactions. In 136 B.C., she leased 35 arouras (or a portion thereof) of land belonging to a temple of Hathor (*P. Giss.* II 37). Two documents that must be dated before 135 B.C. indicate that she planted grain. One (*P. Heid. dem.* 739a = *P. Heid.* N.F. IV 25) records her loan of grain to a veteran, and another (*P. Grenf.* I 15, 16 verso) is an account of Senmonthis concerning barley.[68] Four years later, she made a loan of 35 artabs of wheat to her sister Heraïs and her brother-in-law Apollonius (*P. Grenf.* I 18). The scale of this loan can be appreciated when it is known that one artab of wheat was the average monthly ration for a man.[69] As was normal, if the loan were not paid back by the date specified, five months later, the borrowers were to pay her, as a fine, one and one-half times what the grain was worth at the current market price.[70] She apparently made money. Three years later (*P. Grenf.* I 19), she made some small loans: she loaned 1 talent and 5,030 copper drachmas; and two years later she made a loan of 1 talent and 4,000 drachmas (*P. Grenf.* I 20). As was usual in such transactions, if the loan was not repaid by the date specified, the borrowers were to pay immediately one and one-half times what they owed, plus interest.

Dryton was financially comfortable. There are no indications in the archive that he ever had difficulties meeting financial obligations. Seven is the maximum number of slaves mentioned in any Ptolemaic will[71] (though more are mentioned in other kinds of documents), and Dryton had four. Since ownership of slaves was peculiar to the Greeks, Dryton's holding such a large number must have been particularly ostentatious in the Egyptianized milieu of Pathyris. He could well afford to dower five daughters. He directs in his will that 12 copper talents (i.e., 144 silver drachmas) be paid as dowry to his daughter Tachratis. This dowry was not a generous one. In giving his daughter cash, rather than land, Dryton was following the practice of Greeks in Ptolemaic Egypt. Land is not a constituent of any dowry mentioned in Greek documents before the Roman period, although private land like Dryton's (unlike cleruchic land) could legally be owned by women.[72]

Tachratis married her husband Psenesis soon after 126 B.C., when her father mentioned her dowry in his will. By 124/123 B.C., she was divorced (*P. Bad. dem.* 7). Another document records that one of Dryton's daughters (whose name is not visible) obtained a divorce from her husband, Erienupis (*P. Bad. dem.* 8). In 100/99 B.C., Dryton's granddaughter, Apollonia, was divorced from her husband Pamenos, a Greek born in Egypt. The female descendants of Dryton were particularly unfortunate in their marriages, since three of the four divorces known from the second century B.C. occurred in this family.[73] The marriage of Apollonia and Dryton, perhaps, had set a bad example.

There is no evidence that the three youngest daughters married, unless the divorce document in which the wife's name cannot be read refers to one of them (*P. Bad. dem.* 8). An ostracon from 100 B.C. shows them paying tax together (*W.O.* 1618). Their eldest sister, Apollonia, also called Senmonthis, paid separately in a different month of the same year (*W.O.* 1617). They were paying a tax on dovecotes, probably the ones that Dryton mentioned in his will.[74] These dovecotes were on the land that their father had left them. Doves were—and still are—a favorite food of the Egyptians as well as a source of fertilizer. Although some people preferred to have their dovecotes near, or even adjacent to, their home so that they could look after the birds, Dryton, being a Greek and a man from a city, preferred to keep these noisy and dirty little birds on his agricultural property.

There was not much fertile land on the right bank of the Nile, where Dryton's property was located.[75] The expression *psilos topos* ("waste ground") recurs in his own description of his property (*P. Grenf.* I 21. 9–11, 14). Although he was a soldier, not a farmer, Dryton took steps to improve his land. That he really cared about it and suspected that his heirs did not is evident from his last will, in which he sternly directs his heirs to contribute funds to build a dovecote "until they finish it" (*P. Grenf.* I 21.16–17).

Dryton's country place was a typical rural establishment. Dwellings like his, with brick arches (a characteristic feature of Egyptian architecture), dovecotes, and brick walls, have been excavated[76] (see Plate 10). His daughters, as we shall see, did not move there, but they kept the property. That they were able to pay the high taxes on the dovecotes so many years after their father's death suggests that they were able to maintain the comfortable living standard established by their parents. At the time when the daughters paid the tax, their mother may have been dead, too, and they probably had inherited her property.

Dryton died between 113 and 111 B.C., at the age of eighty or older. His property was distributed according to the provisions in his will. His daughters inherited their share, including a vineyard of $2\frac{1}{2}$ arouras and other land. They lived on the west bank of the Nile, but the property was on the east. Due to disturbances in the neighborhood, they were unable to look after their land. The two eldest sisters petitioned the strategus in behalf of all the sisters, complaining that a certain Ariston from Thebes

10. Roman mosaic showing the Egyptian countryside. Note the rural dwelling with a dovecote in the lower right-hand corner and the towers (*pyrgoi*) in the middle. *Palestrina. Palazzo Barberini. Photo courtesy of Eleanor Winsor Leach.*

on the east side of the Nile had taken possession of their land. The sisters wrote that the culprit had taken advantage of them because he "knew that we were women and lived in another place" (*P. Lond.* II 401, p. 13 = *Chrest. Mitt.* II 18). Other women landowners had similar experiences. In the preceding generation, Apollonia and her sisters complained that their great-uncle and his two sons had taken possession of property left them by their father (*P. Stras. dem.* W. G. 16; *P. Heid.* inv. 1280 + *P. Grenf.* I 15 + 17 = *SB* I 4638 [137/136 B.C.]). Unlike Dryton (who wrote so many), their father had not been careful to write a will (*SB* I 4638.5).

Esthladas did not join his sisters in their complaint. Although he had inherited adjacent property, he may have sold it fairly quickly, preferring to have cash. In fact, he does borrow and lend cash (*P. Grenf.* II 26; *P. Bad.* II 6; *P. Lond.* III 889). For this reason, Dryton left the vineyard and whatever farming equipment he had to his daughters. They continued to hold their property in common, as Dryton had foreseen they would. The land may not have been readily divisible, owing to irrigation arrangements. Certainly it would have been difficult to divide two slaves, a cow, and two dovecotes into five equal portions. It was reasonable for the sisters to manage the property as a whole and then to share the profits. In the preceding generation, their mother Apollonia and her sisters likewise had held in common the land that they had inherited from their father (*P. Giss.* II 36 + 108 = Meyer, *Jur. Pap.* 29; *P. Heid.* inv. 1280 + *P. Grenf.* I 15 + 17 = *SB* I 4638).

*Language, Literacy, and Law*

The archive of the family of Apollonia and Dryton is bilingual, but whether the members of the family were also bilingual—and, if so, to what extent—is not easily determined. The investigation is complicated not only by the wretched state of our knowledge of bilingualism in Ptolemaic Egypt, but by questions of literacy and the dual legal system. Whether the people being discussed are male or female must constantly be kept in mind as the evidence is reviewed.

Dryton's native language was Greek. The documents testify

that he was literate in Greek and that he retained this literacy even after living many years in Pathyris. In 136 B.C., he wrote in Greek, in his own legible hand, a document recording a loan for two people who were illiterate (*P. Grenf.* II 17 = *Chrest. Mitt.* II 138; *BL* I, p. 186). There were not many others in Pathyris who were literate in Greek, for, in 126 B.C., Dryton had to resort to men who were literate in Demotic to witness his will (*Pap. Lugd. Bat.* XIX 4). Dryton may have learned to speak the native language both by living in upper Egypt and by dealing with native soldiers. In this context, it is interesting to recall Plutarch's observation that none of the Ptolemaic kings ever learned to speak the native language. Cleopatra VII was the first to do so.[77] At any rate, there is no evidence that Dryton learned to read or write Demotic. A letter containing a blessing for him is written and addressed to him in Demotic (*P. Heid. dem.* 742a).[78] But the use of this language should be attributed to the fact that the Egyptian priests who wrote the prayer would naturally have used Demotic.[79] The mere presence of Demotic documents in his archive does not guarantee that he was literate in this language. People who are thoroughly illiterate still hold on to their documents.

Apollonia is nowhere labeled illiterate.[80] The documents recording her transactions either did not require her signature or are fragmentary in the section where she might have signed. She may have been literate in Greek. In his note on *P. Grenfell* I 15 (137/136 B.C.), the editor remarks that on the verso of this document there is an account of Senmonthis concerning barley. He describes it as "hopelessly illegible." Illegible penmanship is not tantamount to a low level of literacy, or many scholars would be so labeled. Three of Apollonia's loans are recorded in Greek (*P. Grenf.* I 18–20), but one is in Demotic although the borrower is a Greek veteran (*P. Heid. dem.* inv. 739a = *P. Heid.* N.F. IV 25).

The litigation that Apollonia and her three sisters engaged in over the 35 arouras of land they had inherited from their father is recorded in both Greek and Demotic (*P. Stras. dem.* W.G. 16; *P. Giss.* I 36 + 108 = Meyer, *Jur. Pap.* 29). Some phrases in the Greek reveal that the Demotic was written first and the Greek is the translation. Since the language of the document tended to determine the venue, this order suggests that their first choice was to use the Egyptian legal apparatus.[81] Nevertheless, in the Demotic version, Apollonia refers to herself as a "Greek woman" (*P. Heid. dem.* inv. 739a.5 = *P. Heid.* N.F. IV 25) and, in the Greek document, Ammonia likewise describes herself as "*gyne Hellenis*" (*P. Giss.* I 36 + 108.10).

There are distinct differences in the language preferences of Apollonia's and Dryton's children. Esthladas must have attended school in Ptolemaïs before moving with his father to Pathyris. Not only can he sign his name (*P. Cairo* inv. 10388 = *Archiv* 1 [1901], pp. 63–65), but he is literate enough to write a letter (*P. Louvre* inv. 10594 =*Chrest. Wilck.* 10), albeit his style is laconic. There are no Demotic documents recording his affairs, though we may speculate that he spoke with native soldiers in the same ways that his father may have. He did mingle with Egyptians and Egyptianized people. An Egyptian priest made a payment on his behalf to a woman with both a Greek and an Egyptian name (*P. Lond.* III 889).

There is no evidence that the female descendants are literate in any language. Moreover, in further contrast to Esthladas, they use both languages for their various transactions: their divorces are in Demotic (*P. Bad. dem.* 6–8), but the daughters' petition (*P. Lond.* II 401 = *Chrest. Mitt.* 18) is in Greek. In their petition, the daughters use both their Greek and Egyptian names. Approximately twelve years later, when they pay taxes, they again employ the Greek language, but they use only their Egyptian names. The choice of the Egyptian name, when only one name is necessary, is evidenced for Egyptianization of Greeks in Egypt at this time.[82]

The three divorces in this archive are in Demotic (*P. Bad. dem.* 6–8). P. W. Pestman has pointed out that even the women in this Greek family preferred to use Demotic because of the position of women in Egyptian matrimonial law.[83] There was no standard marriage contract, but the return of the dowry in case of divorce is a provision that does appear in most Greek documents. In Egyptian law, the husband not only returns the dowry, but if he repudiates a wife who has not committed adultery, then he must pay her a fine. If he remarries while the repudiated wife is still alive, the fine is doubled. Moreover, Greek law required that women act with a male as *kyrios*. Egyptian law regarded women as capable of acting in their own behalf.[84] The state was neutral concerning the use of a guardian. For example, if a woman petitioned the government to appoint a guardian for her, the request was granted. On the other hand, if a woman desired to act without a guardian, she was permitted to do so and her transactions were valid.[85] Both legal systems were open to all members of the population. However, if we posit that, despite its attractions and the availability of bilingual scribes, no woman would choose to use the Egyptian system unless she also spoke the language, then we must regard the Demotic documents as further evidence that Apollonia and her sisters, daughters, and granddaughters were all bilingual.

On the other hand, perhaps this assumption is not valid. In the twentieth century, Americans have visited foreign countries such as Mexico and the Dominican Republic to take advantage of their matrimonial laws. Apollonia was able to employ Dryton as a *kyrios* when he was available. In fact, he may have insisted that she employ Greek law whenever he was present. Yet when he was away on military duties, or perhaps looking after his land in Diospolis, Apollonia had no other immediate male relatives to whom she could turn. Male relatives most frequently acted as *kyrioi*. Her father was dead, she had no brothers, and Esthladas may not have been available. Rather than have a Greek court appoint a guardian, it was more convenient to act under Egyptian law. This is what she did when she made a loan to a Greek veteran. Apollonia was a Greek or a Hellenized Egyptian; by marriage, if perhaps not by birth, she was a member of the ruling class. Yet, as an enterprising woman transacting business, she had nothing to gain by enduring the constraints that Greek law imposed on women.

The women in Apollonia's family were capable of conducting their affairs. Dryton himself was aware of this, for although he had appointed a guardian for his minor son Esthladas and any children he would have in the future with Apollonia, in an earlier will (*P. Grenf.* I 12.21–22) he did not appoint any guardians for the women named in his final testament—not even for his younger daughters.

Employing scribes as men (both literate and illiterate) might, the women wrote their various petitions concerning their land. In fact, in only three documents does a woman employ a *kyrios*. These are three loans made by Apollonia (*P. Grenf.* I 18–20).

In contrast to women like Apollonia, some women who were not members of the ruling class adopted the legal disabilities of Greek women as part of the process of assimilation. Thus, Jewish women living in Egypt acted with a *kyrios*, although Jewish law, which they were permitted to use in Egypt, did not require women over the age of twelve to employ guardians.[86] Eventually, even Egyptian women appear acting with *kyrioi*.[87]

*Ethnicity and Gender*

Isocrates declared that being a Greek was no longer dependent on blood, but rather on participation in Greek culture.[88] *Paideia* refers to both culture and formal education. Greek boys like Esthladas, whose parents could pay tuition, were educated as a matter of course. Ambitious Hellenized Egyptians probably enrolled their sons in Greek schools so that they might acquire the education necessary for advancement in the public sphere. Girls were more likely to receive an education in the Hellenistic period than in earlier periods of Greek history, but they were never educated with the same frequency as boys. Because girls were not groomed to make their way in public life, it was not incumbent on parents to educate daughters. Thus, as the papyri show, in proportion to their total numbers, fewer women than men are able to sign their names. Moreover, girls could be enrolled in schools, but they were excluded from those aspects of *paideia* that demanded attendance at the gymnasium. Women as well as men who lived in Greek cities had access to Greek culture in the form of theatrical representations and festivals. Nevertheless, it is fair to say that, insofar as Hellenization is defined in terms of *paideia*, women at all times were less qualified to be called Hellenes. Since most girls were denied the education that is the distinguishing characteristic of Hellenization, they were more likely to pick up their attitudes and customs from their mothers, neighbors, and playmates. In a place such as Pathyris, these were Egyptianized Greeks or Egyptians.

Moreover, girls probably followed their mother's example because men like Dryton remained aloof from their daughters.

Women can preserve their own traditions from generation to generation. For example, Herodotus describes the foundation of Cyrene by Greeks who married native women. The women of Cyrene continued to practice their own dietary customs. He also writes of the union of Amazons and Scythians, where the Amazons preserved their own language and customs among themselves.[89] In Chapter 1, we have observed the continuity of warrior traditions in the female line in Macedonian history from Audata-Eurydice (wife of Philip II) to Cynane to Eurydice (wife of Philip Arrhidaeus).

The documentation for the children of Apollonia and Dryton is thin, but it is clear that the daughters chose to use Egyptian law when it was to their advantage, and, when needing to be brief, used only their Egyptian names. Esthladas, in contrast, was apparently unaffected by his years in Pathyris. Like his father, as a young man he made a loan, and, of course, not only used his father's ethnic and demotic, but followed in his footsteps as a soldier. Thus, the parents' traditions were transmitted to the children of the same sex.

There was a large difference in the ages of Apollonia and Dryton, but young wives are often able to charm elderly husbands. She had, it is true, failed to produce a son and managed to rear a remarkable number of daughters. Yet, more than anything else, Apollonia's behaving like Egyptian women may have been responsible for the marital rift. Contrary to what was appropriate for Greek women, during Dryton's lifetime Apollonia made a loan to one of Dryton's fellow soldiers on her own, without a guardian (*P. Heid. dem.* 739a = *P. Heid.* N.F. IV 25). In leasing the land belonging to a temple of Hathor, Apollonia was also an exception. In Greek papyri, women far more commonly appear as lessors than as lessees.[90] Moreover, in the Ptolemaic period, women with Greek names were more likely to deal in private land, while women with Egyptian names were more likely to deal in sacred land. Apollonia surely could not be faulted for inheriting sacred land, but, in choosing to lease land in a precinct of Hathor, she was behaving like an Egyptian woman. Furthermore, women who are agricultural entrepreneurs tend to cultivate vineyards, gardens, and orchards (see Chapter 5). In growing grain, Apollonia flouted the strict demarcation in sex roles which was a fundamental feature of Greek society and behaved in what Greeks would consider a masculine manner.

On the basis of the fact that Dryton wrote his will in 126 B.C. at Pathyris rather than in a Greek city, Pestman conjectures that he was snubbed by the Greeks.[91] Moreover, Dryton could not find enough Greeks at Pathyris to serve as witnesses; therefore, four of his five witnesses could sign only in Demotic. It may have been Apollonia's activities that led to Dryton's ostracism by the Greeks. Since he himself did not approve of what she was doing and considered the possibility that she would not be "irreproachable" once he had died, other like-minded Greeks could have felt the same. Yet shame that he had bequeathed nothing to his wife may also have motivated him to show the will to only one witness who could read it.

The history of this marriage depicts a lack of harmony even among the well-to-do. Of course, we cannot ignore the personal factor—although it is impossible to evaluate. Apollonia and Dryton may simply have been difficult, uncompromising people. Unfortunately, this kind of documentation does not exist for any other couple of similar background in the pre-Christian period. The marital stress may have arisen from the fact that Dryton lived according to Greek mores which were never adulterated despite his residency in Pathyris. Apollonia, in contrast, at times exhibited behavior appropriate to a Greek woman and at other times behaved like an Egyptian.

Certainly marriages between Greek men and Egyptian women did occur.[92] In the Greek world, the sex ratio was often skewed, and among migrants in the Hellenistic period, unmarried men predominated.[93] This factor alone made it most unlikely that a Greek woman would be given in marriage to an Egyptian man. The ruling class would have regarded such an alliance as dishonorable, and a marriage in which the wife was of higher status than the husband would have been anomalous. On the other hand, some Greek men, of course, married non-Greek women (and such marriages may have fanned the hostility of Egyptian men). The Ptolemies—unlike the Romans in Egypt later, who penalized those who married outside their own ethnic group— did not care whom their soldiers married, but they did encourage them to wed. As an incentive to settlement, Philadelphus granted relief from a tax on animals and slaves to his troops in Syria and Phoenicia who married native women.[94]

Historians often have raised the question of whether Hellenistic culture was actually comprised of two cultures—Greek and barbarian—existing separately, side by side, or whether the culture was mixed. Mixed marriages have drawn attention, since they had the potential to create a mixed culture. W. W. Tarn declared that mixed marriage did not matter, for Greek culture was dominant and "could absorb a good deal of foreign blood."[95] J. P. Mahaffy, in his publication of the testaments of Greek cleruchs, observed with pleasure that some Greeks in Egypt managed to marry Greek women, for thus their children had mothers who were able to preserve the purity of the Greek language.[96] Though the style of his statement appears quaint nowadays, Mahaffy did recognize that women's role was critical in the transformation and transmission of language.

In 1927, E. R. Bevan suggested that Dryton's daughters must have had an Egyptian mother, since they were given both Greek and Egyptian names.[97] In 1953, A. Swiderek deduced that, in cases where a father with an Egyptian name had a son with a Greek name, an Egyptian man must have married a Greek woman.[98] In recent times, more sophisticated theories have been advanced to explain the occurrence of Greek and Egyptian names in papyri.[99] It is nowadays generally accepted that names alone are a fairly safe guide to ethnicity only in the first century of Ptolemaic rule. After that, Greeks adopt Egyptian names and vice versa, and many people bear double names. Occupations and activities may distinguish Greeks from Egyptians. However, such guidelines cannot be applied to women, for few are identified with métiers. Yet the number of mixed marriages may be exaggerated, because of the way in which gender affects our perception of ethnicity. The archive of Apollonia and Dryton gives evidence that, in important characteristics which aid scholars in determining ethnicity (that is, names, language, law, behavior, and *mentalité*), there is some tendency for women to appear as more Egyptianized and men as more Hellenized.

Chapter 4

𝕲𝕽𝕽𝕽𝕽𝕽𝕽𝕽𝕽𝕽𝕽𝕽𝕽𝕽𝕽𝕽𝕽𝕽𝕽𝕽𝕽𝕽𝕽𝕽𝕽𝕽𝕽𝕽

# Slaves and Workers

SOME form of bondage existed in every Greek society. The proportion of unfree to free in the population varied through time and from place to place. The sex ratio within the slave population, the methods of acquiring slaves, their employment, the slaveowners themselves, and countless other factors varied as well.

## THE NUMBER OF SLAVES

The extent of slavery in Ptolemaic Egypt has been much debated.[1] In the twentieth century, William Linn Westermann and Michael Ivanovich Rostovtzeff are the chief representatives in the West of the opposing views—Westermann[2] asserting that there was little slavery, Rostovtzeff[3] maintaining the opposite. Both had the same raw material available to them for the study of slavery, but Rostovtzeff supplied the missing pieces of the jigsaw puzzle of history by introducing evidence from the Hellenistic world beyond Egypt. Westermann, more impressed by the diversity of the individual pieces and by the uniqueness of Egypt, was wary of generalizations. For example, although the only evidence—albeit not incontrovertible—for the employment of female slaves in textile manufacture in the Ptolemaic period consists of documents concerning the workshop at the Memphite estate managed by Zenon and a list of women workers which will be discussed in Chapter 5, Rostovtzeff deduced that many other such workshops must have existed in Egypt.[4] After

125

all, it was Greek practice to employ slaves in manufacture and craft industries elsewhere. In the same tradition, P. M. Fraser, a historian who has investigated areas outside of Ptolemaic Egypt and who prepared the second edition of Rostovtzeff's *Social and Economic History of the Hellenistic World*, gives the highest of current estimates of the slave population at Alexandria. According to Fraser, out of a total population of 1,000,000 persons, 600,000 were free and the rest were slaves.[5]

Westermann's views on the numbers of slaves in Ptolemaic Egypt are consistent with those of the specialists on Egypt who preceded and followed him. In his first major publication on the subject, *Upon Slavery in Ptolemaic Egypt*, Westermann criticized Rostovtzeff and cited U. Wilcken's view that slaves played a negligible role in industry and agriculture, and were employed mainly as domestics.[6] Rostovtzeff later changed his mind and admitted that his notion of large factories of weavers was "highly problematic" and that "slavery as an economic factor was of far less importance in Ptolemaic Egypt than in other parts of the Hellenistic world."[7] He nevertheless continued to believe that Westermann had underestimated the number of slaves in early Ptolemaic times.[8] More recently, Iza Biezunska-Malowist, in an admirable series of publications, has come to the same conclusion as Wilcken.[9] The assertions of both Rostovtzeff and Westermann have tremendous implications for the study of women slaves in Egypt. Though they disagree about the numbers, both scholars are talking primarily about female slaves, whether as textile workers or as domestics.

The reason for the debate on the numbers of slaves is the difficulty in identifying them. Many of the commonly used Greek words connote either youth or slave status. Thus, *paidiskē* can refer to a young girl or to a female slave of any age, while *pais* or *paidarion* can mean a child or a male slave of any age. Similarly, the Romans used the same word, *liberi*, to refer to children and slaves. In a fully developed patriarchal family structure such as the Roman, unemancipated children had a status analogous in many ways to that of slaves. In Ptolemaic Egypt, words like *paidiskē*, *pais*, and *paidarion* were also used of free people who performed menial tasks. (Today, some people refer to female domestics of any age as "cleaning girls" and to adult males who deliver groceries or clear tables as "delivery boys" or "busboys.") When ambiguous Greek words appear in bills of purchase or sale, or in testaments declaring people to be free, or in literary sources, or when other words that indubitably refer to slaves are used, then there are few problems with determining the status of the individuals. But when people are named briefly in a document such as an accounting list and are not known from other sources, scholars can variously argue that they are slave or free. Thus, in his early work, Rostovtzeff took *paidiskē* to mean slave and found a large number of female slaves in Ptolemaic Egypt. Biezunska-Malowist, in contrast, notes that *paidiskē* in Zenon's documents most often connotes a slave, but at times refers to a free young girl.[10]

In the older Greek settlements, free women who needed money worked for wages. Their jobs were often menial and were also performed by slaves. Women spun and wove, worked in vineyards, and took jobs as wet nurses.[11] That free but needy women in Ptolemaic Egypt would also seek to work for wages is obvious. Common sense leads us to conclude that there was a category of free female workers who, due to their lowly status, probably appeared in the papyri along with slaves as *paidiskai*.

The employment of slaves varied geographically. As we have observed, Fraser estimates that there was a high percentage of slaves in the population at Alexandria. The city was Greek, and many inhabitants enjoyed a luxurious way of life. Yet, since the only occupation of slaves attested in Alexandria was domestic service, and it is difficult to imagine that such service required a ratio of two slaves to every three free persons, Fraser's estimate seems rather inflated.[12] There also must have been a fair number of slaves in the other Greek cities, but few in the Egyptian countryside, where, as we have noted in Chapter 3, Dryton's four slaves would have been conspicuous.

The numbers of slaves varied over time. They were used more in the earlier years of Greek occupation, for Greeks like Zenon were accustomed to using slaves as both domestics and artisans. As the Greek population became more acclimatized, they employed fewer slaves. Biezunska-Malowist asserts that, at Alexandria, as the employment of domestic slaves spread, their employment filtered down from the wealthy to the classes beneath.[13] Because she adduces Augustan documents as evidence for the late Ptolemaic, her hypothesis, though likely, must remain unproven, for there were changes in the acquisition of slaves in the Augustan period (see pp. 138–39 below).

Sources of labor other than slaves were available to the Greeks in Egypt. The native population worked for the ruling class. In addition, the Greeks had their children. As I shall argue below, the Greeks in Egypt raised their children, unlike Greeks elsewhere and at other times who practiced child exposure. The case of Ptolemaic Egypt suggests a correlation between slavery and child exposure. In agricultural societies where there is little slavery, there is little child exposure. This axiom can be applied to both Greek and native populations. Aristotle pointed out that the poor used their wives and children as slaves.[14] Parents did not need to be destitute to put their children to work—particularly when they did not own slaves.

## WOMEN AS SLAVE OWNERS

The preceding chapters have introduced several women who owned slaves. The usual pattern is that women owned female slaves. Another reason for women to own female slaves may be deduced from Herodas, *Mime* 5. (Herodas was probably born in the third century B.C. on Cos, an island under the Ptolemaic sphere of influence). Bitinna of Ephesus, the protagonist in the mime, owns a male slave who is also her lover. She berates him for not being satisfied with her and for his involvement with another woman.

The women who are known as owners of slaves received them primarily through dowry or inheritance. For example, in 238/237 B.C., Philon of Cyrene bequeathed all his property, including two female slaves and two (?) males, to his wife and daughter (*P. Petrie* III 7, p. 14 = *C.P.Jud.* I 126). Philon had no son. Approximately a century later, Dryton bequeathed two female slaves to his five daughters (*P. Grenf.* I 21) (see Chapter 3). According to a marriage contract of 173 B.C., the Macedonian Olympias brought with her to the marriage a female slave named Stolis and her infant son (*P. Giss.* I 2). How Olympias came to possess these slaves is not stated, but it is most likely that they were given to her as dowry. Her father was alive, so it is unlikely that she inherited them. Least likely is the possibility that she had purchased them. Most women would not have had the cash necessary for purchasing a slave. (For an exception, see the purchase by Thaÿbastis discussed on p. 131.)

## ACQUISITION OF SLAVES

One of the earliest deeds of sale of a slave from Ptolemaic Egypt records Zenon's purchase of a girl who was approximately seven years old (*P. Cair. Zen.* I 59003 = *C.P.Jud.* I 1). She was of Sidonian[15] origin and bore a typical slave name, Sphragis ("Seal" or "Gem").[16] Zenon purchased her in the spring of 259 B.C. in Transjordan from a Greek mercenary serving in the cavalry of the Jew Toubias. She worked at the textile factory at Memphis. Despite her age, she must have been useful. Even a small child can spin. There are, moreover, some intricate tasks in textile work, knotting, and embroidery that are best performed by small fingers.[17] In 256 B.C., Zenon received a petition from a person named Sphragis. She had been robbed on her way to Sophthis in the Memphite nome and had lost two dresses, wool, and some copper coins (*P. Cair. Zen.* II 59145). Sphragis had heard that her property had been found and asked Zenon to see that it was restored to her. It has been questioned whether the letter can be from the same Sphragis who was purchased three years earlier, for she would then have been only ten.[18] She could well have been the same. First of all, her age when she was purchased is only approximate. It is difficult for a young slave without a mother to know her exact age, and certainly the size of young girls varies greatly. Sphragis may have been somewhat older than ten, but even if she were not, running an errand that involves carrying wool is not beyond the ability of a ten-year-old who has not lived a sheltered life. Her youth, however, would have rendered her more vulnerable to an attack by robbers. Furthermore, since Zenon had purchased her himself, rather than through an agent, she probably knew him. She may have gotten to know him quite well on the long journey back to Egypt from Transjordan. This acquaintance, coupled with youthful intrepidity, could have given her the courage to write to him.

Zenon paid 50 drachmas for Sphragis. In the following chapter, it will be observed that a man and a woman skilled in linen manufacture asked for wages of one obol and one-half obol, respectively (*PSI* VI 599). If these wages, which are low, are used as a standard, it appears that Sphragis cost as much as such a man could earn in three hundred days and such a woman could earn in six hundred. The price paid for Sphragis appears reasonable in the context of the values placed on other female slaves mentioned in the Zenon papyri.[19] In an account dating from approximately 259 B.C. (the year of Sphragis' purchase) written by an agent who had been traveling between Syria and Alexandria, the value of a very young girl (*paidiskarion*) was set at 20 drachmas, while a male slave (*pais*) was valued at 112[20] (*P. Cair. Zen.* I 59010). Around 244/243 B.C., Zenon received a mother and daughter from Philon the baker in payment of a debt of 400 drachmas (*P. Cair. Zen.* III 59355). These women were probably skilled bakers themselves. Moreover, prices were higher in Egypt than in Palestine and Syria, where slaves were plentiful. Prostitutes commanded the highest prices of all the female slaves known from the archive. Around 250 B.C., Zenon received a report that a girl was sold in Hauran, in the Arabian desert, for 300 drachmas (*PSI* IV 406).

Many of the slaves whom Zenon purchased for Apollonius, were, like Sphragis, originally from regions east of Egypt, especially Palestine and lower Syria. Coming from regions Hellenized by the conquests of Alexander, they doubtless understood the Greek of their masters but would converse with one another in Aramaic. Apollonius owned at least one Jewish female slave, who was probably purchased in Palestine. Johanna accompanied Zenon in his journey through the Fayum and northern Egypt in 257 B.C. (*P. Cornell* I 1 = *C.P.Jud.* I 7).[21] This journey could well have been pleasant for the slaves, and their work was perhaps less burdensome than usual. Johanna is listed in the accounts as "receiving oil for the lamp of Zenon," indicating that she worked as his personal attendant.

Another means of acquiring slaves was as booty in times of war. In fact, it has been suggested that the Syrian slaves mentioned in the Petrie testaments were prisoners of war rather than purchased slaves.[22] Moreover, indigenous women were enslaved during civil strife. In 197(?) B.C., Thaÿbastis, a thirty-year-old Egyptian woman described as short, honey-colored, and round-faced, with a mark on her right cheek, purchased a female slave named Thasion from the Crown. Thasion is described as eighteen years old, short, dark-skinned, and distinguished by several conspicuous marks. After a rebellion in lower Egypt, the men had been put to death, while female members of their families— like Thasion—were enslaved.[23] Egyptian women were also enslaved during the civil war between Ptolemy VI and Ptolemy VII in the middle of the second century B.C.[24] However, enslavement of the enemy was a rather intermittent and limited source of supply.

The major source of slaves, in addition to purchase, was natural procreation within the borders of Egypt. Children of female slaves took the status of their mothers. At the very start of this discussion, procreation must be distinguished from breeding. Breeding occurs when slaves are encouraged to produce children sooner and at more frequent intervals than would occur without interference.[25] In the American South, after the closing of the international slave trade, some slaves were forced to bear children to supply a market that importation had previously satisfied. The compulsion was not always external. Self-interest could play a role in a slave woman's decision to bear children. According to Herbert Gutman, female slaves understood that producing children made them more valuable to their owners and decreased the probability that they would be sold.[26] Such a notion was not alien to the ancient world. In the first century A.D., the prospect of earning her freedom could encourage a female slave to bear children. Columella wrote that a slave woman had repaid her purchase price by producing four children for her owner.[27] But Rome was a slave society. In contrast, there is no evidence for such external interference with the reproductive lives of female slaves in Ptolemaic Egypt.

The slave trade was regulated, but more probably by taxation than by any absolute prohibition on export. The relevant stipulation on export is given in a papyrus which breaks off just where the conditions of export might be given: "It is not permitted to anyone to sell slaves for export, nor to brand them, nor . . ." (*P. Lille* 29 = *Chrest. Mitt.* 369).[28]

Some female slaves did bear children. They may have done so because they thought they would ingratiate themselves with their owners by increasing their human capital, or because they had no choice. A slave's body was her master's property. Dryton, whom we have discussed in Chapter III, may have chosen to bequeath a female slave and her child to Esthladas because his son had fathered the child. Dryton's household did not include any male slaves, nor is it likely that there were many in the Egyptianized area around Pathyris. Of course, it is always possible that Dryton himself was the father or that the slave in question had had the baby before being purchased by Dryton and that, like the slave in *P. Giessen* I 2, she was permitted to take her child with her when she moved to a new home.

The cleruch coming to Egypt without friends or kin would naturally develop an attachment to his slave concubine and his children by her. Testaments of Greek cleruchs reveal the maximum that a slave who had borne her master's children might attain. In one, Dion of Heraclea, a cleruch, bequeathed all his property to his wife and their sons, while freeing a slave and his son by her (*P. Petrie* III 2 [237/236 B.C.]). The name of the slave, Melainis ("The Black"), suggests that she was of Ethiopian origin.[29] The son was named Ammonius for the ancient Egyptian god Ammon. In another will, Menippus freed a female slave and her six children (*P. Petrie* I 16). Unlike the testament by which Melainis and Ammonius were freed, this document does not explicitly state that the children are descendants of their master; however, the facts that one slave bore so many children, that the master did not sell them but retained an unusually large number of slaves, and that he freed them by testament indicate that they were his own children. While the modern reader may deplore this sequence of events, it is necessary to remember that there is no evidence that any slave was manumitted in Egypt in the Ptolemaic period except by testament. Moreover, no slave—not even one who had borne children by the master or otherwise—could complacently expect that she would be so manumitted. In an analogous situation, Romans often freed their children so that they would enjoy Roman citizenship. The cleruch did not have a similar incentive. We can only speculate about the feelings of the legitimate wife of Dion—not only when she was living with Melainis and Ammonius, but later when she was deprived, by her husband's testament, of inheriting some valuable human property. Dion's declaration concerning Melainis and Ammonius—"Let no one lay hands upon them"—is not a mere formality in his testament but intended as a caution to his legitimate heirs.

According to Iza Biezunska-Malowist, procreation was the principal source of slaves throughout antiquity.[30] By allowing their slaves to bear children, owners easily increased their fortune. Although there is no evidence for the deliberate breeding of slaves in Ptolemaic Egypt, slaves with children are encountered in the papyri. Rearing a slave's baby was advantageous to an owner. The cost of rearing the slave might come to more than the cost of purchasing one, but the payment was extended over several years, and only sustenance, rather than cash, was required. Moreover, as the example of Sphragis illustrates, a slave could begin to work or be sold for cash at a very young age.

It has been wrongly asserted that the Greeks and Romans did not have the minds of modern accountants and could not have calculated whether it was cheaper to rear a slave from infancy or to buy one.[31] Slave owners in antiquity did not have access to modern actuarial tables which give weight to imponderables such as the mortality and morbidity of slave children, the changing costs of maintaining slaves, and fluctuations in the prices of adult slaves. Nevertheless, a talented manager such as Zenon had some figures to guide him. He kept careful records both of the salaries of free workers and of the costs of purchasing and maintaining slaves. His accounts do not give any evidence that Zenon was interested in the rearing of slaves (but see below, on rations, p. 141). However, since slaves were human, we must suppose that some of them bore children. It should not be assumed that Zenon controlled his slaves' sexuality the way an upper-class Athenian controlled that of his slaves. In Classical Athens, according to Xenophon, a master locked his female slaves in the women's quarters at night.[32] Slaves were not permitted to bear children without the master's permission. In contrast, in Ptolemaic Egypt, women—either slave or free—were not assiduously guarded. Although scholars talk of "women's quarters" in houses in Ptolemaic Egypt, it is impossible to find archaeological traces that reveal such a distinction between rooms. According to literary sources, the palace at Alexandria had certain rooms designated as women's quarters and others set aside for men.[33] Grander establishments in the capital probably followed the royal model. In the countryside, there were some multistoried houses tall enough to be called "towers" (*pyrgoi*).[34] (See Plate 10.) It certainly would have been possible to isolate women in one of the stories. In any event, a slave's owner would have to concur if the slave were to bear and keep her child. The owner would have to consider that the pregnant and parturient slave would perform her daily chores less effectively. If she were a highly skilled slave, considerable losses would be incurred. Childbirth might jeopardize the mother's life, and infant and juvenile mortality could erase an investment made in rearing the baby. A person who owned only one slave was not enormously wealthy. When the one slave bore a child, she doubled her owner's human capital. In the second century B.C., a man revealed his concern for his slave and her child by mentioning them in a letter directly after his wife and children:

> Menon to his brother Hermocrates, greetings,
>     If you are well, so am I, and so are Aphrodisia [his wife] and our daughter, and the slave girl and her daughter . . . (*C.P.Jud.* I 135).

If Menon had fathered the child by his slave, then there is an additional reason for his concern.

If it makes economic sense for an owner to raise children of slaves, does it also profit someone to raise a baby to whom no one has laid claim? In the case of one's own slave, certain human principles in addition to economic motives may be operating: first, the baby in question may have been engendered by the master; second, forcing the female slave to abort or to abandon her newborn could have been detrimental to her morale. The modern reader might suppose that humanitarian ideals would prompt a kindhearted person to take in an anonymous abandoned infant; there is little evidence for such compassion in antiquity. Literature, ranging from tragedies about Oedipus to New Comedy, does give many versions of the exposed-infant theme. A baby is turned over to a servant with the command that it be abandoned. The servant either entrusts the baby to another or raises it himself. The parentage of the baby is thus known by a few people. Attic comedy raises the possibility that a woman may not actually give birth but will present to her husband as her own an abandoned newborn smuggled home in a jar.[35] The only other motive for raising an abandoned child was the acquisition of a slave. In Greek law, abandoned infants were presumed to be slaves.

The first question concerning the recruitment of slaves from abandoned infants in Ptolemaic Egypt is whether there was a supply of such infants. Among the native Egyptians, there was no tradition of exposing unwanted infants. Greek historians were struck by this difference between the Egyptians and themselves. Diodorus Siculus observed, "They raise all their offspring."[36] Diodorus also noted that the Jews raised all their children.[37] Hecataeus of Abdera, the probable source of Diodorus' comments, had visited Egypt in the reign of Ptolemy I. Yet it has been proposed that Diodorus' comments are not based on direct observation but rather should be attributed to a system of thought that sought to emphasize differences between Greeks and non-Greeks and tended to idealize the virtue and natural qualities of non-Greeks.[38] Despite such systems of thought, the report of Diodorus on Egypt seems to be true. Certainly his comments on Jewish norms are correct. Moreover, there is no trace of infant exposure in the Demotic papyri.[39] Although, as an aspect of Hellenization, Egyptians and Jews living in Egypt could certainly have adopted the Greek custom of exposing newborns, such people would probably have been so thoroughly Hellenized that it would be impossible to detect their original ethnicity.

Among the Greeks, there was a long tradition of exposing unwanted infants.[40] These infants were, by and large, female. Unequal sex ratios from many areas of Greek settlement traceable as far back as the Archaic period point to the exposure of girls. Some of the distortion in the ratios can be attributed also to the neglect of girls. Women were consistently undervalued in ancient Greek society. Consequently, in the allocation of a family's resources, boys took precedence. The impossibility of marriage without a dowry was a motive for female infanticide. In a settled community, a poor father might hope that a wealthier relative or friend would dower his daughter. However, the Hellenistic period was a time of unrest. Long-standing ties of friendship and kinship were nonexistent for the deracinated Greek in the vast territories conquered by Alexander. Under such ungenial circumstances, the comic poet Posidippus said, as we have noted, that "Everyone, even a poor man, raises a son; everyone, even a rich man, exposes a daughter."[41] The consequence was observed by Polybius: the older Greek cities were becoming depopulated.[42]

Next, it is necessary to consider whether the demographic patterns of the rest of the Greek world can be traced in Ptolemaic Egypt. A law of Ptolemaïs Hermiou attests to the concept of infant exposure in Ptolemaic times. The law is known from an inscription that can be dated, at the earliest, to the first century B.C.[43] Ptolemaïs was founded by Ptolemy I as a Greek city with a Greek constitution. One of the city laws demanded a period of purification before entering a temple after suffering personal misfortune, or after sexual intercourse, menstruation, childbirth, abortion, or child exposure. The idea behind such a law would have come from a similar law in one of the older Greek cities. G. Plaumann cites parallels for most of the stipulations, except the one on child exposure.[44] The only other Greek law that mentions purification after child exposure is one from the second century A.D. regulating the cult of Dionysius Bromius at Smyrna.[45] The existence of such a law at Ptolemaïs does not imply that child exposure was a regular rather than potential occurrence. Nor does it imply that child exposure was any more offensive than the other natural processes for which purification was prescribed.[46]

Statistical data for the study of demography in Classical antiquity are rare. Nevertheless, inscriptions listing a thousand names have made it possible to examine the composition of families who were granted citizenship by Miletus mostly in the last quarter of the second century B.C., and to posit female infanticide as an explanation for the skewed sex ratio.[47] Census lists have yielded information on family composition in Roman Egypt, but, since the papyri are often torn, these documents do not give consistently reliable evidence for sex ratios within families. Using this census data, M. Hombert and C. Préaux found a ratio of 51.33 percent males to 48.67 percent females and explained the disproportion by the neglect of women and young girls and a higher rate of infant mortality among girls than boys.[48]

The situation of Greeks in Ptolemaic Egypt would seem to have discouraged the exposure of, at least, healthy children. Greek fathers did not need to be obsessively concerned about finding bridegrooms for daughters. With Egypt as the magnet, unattached Greek men seeking military, commercial, or administrative posts were abundant.[49] They were not all able to find Greek wives. Some married native women or took foreign slaves as concubines. Moreover, the Greeks comprised the ruling class. They were relatively prosperous and in a position to furnish dowries for their daughters. As we have observed in Chapter III, the supply of Greek brides was so limited that fathers were not required to supply substantial dowries to attract bridegrooms. Greeks living in the Egyptianized areas would have observed that the Egyptians frowned upon child exposure.[50] In such a milieu, Apollonia, herself one of four sisters, raised five daughters—even if her husband Dryton, who was a citizen of Ptolemaïs, might have considered the girls excessively numerous. Although the Greeks in Ptolemaic Egypt did not employ exposure as a family-planning device on a large scale, mothers in unfortunate circumstances doubtless resorted to exposure when attempts at abortion were ineffective, as they did elsewhere and at other times. In his second idyll, Theocritus describes the plight of Simaetha: Abandoned by her lover, Simaetha resorts to magic to try to bring him back and to punish him. If a real woman in Simaetha's circumstances had conceived as a result of this escapade, and abortifacients were not effective, she probably would have abandoned the infant.

The second part of the inquiry on the exposure of infants as a source of slaves concerns those foster parents—i.e., slave dealers—who collected abandoned infants. From the preceding discussion, it will have been concluded that, in comparison with the rest of the Greek world, Ptolemaic Egypt would have furnished a small number of such infants.

In the only wet-nursing contract from the Ptolemaic period, a father engaged a nurse for his own son (see p. 162). The mother had perhaps died in childbirth or had trouble nursing her baby. In contrast, from the period of Roman occupation as early as the reign of Augustus, there are contracts in which people engage nurses to look after infants who are not their offspring.[51] The high prices of slaves attested for this period show that the investment made in paying a wet nurse would bring a profit to the child's owner.[52]

All the evidence for the rearing of abandoned infants as slaves begins in the Augustan period.[53] The famous letter of Hilarion to his wife (*P. Oxy.* IV 744) dates from 1 B.C.: "If, by chance you give birth, if it is a boy, let it be; if it is a girl, get rid of it."

Claire Préaux cites the letter of Hilarion and the *Gnomon of the Idios Logos*—both from the Roman period—in support of her statement that infants were exposed in the Greek period.[54] Iza Biezunska-Malowist uses the Augustan nursing contracts for abandoned infants as evidence for late Ptolemaic practices.[55] In the last century of Ptolemaic rule, Egypt did not enjoy its former prosperity, and historians quite rightly expect Greeks in unfortunate circumstances to expose their children. But the evidence indicts the Romans rather than the last generations of the Ptolemies.

Although the Greeks had long practiced child exposure, in

Egypt it was under Roman rather than Greek domination that the practice appears. If this change is not simply an artifact of the haphazard preservation of papyri, then an explanation must be sought. Surely the exposure of infants is a symptom of increased hardship for some residents in Egypt under the Romans. Not only did mothers abandon their infants, but other women—some free—turned to wet-nursing for income (e.g., *BGU* IV 1112; *BGU* IV 1106 = *C.P.Jud.* II 146). As we shall see, wet-nursing was not a desirable means of earning an income. On the other hand, the high prices paid for slaves point to the prosperity of some segments of the population. Under Greek rule, then, Egypt was exceptional; under the Romans, there is continuing evidence for the exposure of infants as a source of slaves.

Whether an owner had acquired slaves through purchase or raised them from birth, they embodied a substantial investment of capital. It was therefore in the owner's interest to see that slaves were adequately maintained. It may be observed from the letter of Sphragis that this young slave owned at least two dresses in addition to the one she wore. She probably took some bread from home with her on her journey, but she also had some pocket money in order to purchase what she needed. Slaves were given a small cash allowance so that they could purchase necessities, including oil and some fish or lentils with which to vary their diets.[56] Occasionally there was a holiday and a feast. But the major source of sustenance for a slave such as Sphragis was a grain dole.

Since grain was raised on the estate of Apollonius, it made more sense to distribute it directly to his slaves rather than to give them money with which to purchase it in a market at a price that included profit for the seller. Moreover, slaves who were given grain rather than cash were more likely to use the grain for the purpose intended, although it was always possible to sell or trade it for other items. It should be noted here that the solution of feeding all the slaves in common mess halls scattered throughout the estate was not adopted, for it would have been difficult to control the portions. Instead, each slave received an individual dole.

The archives of Zenon contain several lengthy documents re-

cording grain distributions to workers (slave and free or unde-
termined) on the estate of Apollonius. According to T. Reekmans' study of these papyri, the amount of grain allocated to
individuals was determined by three criteria: age, sex, and inten-
sity of labor.[57] Whether a worker was a slave or free or in an
inferior or superior place in the hierarchy did not influence the
quantity of grain distributed. However, the quality of grain
varied, so that a few favored workers received enough to assure
them of white bread, while the majority made do with ordinary
durum wheat.

There were three categories: children, women and boys, and
adult men. The allocation to women and boys assured them of a
daily intake of 2,420 calories. Adult males received the equivalent
of 3,780 calories.[58] These amounts exceeded the amounts recommended by Cato approximately one hundred years later.[59] Cato's
ration would have given 3,000 calories to adult males, but, of
course, Cato was notoriously ungenerous with his slaves.[60]

After 248/247 B.C., the rations on the estate of Apollonius
were reduced, probably because grain production on the estate
decreased. At that time, women were allocated the equivalent of
only 1,890 calories and men received 2,838.[61] Since it was unlikely that the amount of cash distributed was increased in compensation, at this time the slaves had an inadequate diet, falling
below both Cato's allowance and the 2,500 calories per woman
and 3,600 per man recommended for very active members of a
modern population.[62] Nevertheless, on the average Zenon's
slaves were still slightly better fed than free villagers in Egypt
more than a century later. The average caloric intake at Cerceosiris in the last quarter of the second century B.C. was 2,279.
This figure was based on grain consumption alone. Such a diet
was often augmented by lentils, beans, and vegetables.[63] According to Robert William Fogel and Stanley L. Engerman, the
American slave in 1860, on a diet consisting mostly of corn and
pork, received 4,185 calories, while the total population in 1879
received 3,741.[64] As one of Fogel's and Engerman's critics has
pointed out, a high caloric allocation can be evidence of hard
physical labor on the part of the slave rather than generosity on
the part of the owner.[65]

Four women in Zenon's account were given men's rations.[66] This largesse may have been due to their engaging in more intense labor than most women or, according to the principles on which grain was allocated, engaging in work classified as men's work. However, Choirinē, like other women, was a weaver, and Isidora probably was a baker. The jobs of the other two women are not known. It seems more likely that they were given increased rations because they were pregnant or lactating. The modern recommended dietary allowance for women is increased by 200 calories a day for pregnancy and 1,000 for lactation.[67] There need not be any implication here that Zenon rewarded these women for breeding; rather, he simply recognized that they were feeding two bodies rather than one. The principle of "mothers' rations" appears as early as 489 B.C. in Persepolis in the amounts of wine, beer, and grain awarded to Ionian women with infants.[68]

## JOBS OF SLAVES

Nutrition affects the capacity to work. Zenon's allocation of grain suggests that some jobs were designated as women's and others as men's. The division of labor between the sexes traditional among the Greeks extended to slaves, but, as we shall observe in the discussion of weaving in Chapter 5, in Egypt the gender associations of jobs were not so rigid as they had been in older Greek settlements.

In Chapter 5 we shall also observe that some slave women in the textile industries made a contribution to the economy. Most, but not necessarily all, the women in one textile workshop were slaves (see p. 170). The owner of the factory may not have owned all the slaves who worked for him; some may have been leased to him. Regardless of their status, the women were paid the same salaries. The difference was that the slave's owner would take her earnings, while the free woman would keep her own.[69]

The vast majority of female slaves in Egypt were domestics. They lived in households boasting four or five slaves, at most, and performed work traditional to women.[70] According to Biezunska-Malowist's theory, the expansion of slavery in late

Ptolemaic Egypt should be attributed to an increased employment of slaves in relatively modest households.[71] It became natural to have a slave girl perform the daily chores. The brick houses in Egypt today are not very different from the houses of Ptolemaic Egypt, and the tools used for cleaning them remain the same. Natural fibers such as reeds and palm were fashioned into brooms and baskets of all shapes (see Plate 11a–f).

All housework is endless; the same task must be repeated day after day. Among these tedious chores, one of the most burdensome was the provision of water for the house. Water was used not only for cooking, cleaning, and sponge baths, as had been the case in the older Greek settlements, but also for immersion baths. Excavations reveal that some of the private homes had small rooms designated for bathing.[72] These rooms were not heated as were Roman bathrooms, but since the temperature is high in Egypt for most of the year, a cold bath would not have caused much discomfort. Even if a free woman could have managed to do all her other housework, she would want to have a slave girl to carry water to the house. The myth of the Danaïds offers an interesting perspective on this chore of housewives, a chore that not only is physically demanding but—unlike weaving—leaves no permanent result. Forty-nine daughters of Danaus killed their husbands on their wedding night in rebellion against a marriage that was being forced on them. Appropriately enough, the Danaïds who had refused to become wives were condemned to carry water in leaky vessels in the underworld.

Praxinoa, in Theocritus' *Idyll* 15, expected her slaves to keep the house clean, look after the baby and the dog, spin wool, help their mistress wash and dress, and accompany her on expeditions. Her husband was fussy, so Praxinoa had to look after the cooking herself.

There could be little job specialization among slaves, except in larger households. Even a grand establishment such as that of Appolonius does not display the degree of job specialization that is attested for the slave familiae ("slaves of a household") of Rome, where female slaves bore distinct job titles as clothes folders, readers, or mirror holders.[73] The household of Apollonius, a man of high rank, did include a cithara player, Satyra.[74]

She wrote to Zenon complaining that she and her mother had not received their clothing allowances and would soon be naked (*P. Cair. Zen.* I 59028 [258 B.C.]). The next year she did receive at least one linen chiton (*P. Cair. Zen.* I 59087.23 [258/257 B.C.]).

One of the common nouns used in papyri to connote slave is *soma* ("body"). Slaves have always been available to provide sexual services to their owners, as well as to those to whom their owners offer access, whether as a primary or a secondary function. The concubines of Greek cleruchs have already been mentioned. A slave such as Satyra could be expected to entertain Apollonius or his guests sexually as well as musically. In this household, young male slaves were available as well to suit homosexual fancies. The Jewish chieftain Toubias had sent as a gift to Apollonius four boys in the company of a eunuch. Two of the boys were ten years old, one was seven, and one was eight (*P. Cair. Zen.* I 59076 = *C.P.Jud* I 4).

Concubines must have performed domestic work in addition to providing sexual services, for their masters did not own other slaves until these women gave birth to some. The Syrian Elaphion, in contrast, was evidently a professional *hetaira,* either slave or free. She is known from two documents of the early third century B.C. In the first, Elaphion, with her guardian Pantarces, paid 300 drachmas to Antipater for *tropheia* ("maintenance"?) on the condition that he renounce all claims against her (*P. Eleph.* 3). Five months later, acting with another guardian, Dion, Elaphion paid 400 drachmas to the aforementioned Pantarces for *tropheia* on the same conditions (*P. Eleph.* 4). O. Rubensohn, the first editor of the papyri, suggested that Elaphion was a free *hetaira* who passed from one soldier to another among the garrison at Elephantine. Each time, the new lover compensated the previous one. It has also been suggested that she was not a slave, but that she was shared by two men and was buying a release from her agreement with them.[75] The papyri give no indication that the new lover is given any rights over Elaphion that ought to justify his paying for her. Therefore, Elaphion may have been a slave belonging to two masters, Antipater and Pantarces.[76] Elaphion bought her freedom first from Antipater and then, when she had amassed enough money, from Pantarces. Sharing a slave for sexual purposes was not

**Palm broom**

**Palm-leaf baskets**

11. Artifacts from Caranis in the Kelsey Museum of Archaeology, University of Michigan

Rag doll

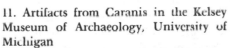

Palm sandals

unusual. Opponents of Neaera in fourth-century Athens asserted that she had been the property of a select group of men. Some of them had lent her money to purchase her freedom.[77] Similarly, Elaphion could have obtained the large sums required for her emancipation from other soldiers at Elephantine. She would have been able to repay the loans with money earned as a freelance *hetaira*.

The homosexuality of the Greeks has been overemphasized by modern scholars. There was a steady market for heterosexual experience as well.[78] Elaphion cost 700 drachmas, but she would have been able to repay the money she had borrowed. Prostitution was a profitable profession, and the earnings of prostitutes justified the high prices paid for them. An artist who corresponded with Zenon expressed his own preferences succinctly: "Wine and prostitutes forever!" (*PSI* IV 352).[79]

Zenon's archives include a complaint about a certain Dionysius and the coachman Drimylus, who dealt in female prostitutes (*PSI* IV 406). They took one girl, provided her with an outfit according to their means, and established her with a border guard. They dragged another from Ammon in eastern Palestine and sold her in Ptolemaïs on the coast. They brought a third to Joppe to serve as a sacred prostitute. They sold another girl at Hauran in Arabia, east of Palestine, for 300 drachmas. It was also reported that these two entrepreneurs bought a girl, sent her streetwalking every day, and "profited gloriously." They then sold the girl—along with a donkey and an ass.

This brief document offers a glimpse of the fate of most of the female slaves who worked as prostitutes throughout Greek history. The girls may not have been slaves to begin with, but they were kidnapped and carried away before their families could find them. The document nowhere indicates that the two men bought the girls and then resold them. Their action in regard to the first one is described as *proschrēsamenos* ("availing himself of," or "abusing").[80] Each victim is referred to by the term *paidiskē*. As we noted at the beginning of this chapter, this word does not necessarily imply youth, but rather connotes inferior status. However, young girls were more valuable than mature women as prostitutes. Therefore it is proper to refer to them as "girls" rather than "women." The two men turned the first girl over to a border guard.[81] In this location, there would be frequent traffic and plenty of customers. For this reason, inns often served as houses of prostitution. They brought the next girl across Palestine to sell her at a center of trade. Ptolemaïs is south of Tyre, which, Herodas reports, was the point of embarkation for prostitutes brought to Egypt.[82] One of the girls became a sacred prostitute, probably in a temple of Astarte.[83] Actually, for the girl involved, sacred prostitution was no better than the secular kind. The only difference was that a temple rather than an individual owned the slave and reaped the profits. Dionysius and Drimylus themselves acted as pimps for the fifth girl and made some quick cash before selling her along with a couple of animals.

All *hetairai* and prostitutes need not have been slaves or ex-slaves. Doubtless there were numerous women who voluntarily flocked to settlements where they found soldiers and other men with ready money. In the first year of the reign of Ptolemy Philopator (221 B.C.), Sopolis petitioned the king (*P. Enteux.* 49):

> I have been wronged by Demo who lives in Crocodilopolis in the Arsinoite nome. She is a prostitute. . . . She persuaded my son Sopolis, who is still a minor, to sign a contract for a loan of 1,000 drachmas. I beg of you, King, to order Diophanes the strategus to summon Demo and the man who acted as her guardian on this contract and to make a complete inquiry. If it is established that no money was given at all and that the deed took place without dishonest intentions, force her to return the document to us. As to herself—let Diophanes the strategus decide.

In the smaller settlements in the countryside, a *hetaira* was more of an anomaly. In a list of payments that may be connected with the beer monopoly, eleven women are named (*Pap. Lugd. Bat.* XX 63). They may have been brewers or retailers of beer. One of the women may be identical with an innkeeper known from another document.[84] However, the only one whose profession is noted is Taësis the *hetaira*. This notation may well have been a stigma. In contrast, in the capital—where a mistress of Ptolemy II had been deified—it was less easy (and often less important) to distinguish respectable women from the others.

Chapter 5

━━━━━━━━━━━━━━━━━━━━━━━━━━━━━━━━━━━━━━━━━━━━━━━━

# Women's Role in the Economy

THE role of land ownership in the ancient world cannot be overestimated.[1] The possession of land was the primary objective in the various revolutionary reform movements in the Hellenistic period.[2] Land was a precious commodity in Ptolemaic Egypt, a country that, like most other ancient states, was decisively based on an agricultural economy.

## AGRICULTURE

Despite the wealth of documentation, the system of land tenure under the Ptolemies remains a controversial subject. Some of the land was held by private owners, some belonged to cities and temples, and the rest remained royal domain.[3] There were several subcategories of royal land. The Ptolemies allowed royal land to be leased to peasant farmers. They also distributed it for long-term possession as renewable gifts and as *kleroi*, or allotments, to men who would be available for service in the army. The proportions of each category of land varied through time and from place to place. There are few statistics. According to Diodorus Siculus, the land of Egypt was divided into thirds: one-third was held by the king, one-third by the priests, and one-third by the soldiers. Diodorus probably got his information from Hecataeus, who wrote a history of Pharaonic Egypt in the time of Ptolemy I.[4] Diodorus does not know of the existence of private land. This is because he was following Hecataeus, who was describing land tenure in an earlier period.

The *Prosopographia Ptolemaica* lists the people who had dealings connected with land.[5] Some are laborers, but the majority are in possession of land either as lessees or owners. These people are classified according to the category of land with which they were involved (e.g., royal, gift, private, cleruchic, or sacred). Most of the statistics in the following discussion of women and land are based on the entries in the *Prosopographia Ptolemaica*. The figures are approximate, because some Egyptian names were borne by both women and men. However, whatever errors exist are likely to have had the same effect on the figures relating to the various categories of land. In any event, the potential for error is not important, since in the following discussion our conclusions will not be based on absolute numbers. (In fact, since some of the women were involved with more than one category of land, the totals of the four categories should not be added.) Rather, attention should be paid to comparisons such as those between women with Greek names and women with Egyptian names, and to the changing proportions of women possessing the various categories of land in the three Ptolemaic centuries. Here the results of the survey are so decisive that adding or subtracting a few women in every category would not make any difference.

### Cleruchic Land

As we have pointed out in our discussion of soldiers' wives, the early Ptolemies offered land to encourage their own troops and unaffiliated mercenaries to settle permanently in their country. In the early period of Ptolemaic rule, land in Egypt was more attractive to many soldiers than pay in currency offered by rival Hellenistic kings.[6]

Because the cleruchic land was encumbered by the obligation to serve in the army, women were not permitted to hold it. In excluding women from all land that was designated as cleruchic, the Ptolemies were acting according to both Pharaonic and Greek traditions. The Pharaohs in the Third Intermediate period had settled soldiers on their land.[7] Among some of the

Greeks, there was a connection between a man's ability to defend the land and his right to possess it. In Athens and Delos, for example, only male citizens could own land. It was mortgaged by men as sureties for dowries, but no woman actually owned such land.[8]

A cleruch was not tied to his land as a peasant might be. Many cleruchs lived in Alexandria and other centers of Greek population, and functioned as absentee landlords.[9] Because they were responsible for taxes on their land, they were obliged to keep it under cultivation. From the middle of the third century B.C., the cleruchs had the right to lease their property.[10] There are 372 known exploiters of cleruchic land belonging to others. Of these, only three are women. Two from the third century bear Greek names,[11] while one from the first bears an Egyptian name;[12] all the documents are in Greek. The locations are Philadelphia, Coite (of the Heracleopolite nome), and Oxyrhynchus. The three documents prove that it was not illegal for women to lease cleruchic land. One of the reasons that so few women did avail themselves of the opportunity must have been the tradition that such land was the property of men. This attitude continued even in the Roman period. *P. Iandanae* VII 137, a fragmentary list of taxes from Theadelphia from the first half of the second century, shows women paying at a higher rate on transfers of catoecic land (i.e., land originally designated for military colonists). Sir Harold Idris Bell follows the editors of the papyrus in suggesting that the higher rate indicates that the origin of catoecic land as military *kleroi* had not been forgotten with the passage of time.[13] However, the tax rate did not deter women from owning land in this category in the Roman period.[14]

In the second century B.C., when Egypt's ability to lure new recruits declined, administrative changes had to be made if the numbers of soldiers were not to decrease. Rather than let land be abandoned, risk famine, and lose the taxes on land and produce, the Ptolemies gradually revised the system of land tenure.[15] Small *kleroi* were distributed to natives who were, from the time of the battle of Raphia (217 B.C.), recruited for military service. In our discussion of soldiers' wives, we have noted that after the Seleucid invasion the government attempted to compel the population to cultivate land that had been abandoned. We have observed that, although soldiers' wives were exempt from this obligation, less privileged women were susceptible to it. Claire Préaux has pointed out that, after the indigenous population began to serve as soldiers, the number of men available to farm the land necessarily decreased.[16]

As the state grew weaker and needed to placate its soldiers, cleruchies began to be treated as private property. By the third century, it was not uncommon for soldiers to bequeath their *stathmoi* (billets) not only to sons but to wives.[17] In the second half of the second century B.C., the military allotments became hereditary in the male line. The land and the concomitant military obligation could thus pass from father to son to assure the presence of a permanent Greek army in Egypt and to reduce the need to recruit soldiers abroad. Finally, in the first century B.C., a brotherless girl inherited her father's *kleros*.[18]

### Gift Land, Royal Land, Sacred Land, and Private Land

The Ptolemies distributed large parcels of land as renewable gifts to those who were their favorites and had performed services for them. Apollonius, the dioecetes ("chief financial official") whose estate Zenon managed, was the recipient of such a grant. There are no women in this category.

Of the 449 names connected with royal land, only 7 are women. Six of them bear Egyptian names.[19] The seventh is Eirene, of whom we shall have more to say in this chapter.[20] Five of the seven are named in Demotic documents and are from Apollinopolis.

Sacred land was owned by temples, but it could be leased or purchased by secular individuals. We have already noted that Apollonia, wife of Dryton, and her three sisters engaged in a dispute over a parcel of land. The sisters asserted that their father had purchased the land and that they were his heirs. This property was located on sacred land. We have also observed that Apollonia leased 35 arouras in the precinct of Hathor.

Of 539 people known to have engaged in dealings concerning sacred land, 49 are women. The majority of the documents come not from the Fayum but from places farther up the Nile, including Pathyris, Apollinopolis, Latopolis, Lycopolis, and Diospolis Magna. As one would expect in documents dealing with sacred land, the majority are in Demotic. Nevertheless, a substantial number are written in Greek. Thirty-six women bear Egyptian names,[21] nine Greek names,[22] and Apollonia and her three sisters bear double names.[23] Some of the women with Egyptian names may have actually had a Greek name as well, but may not have used it when their dealings concerned land in the precincts of Egyptian gods, particularly when the documents were written in Demotic.

Of the 664 exploiters of private land, 51 are women. This number includes the five daughters of Apollonia and Dryton, who inherited a vineyard from their father. Some of the sources, whether for private or sacred land, do not state what was grown on the land. Several, however, do show that women possessed sacred and private lands with vegetable gardens and orchards planted with olives, date palms, and sycamores; the same is true of royal women. Among women who possessed private land, by far the largest number (24) owned vineyards, either exclusively or along with other property. Like the sacred land held by women, the vast majority of the private land was up the Nile, beyond the Fayum.

In contrast to the holders of sacred land, the majority of women (29) who possess private land bear Greek names.[24] Eighteen bear Egyptian names,[25] while the five daughters of Apollonia and Dryton—and one other woman—bear double names.[26] The employment of Greek names may be attributed to the fact that the vast majority of documents in this survey were written in Greek. Yet the conclusion that Egyptian women or Egyptianized Greeks preferred to deal in sacred land, while Greek women or Hellenized Egyptians tended to deal in private land, is so obvious that it should not be automatically discounted on the theory that, after the first century of Ptolemaic rule, names do not indicate ethnicity.

*Location*

The first Ptolemy and his son reclaimed the Fayum from Lake Moeris.[27] Philadelphus named the province, previously called "the marsh" or "the lake" (*limnē*), after his sister Arsinoë II. He was able to settle many of his soldiers there and avoid dislodging Egyptians to make room for them. By settling the area with soldiers, he also gave it a population of men able to make the physical effort required to remove brush and stumps that were left by the lake and to install an irrigation system which transformed the Fayum into one of the most fertile areas in the Hellenistic world.

The majority of the parcels of land cultivated by women was located south of the Fayum. The distribution of various categories of land throughout the country is not known. Perhaps there was more private and sacred land available in these areas. As was noted above, women seem to have been reluctant to lease cleruchic or royal land. If this type of land predominated in the Fayum, then there would be some reason for the lack of women's transactions in land in this region. In the village of Cerceosiris in the Fayum in 118 B.C., 52 percent of the land was royal; 33 percent was cleruchic; and 6 percent was sacred.[28] The rest consisted of orchards, untaxed land, and the village and its surroundings. There was no private land. Much of the sacred land was infertile, but women did not attempt to compensate for the lack of private land by contracting to cultivate cleruchic or royal land. Only one woman, Thaësis, is recorded as leasing cleruchic land, and this lease was made only as late as the middle of the first century B.C.

The sort of women, generally speaking, who lived in the Fayum differed from women farther south in their attitudes toward land cultivation. The Fayum was heavily settled by Greeks and Greek customs flourished more vigorously there. The areas in the south were less Hellenized. Therefore, women in the Fayum may have subscribed to the traditional Greek attitudes that associated land cultivation with men. In contrast, the Egyptian way of life did not discourage women from agricultural enterprises. Thus, women living in the more Egyptianized areas, whether they were Greeks or Egyptians, were more likely to engage in these activities.

All women, whether Greek or Egyptian, were less likely to lease cleruchic or royal land than land of other categories. To have done so would have brought a woman in contact with Greek men who were cleruchs, or with Greeks or Hellenized Egyptians in the bureaucracy. Greek women in Egypt were not secluded; nevertheless, Greek tradition would discourage them from business contacts with strange men. Egyptian women, on the other hand, though not inhibited from associating with men, would tend not to be part of the milieu in which important men—cleruchs and bureaucrats—were found. They would be more comfortable dealing with owners of small private plots and with priests in their local temples.

*Crops*

The type of crop grown on the various categories of land may have influenced women. Although some grain was raised, private land for the most part was planted with vineyards, orchards, and gardens. The bulk of the grain which made Egypt a leading producer in the Hellenistic world was grown on land controlled by the state. These categories were not exclusive. As the discussion of Eirene's activities later in this chapter will show, orchards and vineyards were planted on royal and gift land. The Revenue Laws of Ptolemy Philadelphus cover cleruchies and gift land that include vineyards and gardens.[29] Indeed, the Egyptian farmer even today often mixes the crops on any given plot—for example, planting vegetables under fruit trees. Grain was a more profitable crop than fruit.[30] Yet women may have tended to avoid it because, in the short run, it required more labor—both human and animal—and closer supervision than fruit. To grow grain, one needed a plow and a large animal to pull it. There is abundant evidence for women's possession of small animals such as goats and sheep, but not for large animals.[31] Close obedience to an imperious calendar of agricultural chores announced by the state was required. Short fallow was mandatory to assure that sufficient grain was produced to support those inhabitants of Ptolemaic Egypt who did not produce their own food. Vineyards and orchards do not require the same backbreaking labor as fields of grain. Even when neglected for years—barring calamities such as floods—trees and vines continue to yield a crop. Most of the chores in vineyards and orchards can be performed at the owner's discretion. If her child was ill and a woman had to delay pruning her olive trees, no harm would be done. A woman could also hire a day laborer from time to time to perform the chores or, if she could not afford the wages, she could perform the tasks herself. That such work was not considered intrinsically unwomanly and even a respectable woman could perform it if she had to is indicated by a speech of Demosthenes (57.45) in which it is asserted that, during the hard times after the Peloponnesian War, many women had to become wet nurses, workers in wool, or laborers in vineyards. Along with members of her family, a woman might harvest the fruit. Descriptions of the vintage in Greek poetry indicate that it could be regarded as a pleasurable occasion.

Women performed all kinds of agricultural labor. Female slaves even had to work at "men's" tasks, such as clearing away tree stumps and brush. One of them, in fact, complained about the work to Zenon. She wrote that she no longer had the strength to work, but did not wish to flee as the others had done (*PSI* VI 667). Obviously, it was best to be an owner of land, although with ownership came the responsibility for paying taxes. Women paid the same taxes on land and crops as men did. That most women preferred not to deal with the ordinary requirements of farming—and either performed the chores themselves or hired others to do them—is indicated by the fact that they appear in contracts more often as lessors than as lessees.[32] On the other hand, as we have noted in Chapter 3, under certain circumstances—for example, a dearth of males—women were compelled to perform agricultural labor.

The behavior of women in Ptolemaic Egypt vis-à-vis agriculture is consistent with women's behavior in other times and places. Ester Boserup has identified factors that influence women's participation in farming. Where work is centralized under a bureaucracy and the cultivation of land is intense, requiring that short-fallow and plow agriculture be practiced, the level of women's participation in farming is low.[33]

### Changes over Time

Women's ownership of land changed during the three Ptolemaic centuries and changed in ways different from men's. The most dramatic change was in relationship to cleruchic land. Though women were at first totally excluded from owning cleruchic land, as noted above, by the first century B.C., daughters could inherit it. Women's dealings with sacred and private land also changed. Of the women in our survey whose dates are known and who exploited sacred land, more than half belong to the second century B.C. and nearly one-third to the third; the first is most poorly represented.[34] Of the women who exploited private land whose dates are known, more than half belong to the second century B.C., nearly one-third to the third, and few to the first.[35]

A survey of men who exploited sacred land shows results similar to the survey of women.[36] There are approximately twice as many men in the second century B.C. as in the third, with few in the first. An analysis of men's ownership of private land yields different results. Here the number of men in third-century documents exceeds those in the second century. The fewest are again in the first century.

The documentation for the last century of Ptolemaic rule is thin in general. Therefore, the significant point in this survey is the increase in women's ownership of private land in the second century, when men's ownership of such land decreased. A possible explanation for the difference is that women took advantage of the turmoil of the second century to improve their economic situation. When native men began serving in the army, they may have sold their land for a low price or even abandoned it. Small *kleroi* were allocated to the native soldiers, making it less necessary for them to compete with women for private land.

*Acquisition of Land*

Although land was a constituent of dowries in other parts of the Hellenistic world, it is not mentioned as part of a dowry in any Greek marriage contract in Ptolemaic Egypt.[37] It should, however, be admitted that the documentation for dowries in the Ptolemaic period is not ample and subsequent discoveries may alter some of the interpretations expressed in this chapter. The earliest example of a Greek marriage contract from Egypt showing a dowry that includes land comes from A.D. 42 (*P. Mich.* II

121. recto ii 2, Tebtunis). Apparently land was also excluded from dowries among the native population, for it is not mentioned as part of matrimonial property.[38]

Inheritance was the means by which most women became landowners.[39] As we have seen, Apollonia and her three sisters and then Apollonia's five daughters inherited land from their respective fathers. In contrast to marriage contracts, numerous wills, both Greek and Demotic, show that parents and husbands regularly bequeathed land to women. However, according to Orsolina Montevecchi's analysis of the Greek testaments, many more sons than daughters are mentioned as beneficiaries.[40] Married daughters are seldom mentioned, since many of them would have taken their portion of the patrimony as dowry and gone off to live away from their natal family. The women in Apollonia's family do, however, remain in Pathyris and claim their legacies (see pp. 113–17).

The disturbances of the second century B.C. must have increased women's opportunities to inherit land. As men were dying or going into anachoresis (withdrawing or hiding) to avoid obligations to the state—including military service and taxes—women would inherit larger shares of the family property. Just as a brotherless girl inherited her father's *kleros* in the first century B.C., so many brotherless girls or widows may have inherited property one century earlier.

Women's possession of land was a symptom—though surely not a cause—of the decline of the system of land tenure that the first two Ptolemies had designed for Greek rule in Egypt. Women were permitted to possess cleruchic land and increased their holdings of private land only when it was being abandoned and the interest of the state required that it be kept under cultivation by any possible means. In Egypt, weakness in government brings about a decline in the irrigation system. Thus, women came into possession of land at a time when farming was difficult and the economy was deteriorating. But it was better to hold land than to possess the unreliable currency of the later Ptolemies. Even the waste land belonging to the daughters of Dryton on the less fertile side of the Nile near Thebes was attractive enough for someone to seize it in the daughters' absence. Those who owned land in adverse circumstances were better off than those who were obliged to live off the land of others. Thus, the demise of the cleruchic system and the growth of private property brought about an improvement in women's economic position and gave them an opportunity to share equally with men in the chief means of production in Egypt.

### Eirene, Agricultural Entrepreneur

Eirene, a Macedonian, daughter of Orphis and wife of Agamemnon, exploited land in the Fayum.[41] Both Eirene and Agamemnon were descended from important families. Eirene's father is known from his correspondence with Zenon. Agamemnon was the son of Chrysermus, an official in Cilicia. Although Agamemnon, when required, served as his wife's guardian, there is no need to assume that Eirene delegated to her husband any of the actual work arising from her landholding.[42] In fact, it seems more natural to assume that—like Apollonia, wife of Dryton—Eirene personally supervised her business.

As has been pointed out in the first part of this chapter, it was relatively unusual in the Ptolemaic period for a Greek woman to deal in land in the Fayum. Furthermore, Eirene's holdings were unusually extensive for a woman. It was also uncommon for a woman to rent crown and gift lands, although she did so. Eirene was also an exception to the rule that most cultivators of royal land were Egyptians, not Greeks.[43] Her high status must have rendered her fearless in dealing with the bureaucracy in charge of state-owned land. However, in the variety of the crops she cultivated, in her management of cash and produce, and in her business relationships with men, her activities were typical of women landholders—though on a larger scale.

Eirene has been called "wealthy" and her land referred to as an "estate" and compared to the property of Apollonius the dioecetes.[44] Yet not only was Apollonius' estate grandiose (10,000 arouras), but it was conferred on him as a gift by Ptolemy Philadelphus. Apollonius employed Zenon—no negligible person in his own right—to manage it. In contrast, Eirene inherited some property and a dovecote from her mother, but she had to rent most of her land from the state and manage it herself.

The documents give some information about the financial transactions of Eirene from 185 B.C. to 178 B.C. She owned outright only a dovecote and some undescribed property that she had inherited. By 185/184 B.C., she had rented gift and crown lands from the state. The bulk of her income was derived from these properties. Her land included a vineyard, a garden, caraway and henna plants, and an orchard of olives, figs, and pomegranates. She rented out the property she had inherited. In 183/182 B.C., she leased the crops of her orchard to a consortium of three men organized by Leontiscus. They, in turn, agreed to pay the rent due on the orchard directly to the state. By this transaction, Eirene not only turned over the profits on the orchard to the consortium, but also freed herself of the responsibility for paying the state. In other words she became a "middleman" without any profit. Perhaps she had tried to manage the harvest of the orchard for a year and was not pleased with the results. Since the leases on state-owned land ran for several years, she could not simply turn back the land. In this situation, the best arrangement she could make was to place the responsibility for paying the rent on others. In January 182 B.C., Eirene borrowed 44 talents, 4,800 copper drachmas from Nicander, a Syracusan who had a cleruchy of 80 arouras.[45] She again leased out the crops of her orchard to the consortium of three. At this time, she may not have known that they had failed to pay all the rent due to the state for the preceding year.

Eirene's total income from all her properties for one year (181/180 B.C.) was less than her debt to Nicander. She must have held more property in 182 B.C., since the consortium of fruit-pickers agreed to be responsible for the debt to Nicander. At this time, Eirene herself probably remained responsible for the rent owed to the state. Leases of royal land often ran for five years. Eirene must have divested herself of part of the orchard as soon as she could. Her accounts of 181/180 B.C. show no income from olive trees, though she did have olives in 182 B.C.

What prompted her to borrow such a large sum from Nicander? The orchard with its fruits leased in return for the payment of rent should not have been responsible for this debt. Rather, Eirene must have needed the money for the vineyard. Like the other women landholders whom we have discussed, she held orchards and vineyards but had a particular affinity for the latter. She did not subcontract for the vineyard, but managed it herself. Her agricultural accounts of 181/180 B.C. are extant. She seems to have been able to sign her own name (*P. Mich.* III 183). Perhaps she kept her own accounts, too. Her accounts give day-by-day entries for the expenses incurred in hiring laborers for the vintage.

Eirene's accounts for 181/180 B.C. show a total income of 28 talents, 4,990 drachmas on the copper standard. From this she paid rents, taxes, and the debt to Nicander, which had been left in default by the consortium of three. These payments totaled 16 talents, 5,940 drachmas. The remainder was 11 talents, 5,050 drachmas. From this remainder, Eirene would have had to pay the expenses incurred in cultivating her vineyard.

Although Eirene dealt in large amounts of land, cash, and produce, most of the time payments due her were outstanding and she herself was in arrears. Such cash-flow problems were common and need not indicate that she lacked business acumen. She was overextended at first, but, as soon as she could, she reduced her holdings. We can only speculate about her reasons for maintaining her relationship with the various consortia organized by Leontiscus, for they were continually in arrears. Inertia and timidity are not likely to have inhibited Eirene from changing her subcontractors. It is more probable that she realized that she would never collect from them unless she maintained the relationship and that no one more competent was available. Her prestige in the community was such that, after she had been cultivating state land for at least three years, she was able to borrow a substantial amount of cash from a cleruch. Whether her agricultural transactions brought her a net profit or a loss remains unclear.

## DOMESTIC AND INDUSTRIAL JOBS

Agriculture offered respectable women the greatest opportunity to make money in Egypt, but there were other ways as well. Plenty of women owned immovables, including houses or sheds or parts of buildings. This property could be rented or sold.[46] Women with sufficient resources, like Apollonia, wife of Dryton, made loans of commodities and cash for profit. At another economic level of society, women worked in commerce and industry. The historical sources give us the names of relatively few women who worked at specific wage-earning jobs. There are scattered mentions of women pursuing the same means of making a living as women had done in the older Greek cities. These include a linen seller,[47] a general dealer,[48] and weavers of garlands and fillets.[49] Doubtless there were plenty of others, but their activities involved small sums or were not taxable, so they are not recorded on a scrap of papyrus or an ostracon. The women we do know most about worked at food preparation, clothing manufacture, and wet-nursing. These jobs were traditionally performed by women in the Greek world, but in Egypt only wet-nursing was, necessarily, confined to women.

Praxinoa in the idyll of Theocritus had one slave who performed general housework and baby-sitting.[50] Praxinoa kept her clothing in a locked chest, but she did not hesitate to leave her baby in the care of her slave with whom she was not totally satisfied. Some Greek women who could afford them employed women who specialized in wet-nursing or baby nursing.[51] In the older Greek cities, these jobs were performed by slaves or by free women who needed the money. Terracotta figurines depicting women holding babies and leading toddlers by the hand are the best Hellenistic evidence for these.[52] In contrast to the glamorous, well-dressed women on other Hellenistic figurines, the nurses appear, at least to the modern viewer, to be middle-aged. However, since some of them are carrying young babies who must have been still suckling, the nurses must be younger than they look, and their aged appearance must be attributed to a life spent at hard work.

The wealthier women who lived in Alexandria probably used their own slaves as wet-nurses and baby nurses. If they had made a contract with a free woman, such a contract on papyrus would not have survived—except through incorporation in cartonnage—since the climate of Alexandria was unfavorable to the preservation of papyri. The names of several nurses are extant. Cosmia is listed in a tax declaration of 240 B.C. (*Chrest. Wilck.* 198.4).[53] The family for whom she works has four sons, ranging from five to fifteen years old. Like the nurse, the boys and their parents all have Greek names. Tryphaena, the nurse of Ptolemy XIII, is the subject of an inscription of 60/59 B.C.;[54] and, as mentioned in Chapter 2, Agathoclea was the nurse of Ptolemy V.

Although there are numerous papyrus contracts for wet-nursing from the Roman period, I know of only one that has been published from the Ptolemaic period. This contract is in Demotic (*P. Cairo dem.* II 30604 [233/231 B.C.]) with a Greek docket (*P. Tebtunis* II 279 = *UPZ* I, p. 603, no. 2). Sponnesis agreed to serve as a wet nurse for a boy for three years.[55] She was to live in the baby's house in Tebtunis and provide milk from both breasts. She received her board and earned a salary of 350 drachmas and oil. The baby's father and grandfather have Egyptian names, and, since the contract is in Demotic and dates from the first hundred years of Ptolemaic occupation, the names signify ethnicity. Two years is the normal duration of Greek nursing contracts. Although, among Greeks, boys were suckled longer than girls, three years would have been an exceptionally long time span for them. Thus, viewed by Greek standards, this baby appears to have been of great value. However, the nursing practices of the Egyptians are not known.

The Greek contracts from the Roman period differ in that often—though not inevitably—the baby to be nursed is not the child of the person making the contract with the nurse.[56] Rather, it is a foundling who will be brought up to be a slave. Furthermore, the nurse takes the baby to her own house. This circumstance gave rise to allegations that the nurse had substituted babies. Moreover, it was usual to include a stipulation that the nurse refrain from sexual intercourse—which, of course, might lead to pregnancy and the cessation of lactation.[57] This stipulation is found even in contracts in which the nurse is a free married woman and her husband is her guardian.

Women prepared and sold food.[58] They also brewed and sold beer. The brewing of beer was known in Egypt as early as Pharaonic times.[59] Women must have participated, since brewing is related to food preparation and the work was performed at home. The home breweries threatened to become an artifact of the past, owing to the intensive effort of the first Ptolemies to restore the beer industry.[60] Even after the government took control of brewing, there continued to be female brewers,[61] and in one case a beer shop was run by a mother and daughter. (The daughter was seduced by a married man and ran away with him.)[62] Government supervision of industry was detrimental to domestic industries.[63] No longer were there family businesses such as breweries that were passed down through the generations. The changes in weaving that occurred in Egypt with the advent of the Ptolemies were even more profound.

Working in wool was the most characteristic occupation of Greek women.[64] In Homeric epic, Helen spins, Penelope weaves, and Andromache is admonished to attend to her weaving. The sixth-century B.C. Law Code of Gortyn recognizes woven goods as the only substantial contribution that a wife makes to the household economy. In case of divorce, the code permits a wife to take half of what she has woven.

In Classical Athens, women of all classes spun and wove—for profit, for pleasure, and for practical reasons. Expensive vases show well-dressed, respectable women as well as *hetairai* working in wool.[65] Weaving also had its place in rituals, such as the replacement of the peplos ("dress") of Athena Polias. The symbolic aspects of weaving definitely associate this task with all that is feminine. For example, the fourth-century poet Erinna titled her poem about girls growing up "The Distaff."[66] In the older Greek cities, clothing was often made from start to finish at home, and all the women in the household, from slaves to the mistress, shared in this labor.

In Athens, clothing was also produced commercially. Men—both slave and free—as well as women were employed in this industry.[67] Interestingly enough, the documentation for commercial production in the Classical period begins only in the second half of the Peloponnesian War and is most abundant for the fourth century B.C. This period is thus a watershed in the transformation of gender roles, marked both by women's entrance into the liberal arts and professions previously reserved for men[68] and by men's engagement in the quintessentially female task of clothing production.

The housewife in Ptolemaic Egypt was not obliged to devote long hours to wool-working. Ready-made cloth was available for purchase. A poem of Theocritus indicates that well-dressed Alexandrian women might purchase cloth and then fashion their own outfits:

GORGO:     My husband's the same. Diocleidas wastes money. Yesterday he spent seven drachmas for dogs' hair, pluckings of old wallets, five fleeces he bought, all dirt, nothing but work. . . .
PRAXINOA (to her slave):   It's always a holiday for the lazy. Eunoa, pick up that spinning. You let it lie around there again, and I'll give you a good lesson. Cats like to sleep on soft beds. . . .
GORGO:   Praxinoa, that pleated dress with the buckle on the shoulder suits you. Tell me, how much did it cost you off the loom?
PRAXINOA:   Don't remind me, Gorgo. More than two minas of pure silver. As for the work, I put my heart and soul into it.[69]

The references to fleeces and spinning in this poem indicate that such women would also spin wool themselves. Rostovtzeff asserted that Greek women in Egypt continued to work in wool at home, as they had done in the older Greek cities. However, the idyll of Theocritus is his only good evidence. In *A Large Estate in Egypt in the Third Century B.C.*, published in 1922, Rostovtzeff cited two papyri in support of his statement that there was no restriction on weaving and making woolen clothes at home in Egypt.[70] One of these documents (*PSI* IV 364 [251/250 B.C.]) is simply a letter to Zenon thanking him for a cloak. Where the cloak was made was not stated. The second document cited (*UPZ* I 29 = *P. Cair. Zen.* II 59170 [255 B.C.]) has nothing to do with weaving, for it is a letter to Zenon concerning the sale of wine. In his great work, *The Social and Economic History of the Hellenistic World,* published in 1941, Rostovtzeff stated that Greek women and their slaves produced ordinary clothing for their households at home, this time giving Theocritus' poem as his sole evidence.[71] Yet Gorgo and Praxinoa had developed their habits outside Egypt, for they, like Theocritus himself, were immigrants from the old Greek city of Syracuse. Later generations of Greek housewives who could afford to purchase cloth and ready-made clothing probably relinquished this chore with relief. We have already drawn attention to the soldier's wife who became embroiled in an altercation while purchasing a mattress in the market at Alexandria (see p. 101). (Earlier generations of Greek housewives had made their own mattresses at home.)[72]

The option of purchasing textiles rather than producing them at home was not a prerogative limited to inhabitants of the city of Alexandria. We have also drawn attention to a marriage contract (*P. Tebt.* I 104) that stipulates that a wife in Cerceosiris must be provided with clothing (see p. 93). This stipulation must refer to the cash required to purchase clothing, for if she were weaving it herself, the husband would not be obliged to provide it.

Rostovtzeff was attempting to make the point that, though the government controlled the textile industries, the control was not so tight as to eliminate private production. In fact, cloth was manufactured in both royal and private workshops, but Rostovtzeff overemphasized private production by bourgeois women. These are the very women who had the cash to purchase beautiful textiles and fashionable clothing. Unlike their counterparts in Classical Athens, they were not obliged to stay at home, and they did not need to fill their hours with wool-working. The pictorial arts bring out dramatically the difference between the occupations of respectable women in Classical Athens and in Hellenistic Alexandria.[73] Respectable women are frequently portrayed on Athenian vases working in wool. Vases and grave stelae show maids presenting a jewel box or a mirror to their late mistress (Plate 12). In contrast, the grave stela of Nico, an *aste* from Alexandria from about 250 B.C., shows a woman in the same pose as the women on the stelae in Classical Athens.[74] However, her maid offers her a lyre (see Plate 13).

Claire Préaux gives a more accurate picture than Rostovtzeff

12. Grave stela of Hegeso from Athens, ca. 400 B.C. A slave offers a jewelry box to an upper-class woman holding a necklace. *Athens. National Museum 3624.*

13. Grave stela of Nico from Alexandria, ca. 250 B.C. A slave offers a lyre to an upper-class woman. *Cairo. Egyptian Museum C.G. 9259. Photo courtesy of the Deutsches Archäologisches Institut, Cairo.*

did of domestic production when she describes the workers as people who were actually employed in other jobs, and who made textiles in their spare time. It is difficult to determine how widespread this cottage industry was. The evidence comes from Zenon's documents. The estate Zenon managed was atypical because of its enormity and because some of Zenon's methods of management, including his employment of slaves, were more characteristic of old Greece than of Egypt. Some women made textiles at home for Zenon. Zenon had organized the entire enterprise in a way that was, perhaps, inimitable. He imported and raised sheep of high quality and supplied his workers with the wool (*P. Mich. Zen.* 13, 16). Whether such women made textiles at other times for anyone else, even for the members of their families, is not clear. One woman, Maiandria, wife of an employee of the dioecetes Apollonius, wove a cloak for Zenon. Her husband was in debt to Zenon, and the price of this cloak was deducted from the sum owed (*P. Cair. Zen.* II 59263 [251 B.C.] and III 59355. 90 [243 B.C.]).[75]

In a declaration of 250 B.C. (*P. Cair. Zen.* II 59295), Zenon wrote that he had 320 women working in wool in Mouchis, 314 at Oxyrhynchus, and 150 at Tebtunis—a total of 784 in the three Fayum villages. Wool was produced for the Greek population; the Egyptians had manufactured linen before the arrival of the Ptolemies.[76] The following letter (*PSI* VI 599) was sent to Zenon from men who sought employment making linen:

> We have come here to work. To be fair, we should be given 1 drachma for each talent that we wash and comb. Weaving costs 3 copper drachmas for one linen cloth—and even that is not enough for us. Each cloth requires three men and one woman, and it is necessary to work for six straight days. If these conditions do not suit you, give each one $1\frac{1}{2}$ obols and to the woman $\frac{1}{2}$ obol. Give us an assistant at 5 drachmas 2 obols [per month] who can do the work, deducting this salary from our wages.

The wages asked are very low and may have been quoted to entice the prospective employer. As was the case at Athens, when wool-working ceased to be confined to the home, it was no longer limited to women. Egyptian men had always worked alongside women in the textile industries.[77] In Ptolemaic Egypt, Greek men also engaged in this work (*PSI* IV 341, quoted below). Not only did men work with women in the textile industries, but, as the letter quoted above shows, they could be paid three times as much as women. It is interesting to observe how the wage differential between male and female workers compares with the differential in salt tax (a universal "head" tax). The annual rates were $1\frac{1}{2}$ drachmas for a man and 1 drachma for a woman until 254/253 B.C., and 1 drachma for a man and 3 obols for a woman thereafter.[78] The pay scale quoted in *PSI* VI 599 was not necessarily intrinsically discriminatory, but may reflect the different skills of the workers. Of course, assigning the lower-paying job to a woman is in itself discriminatory.

Whereas in domestic production each woman was expected to perform all the chores related to clothing production, from preparing the wool to sewing the garments, in commercial production the various stages were performed by specialists. Some prepared the wool, others wove, and still others turned the cloth into garments. Some made particular items of clothing, such as cloaks (*PSI* V 485 [258/257 B.C.]). Others specialized in a full line of women's clothes (*PSI* IV 341 [256/255 B.C.]):

> Greetings to Zenon from Apollophanes and Demetrius, brothers, producers of all kinds of woolen clothing for women.
> If you would like to, and if by chance you have need, we are ready to supply what you want. We have heard speak of the glory of the city [Philadelphia] as well as of the goodness and justice with which you administer it. That is why we have decided to come to you, to Philadelphia, with our mother and wife so that we might be workers. Summon us if you would like us to work. We make, as you wish, cloaks, tunics, girdles, dresses, belts, ribbons, split tunics, trimming, everything to size. And we can teach our trade, if you like. Tell Nicias to provide lodging for us. So that we won't seem strangers to you, we can supply references from people known to you, some from here whom you can trust, others from Moithymis. Farewell.

Free workers were employed in textile manufacture at Philadelphia. These people worked in small domestic workshops. Zenon also ran a factory for the production of woolen fabrics at Memphis. What such a factory was like can be envisioned from Wolfgang Müller's analysis of a papyrus from the second or first century B.C. (*P. Berl.* inv. 1942 = *SB* X 10209):[79]

| | |
|---|---|
| Apollonia | . . . |
| Arcadia | sick |
| Aristonice | preparing wool |
| Gaza | spinning |
| Dionysia | preparing wool |
| Dianoia | preparing wool |
| Demarion | sick |
| Helenis | sick |
| Euthene | spinning |
| Hermione | spinning |
| Eirene | . . . |
| Ebenion | sick |
| Heracleia | sick |
| Theophila | preparing wool |

Because the fragmentary list was alphabetical in Greek, Müller was able to suggest that these women worked in a medium-sized workshop which employed about forty women. He concluded that they were predominantly or exclusively slaves. None of the women has an Egyptian name. Ebenion may be a name used by slaves from Africa.[80] Some are named after places—an onomastic that indicates slave origin. Most of the workers have ordinary Greek names. We may recall that Dryton's female slaves also bore ordinary Greek names. These names do not necessarily indicate Greek origin. Rather, in Ptolemaic Egypt, the people who owned slaves were Greeks, and they tended to call their slaves by Greek names. The slaves who worked in textile factories were probably imported from lands east of Egypt.

Historians have debated whether the Industrial Revolution, which brought women textile workers out of the home and into the factory, was good or bad for women.[81] For workers in Ptolemaic Egypt, the analogous questions are equally debatable. Was it better for a slave to spin wool in a workshop with other women or as the lone slave in a private house like Praxinoa's? Was it easier for a poor woman to take a job in a workshop or to weave at home? Müller's list shows that thirty percent of the women were not working on a given day. He attributes this rate of absenteeism to hard work, insufficient nourishment, and poor lodgings.[82] To these hypotheses should be added the ready excuse of menstruation, which must have affected some of the women. At least it should be noted that the conditions were not so oppressive that these women were forced to work when they felt ill.

The names of more women are attested in connection with textile manufacture in Ptolemaic Egypt than for any other job.[83] Moreover, the textile factories provide the first example in the Greek world of large numbers of women working together. Such factories were, of course, managed by men like Zenon, and men—including the king and Zenon's employer—reaped the profits. The bourgeois housewife must have considered herself a beneficiary as well, for she was relieved of the necessity of providing all the clothing for members of her household. On the other hand, she had relinquished a means of making a tangible contribution to the household economy, and, inasmuch as weaving is an art, she had lost an avenue of self-expression. Of course, a woman might weave as a hobby. But even in this case her husband was no longer dependent on her for clothing the household, while she was dependent on him for the cash with which to purchase clothing. But women such as Gorgo and Praxinoa, or Eirene, or Apollonia wife of Dryton, or Apollonia also called Cellauthis doubtless did not recognize the availability of ready-made cloth as a mixed blessing.

Respectable women participated in the economy of Ptolemaic Egypt to a greater extent than can be documented for any other Greek society and in ways comparable to the activities of women in later Roman society. At the level of royalty, insofar as some Ptolemaic queens enjoyed access to the state treasury, they surpassed their Roman counterparts.

As we have seen, women worked as professionals of many sorts. Of course, the military—the profession most characteristic of the Hellenistic period—was closed to women. However, a few women earned money in the liberal professions, while many more worked in the service professions as nurses, prostitutes, and domestic slaves. They also worked as artisans, especially in textile manufacture, and as vendors selling all sorts of goods ranging from luxury items to necessities.

Women owned the same kinds of property as men did, but owned less of it. They owned immovables, such as buildings and land, and movables, including personal property, small animals, and slaves. As owners, they were responsible for liturgies (public duties) and taxes on their property, and they could pay their own taxes and initiate petitions to the government in their own behalf when their ownership of land or tax liability was at issue. Women also were not exempt merely by reason of gender from the performance of compulsory agricultural services for the state.

Women were active in the money market as both lenders and borrowers. As married women, they possessed dowries and performed domestic services in exchange for maintenance by the husband. In contrast to the situation in Athens, there is little overt reference in Ptolemaic Egypt to the production of children as women's primary contribution to the domestic economy. Nor is there any trace of female infanticide—a practice which reveals that in some societies daughters were considered a financial liability.

The Athenian woman was legally prohibited from entering into a contract independently for an amount greater than the price of a *medimnus* of barley (a *medimnus* could sustain a normal family for six days). Although there is no specific law extant, it is apparent from the documents that a woman in Ptolemaic Egypt, acting under Greek law, similarly needed the consent of a *kyrios* (guardian) for financial transactions of more than a trivial value. However, women in Ptolemaic Egypt had the option of using the Egyptian legal system, in which a *kyrios* was not required. Moreover, the observable fact that Egyptian women were acting without guardians would have demonstrated to the Greeks that all women were perfectly capable of doing so. It is likely that, in such a milieu, the consent of the guardian would become a routine matter, but this cannot be documented. If true, however, such a development would be analogous to the situation in the Roman Republic, where, by the last century B.C., the approval of a woman's guardian (*tutor*) was often merely an empty legal formality.

Thus, in the economic sphere, as in the political and social realms, there was less distinction between the genders in Ptolemaic Egypt than there was, for example, in Athens, or in Greek society in general of an earlier period. Parallels can be found scattered elsewhere, but no other Greek society of the Hellenistic period provides a comparable quantity and variety of documentation for the improvement of the economic status of respectable women.

# Notes

## Foreword

1. Adapted from the translation by Walter Headlam, *Herodas: The Mimes and Fragments*, p. 5.

2. There are many surveys of Hellenistic history. See, e.g., M. I. Rostovtzeff, *The Social and Economic History of the Hellenistic World* (hereafter cited as *SEHHW*), and Claire Préaux, *Le monde hellénistique: La Grèce et l'Orient (323–146 av. J.-C.)* (hereafter cited as *MH*).

3. For the history of the city, especially its intellectual life, see P. M. Fraser, *Ptolemaic Alexandria* (hereafter cited as *PA*).

## Introduction

1. For reviews of scholarly assessments of the status of Greek women, see Sarah B. Pomeroy, "Selected Bibliography on Women in Antiquity," pp. 140–43, and *Women in the Ancient World*, pp. 330–33, and *Goddesses, Whores, Wives, and Slaves: Women in Classical Antiquity* (hereafter cited as *GWWS*), pp. 58–60.

2. See, e.g., Michelle Zimbalist Rosaldo, "A Theoretical Overview," p. 41.

3. On the separation of the sexes at Athens, see Pomeroy, *GWWS*, pp. 79–84.

4. *Pol.* 1.2.12 (1254b) and 1.5 (1259–60); see also *EE* 7.10.8–9 (1242a), 7.3.3 (1238b), and 7.5.5 (1239b).

5. See especially *Rep.* 5 and Pomeroy, *GWWS*, pp. 115–18.

## Chapter 1

1. Material in this chapter was presented in my lecture "Macedonian Queens and the Feminization of Greek Culture."

174

2. N. G. L. Hammond and G. T. Griffith, *A History of Macedonia*, vol. 1, pp. 335, 354, 366; vol. 2, p. 143.

3. For Athenian burials, see Pomeroy, *GWWS*, pp. 42–43, 83–84.

4. Her. 5.18–20. The historian may have invented the "women's quarters" because he knew of their existence in other parts of the Greek world. George Cawkwell, *Philip of Macedon*, p. 24, finds the story of the murder of the Persian envoys "highly suspect."

5. Her. 8.137.2; Curt. 5.2.20; Aristid. 45.55 (Dindorf); Hammond and Griffith, *Macedonia*, vol. 2, p. 154.

6. *Anab.* 7.9.2.

7. Athen. 13.557b–e = *FHG* 3, p. 161, frag. 5. On this passage, see Anna Maria Prestianni Giallombardo, "Diritto matrimoniale, ereditario e dinastico nella Macedonia di Filippo II."

8. For an early description of the tomb, see Nicholas and Jean Gagé, "Treasures from a Golden Tomb." The contents of the tomb have since been published in a number of museum catalogues, for example the guide to the exhibit at the Archaeological Museum of Thessalonike, *Treasures of Ancient Macedonia*, ed. K. Ninou. For the debate on whether the tomb is actually that of Philip II, see, for example, E. A. Fredericksmeyer, "Again the So-Called Tomb of Philip II"; William M. Calder III, "Diadem and Barrel Vault: A Note"; and Anna Maria Prestianni Giallombardo and Bruno Tripodi, "Le Tombe Regali di Vergina: Quale Filippo?"

9. Giallombardo and Tripodi, "Le Tombe Regali," p. 993, draw attention to the feminine quality of the floral decoration.

10. Eugene N. Borza, "The Macedonian Royal Tombs at Vergina: Some Cautionary Notes," pp. 78–79, argues that the armor actually belonged to the king and that the dead woman is the noblewoman Cleopatra. Nevertheless, it cannot be denied that there were a number of warrior women at the Macedonian court—even if it should turn out that the woman in the tomb was not one of them.

11. "Philip's Tomb in Historical Context," pp. 335–36.

12. S.v. "Getia." For a discussion of classical sources on suttee, see Waldemar Heckel and John C. Yardley, "Roman Writers and the Indian Practice of Suttee."

13. 4.71.4; 5.5.

14. Peter Green, "The Royal Tombs of Vergina: A Historical Analysis," p. 145 n. 44, following Satyrus, does not believe that Philip ever married a Scythian princess. On pp. 140–41, Green provides a very useful chart of possible candidates for burial in the royal tomb. The birthdates of Philip's wives are not known, but there is better evidence

for the dates of their marriages. Green calculates their birthdates based on marriage at about the age of twenty. This age is too high for the first marriage of an upper-class woman in antiquity. For example, Adea-Eurydice married Philip Arrhidaeus at the age of fifteen, and Arsinoë II married Lysimachus at the age of sixteen.

15. Polyaen. 8.60. On Cynane and her daughter Eurydice, see Grace Macurdy, *Hellenistic Queens* (hereafter cited as *HQ*); pp. 48–52.

16. Athen. 13.560f. = *FGrH* 2, p. 150, frag. 52.

17. A preliminary analysis of the bones indicating that they are of a woman from twenty-three to twenty-seven years old makes it less likely that Eurydice is the occupant of the tomb. However, bones cannot be dated so precisely as to rule out decisively a person three years younger than the suggested dates.

18. Giallombardo and Tripodi, "Le Tombe Regali," pp. 996–99.

19. 7.110–17.

20. T. Sulimirski, *The Sarmatians*, pp. 34, 105–6.

21. J. K. Anderson, *Ancient Greek Horsemanship*, pp. 115–16.

22. "La position de la femme en Asie centrale, pp. 151–52."

23. Curt. 6.5.23–32. On the letters alleged to have been exchanged by Alexander and the Amazon queen, see Fraser, *PA*, vol. 1, p. 678.

24. Above, note 6, *Anab.* 7.9.2. Cawkwell, *Philip*, pp. 39–40, 114.

25. Plut. *Alex.* 68.3. On Olympias, see the full-length study by Walther Tritsch, *Olympias: Die Mutter Alexanders des Grossen.*

26. *Pol.* 2.6.6 (1269b).

27. On the effects of war on women, see Pomeroy, *GWWS*, pp. 66, 119, 177–81.

28. Donald W. Engels, *Alexander the Great and the Logistics of the Macedonian Army*, p. 18.

29. Arr. *Anab.* 1.24.1.

30. Plut. *Them.* 32.2.

31. For discussion of whether Eurydice became institutionalized as a "throne-name," see Macurdy, *HQ*, p. 25; Waldemar Heckel, "Kleopatra or Eurydike?"; Anna Maria Prestianni Giallombardo, "Eurydike-Kleopatra. Nota ad Arr., *Anab.*, 3, 6, 5"; and, arguing persuasively against this idea, Ernst Badian, "Eurydice."

32. On the four names of Olympias as marking different stages in her life, see Waldemar Heckel, "Polyxena, the Mother of Alexander the Great." Badian, "Eurydice," p. 107, points out that she is never actually referred to by any name other than Olympias.

33. This work has not been replaced as the standard reference on the topic. However, much research has of course been published since

1932, and the reader is cautioned about Macurdy's chronology in particular.

34. Vol. 1, pp. 181–294. See also, *inter alia*, E. R. Goodenough, "The Political Philosophy of Hellenistic Kingship."

35. Préaux, *MH*, vol. 1, pp. 219, 254, 286.

36. On Roxane, see H. Berve, *Das Alexanderreich*, vol. 2, pp. 346–47.

37. 18.41.5–10.

38. 22.20.1–4.

39. *OGIS* 308.

40. 13.576E.

41. *SIG*³ 314. See also p. 53 above.

42. *Pyrr.* 4.4. The influence of Hellenistic queens is also mentioned in inscriptions. See Michael Wörrle, "Epigraphische Forschungen zur Geschichte Lykiens, II: Ptolemaios II und Telmessos," p. 202; *SEG* 4.442; and *IG* 4.750.

43. See Pomeroy, *GWWS*, pp. 38–39, 130–31.

44. Plut. *Pyrr.* 9; Daniel 11.6; *P. Cair. Zen.* II 59251; Macurdy, *HQ*, p. 84.

45. Diod. Sic. 1.52.5–6.

46. See the documents cited in W. Peremans, E. van't Dack, et al., *Prosopographia Ptolemaica* (hereafter cited as P.Pt.): IV 8523, 8524, 8526, 8530, 8531; and Hans Hauben, "Le transport fluvial en Egypte ptolémaïque: Les bateaux du roi et de la reine." For other women shipowners, see p. 54 above.

47. See Pomeroy, *GWWS*, pp. 130–31, 161–63.

48. Hyper. *Euxen.* 19.24–26.

49. *IG* II–III 2¹.1492.46ff.

50. Karl Lehmann, *Samothrace: A Guide to the Excavations and the Museum*, p. 54.

51. Polyb. 5.89.7–8.

52. See Sarah B. Pomeroy, "Charities for Greek Women."

53. Diod. Sic. 19.59.4. Phila also played a judicial role, freeing men who had been accused unjustly. On this exemplary woman, see C. Wehrli, "Phila, fille d'Antipater et épouse de Démétrius, roi des Macédoniens."

54. *ASAA* 45–46, n.s. 29–30 (1969); Giovanni Pugliese Carratelli, "Supplemento epigrafico di Iasos," pp. 445–53, number 2. Pugliese Carratelli thought that the author was Laodice II, wife of Seleucus II. In "Bulletin épigraphique" (*REG* 84: 502–9, number 621, and *ibid.* 86: 165–66, number 432), Jeanne and Louis Robert have argued convincingly that Laodice III, the wife of Antiochus III, was the correct Laodice.

55. See the full-length study by Gabriella Longega, *Arsinoë II*, and the comments on Longega's work by E. Will and Stanley Mayer Burstein, cited in note 60 below. See also Macurdy, *HQ*, pp. 111–30; E. Kornemann, *Grosse Frauen des Altertums im Rahmen zweitausendjährigen Weltgeschehens*, pp. 110–34; and Hermann Bengtson, *Herrschergestalten des Hellenismus*, pp. 111–38.

56. On this subject, see, most recently, M. Keith Hopkins, "Brother–Sister Marriage in Roman Egypt." See also *P. Vindob. Worp*, p. 5.

57. According to Jaroslav Černy, "Consanguineous Marriages in Pharaonic Egypt," no marriages between full siblings in the Pharonic period can be supported by historical evidence.

58. *HQ*, pp. 111–30.

59. *Arsinoë II, passim.*

60. Stanley Mayer Burstein, "Arsinoë II Philadelphos: A Revisionist View." See also E. Will, "Histoire grecque."

61. Will, "Histoire grecque."

62. *IG* II² 687.

63. *HQ*, p. 119.

64. See Burstein, "Arsinoë."

65. Homer *Od.*, 6.313–15, 7.66–77.

66. For women as a "muted group," see Edwin Ardener, "Belief and the Problem of Women."

67. Jan Quaegebeur is engaged in an exemplary ongoing study of Arsinoë II. Among his publications, see "Reines ptolémaïques et traditions égyptiennes," especially pp. 258, 262; "Ptolémée II en adoration devant Arsinoé II divinisée," especially pp. 204–6; and "Documents Concerning a Cult of Arsinoë Philadelphos at Memphis."

68. "Ptolémée II," pp. 205–6, 208–9.

69. According to the Suda *Life* (p. 116 West.; T 21 Kuchen), Philetas was engaged as tutor for Ptolemy II. On this passage, see Fraser, *PA*, vol. 1, p. 536, and vol. 2, p. 464 n. 19.

70. See Sarah B. Pomeroy, "Technikai kai Mousikai: The Education of Women in the Fourth Century and in the Hellenistic Period," pp. 60–61, for the education of Hellenistic queens.

71. G. Nachtergael, "Bérénice II, Arsinoé III et l'offrande de la boucle."

72. Callimachus *Aitia* IV frag. 110, in Rudolf Pfeiffer, *Callimachus*, vol. 1; Catullus 66.

73. C. Meillier, "Callimaque (P.L. 76d, 78abc, 79, 82, 84, 111c), Stésichore (?) (P.L. 76abc)"; and P. J. Parsons, "Callimachus. Victoria Berenicis."

74. P.Pt. IV 17199 (see note 80 below). G. Coppola, "Callimachus Senex," pp. 284–85, discusses a Callimachean epinician in honor of Berenice.

75. Arist. *Pol.* 2.6.11 (1270a); Plut. *Agis* 4, 7; *IG* 5.1564a; Paus. 3.17.6, 3.8.1, 6.1.6, 5.8.11. See also p. 54 above.

76. Athen. 4.139f.

77. 3.14.11.

78. Alan Cameron, "Two Mistresses of Ptolemy Philadelphos," commenting on *AP* 5.202 and 203. I am grateful to Professor Cameron for showing me this unpublished essay.

79. Hyg. *Astr.* 2.2.4.

80. *IG II²* 2313. The members of this family are all listed in P.Pt. Zeuxo: P.Pt. VI 17211; Hermione: P.Pt. III 5119 ψ VI 17209; Eucrateia: P.Pt. VI 17210; Zeuxo (daughter): P.Pt. VI 12712. On this family, see pp. 43–44 above.

81. Jan Quaegebeur, "Reines ptolémaïques," p. 254.

82. P. W. Pestman, *Chronologie égyptienne d'après les textes démotiques,* (*Pap. Lugd. Bat.* XV) (hereafter cited as *Pap. Lugd. Bat.* XV), p. 28.

83. For the dating prescripts, see *Pap. Lugd. Bat.* XV.

84. U. Kahrstedt, "Frauen auf antiken Münzen," p. 274.

85. T. C. Skeat, *The Reigns of the Ptolemies,* p. 35; *Pap. Lugd. Bat.* XV, p. 66; Fraser, *PA,* vol. 2, p. 216; A. E. Samuel, *Ptolemaic Chronology,* pp. 145–47; W. Otto and H. Bengtson, *Zur Geschichte des Niederganges des Ptolemäerreiches,* p. 47 n. 1.

86. For the date of the marriage of Cleopatra III and Ptolemy VIII, see *Pap. Lugd. Bat.* XXIIA, p. 66.

87. Samuel, *Ptolemaic Chronology,* pp. 149, 151. Fraser, *PA,* vol. 1, p. 123, calls Cleopatra III "almost the most remarkable of the queens who dominate Ptolemaic history."

88. Dorothy Burr Thompson, "More Ptolemaic Queens," p. 182.

89. Skeat, *Reigns of the Ptolemies,* p. 37; *Pap. Lugd. Bat.* XV, p. 76.

90. Skeat, *Reigns of the Ptolemies,* p. 39.

91. *Pap. Lugd. Bat.* XV, p. 82. Quaegebeur, "Reines ptolémaïques," p. 45 n. 1, points out that in B. Porter and R. Moss, *Topographical Bibliography,* vol. 1: *The Theban Necropolis,* part 2: "Royal Tombs and Smaller Cemeteries," Cleopatra VII is listed in the index of kings, although preceding queens are listed as private individuals.

92. For the double dating of Cleopatra's reigns with her brothers, see, most recently, Linda M. Ricketts, "A Chronological Problem in the Reign of Cleopatra VII."

93. For an analysis of the historical sources and bibliography on

Cleopatra, see Hans Volkmann, *Cleopatra: A Study in Politics and Propaganda*. For a favorable portrayal of Antony, see Eleanor Goltz Huzar, *Mark Antony: A Biography*.

94. Pomeroy, *GWWS*, p. 124.

95. For a review of the literature on the paternity and birthday of Caesarion, see P. M. Fraser, "Bibliography. Graeco-Roman Egypt. Greek Inscriptions 1960," p. 144.

96. 49.10.

97. See *Pap. Lugd. Bat.* XV, p. 82.

98. 54.6. According to Volkmann, *Cleopatra*, p. 226, Plutarch used some of the sources hostile to Cleopatra, so his work must not be accepted without scrutiny.

99. J. P. V. D. Balsdon, in his review of H. Volkmann, *Cleopatra*, presents this argument.

100. See M. Keith Hopkins, "Contraception in the Roman Empire," and E. Eyben, "Family Planning in Graeco-Roman Antiquity."

101. For the charges against Cleopatra as a client ruler, see Meyer Reinhold, "The Declaration of War Against Cleopatra."

102. Pliny *NH* 9.119–21.

103. Plut. *Ant.* 27.2–3.

104. Athen. 15.689a and note 45 above.

105. Homer *Od.* 4.220–32.

106. Fraser, *PA*, vol. 2, p. 548 n. 306. An otherwise unknown Cleopatra is the author of an extant gynecological treatise. See Pomeroy, "Technikai kai Mousikai," p. 60. Possibly the real author intended that work to be attributed to Cleopatra VII.

107. J. Gwyn Griffiths, "The Death of Cleopatra VII," argues that there must have been two cobras, representing the double uraeus, a royal, religious symbol.

108. Plut. *Ant.* 85.4. The use of the word *apogonos* ("descendant") rather than *apogonē* ("female descendant") in this context may signify that Cleopatra ruled as a king, descended from earlier kings. For *apogonē*, see *LSJ* and *LSJ Supplement*, s.v. "*apogonos*."

109. The bibliography on Ptolemaic cults is enormous. On queens and female divinities in particular, see Dorothy Burr Thompson, *Ptolemaic Oinochoai and Portraits in Faience: Aspects of the Ruler Cult;* L. Tondriau, "Princesses ptolémaïques comparées ou identifiées à des déesses"; Quaegebeur, articles cited in note 67 above; and Sharon Kelly Heyob, *The Cult of Isis Among Women in the Graeco-Roman World*.

110. Eur. *IT* 1406–7.

111. Plut. *Alex.* 3.2.

112. On the controversy concerning the divine honors paid to Alexander, see Ernst Badian, "The Deification of Alexander the Great." On the divinization of Alexander and his successors in Egypt, see Fraser, *PA,* vol. 1, pp. 189–246; L. Cerfaux and J. L. Tondriau, *Un concurrent de christianisme: Le culte des souverains dans la civilisation gréco-romaine;* and F. Taeger, *Charisma: Studien zur Geschichte des antiken Herrscherkultes,* with extensive bibliography.

113. *Alex.* 2.5.

114. Albert Henrichs, "Greek Maenadism from Olympias to Messalina," p. 143.

115. Thompson, *Ptolemaic Oinochoai,* p. 56 n. 3, reviews the evidence.

116. *Ibid.,* pp. 28, 56 n. 3. On the diadem in the tomb at Vergina, see Calder, "Diadem and Barrel Vault."

117. *Ptolemaic Oinochoai,* pp. 69, 73, 120.

118. See Tondriau, "Princesses ptolémaïques," p. 16.

119. *Idyll* 17.133.

120. Lewis Farnell, *Cults of the Greek States,* vol. 2, pp. 655–57.

121. See Paul Friedrich, *The Meaning of Aphrodite,* pp. 85, 140–41.

122. Robert F. Sutton, *The Interaction Between Men and Women Portrayed on Attic Red-Figure Pottery,* pp. 186–89.

123. 8.21.

124. Apollodorus 3.71–72.

125. 1.614–15.

126. Farnell, *Cults,* vol. 2, p. 656.

127. 5.73.

128. *Amat.* 23 (769).

129. 67.20.

130. Homer *Od.* 19.107–14.

131. Farnell, *Cults,* vol. 2, pp. 658–61.

132. On the development of the female nude figure in art, see Pomeroy, *GWWS,* pp. 142–46. For a provocative, well-documented interpretation of the socio-historical meaning of the Aphrodite figure, see Wiltrud Neumer-Pfau, *Studien zur Ikonographie und gesellschaftlichen Funktion hellenistischer Aphrodite-Statuen.*

133. Cf. Titian's "Sacred and Profane Love" in which both loves are women: Sacred Love is nude and Profane is clothed.

134. F. Lenormant, "La Vénus de l'Esquilin et le Diadumène de Polyclète," pp. 145–46, similarly interpreted by W. Fuchs, *Die Skulptur des Griechen,* p. 243. According to Christine M. Havelock, "The Por-

trayal and Significance of the Goddess Aphrodite in the Hellenistic Period," the proliferation of nude Aphrodites can be traced ultimately to the influence of Arsinoë II.

135. Louis Robert, "Sur un décret d'Ilion et sur un papyrus concernant des cultes royaux," p. 198. Fraser, *PA,* vol. 2, p. 379 n. 318, has misread Robert. The goat is not prohibited in sacrifices to Aphrodite Pandemus, but it is prohibited in the cult of Arsinoë.

136. In an epigram of Dioscurides (*AP* 6.290) a *hetaira* dedicates a fan to Urania. A. S. F. Gow and D. L. Page, *The Greek Anthology: Hellenistic Epigrams* (hereafter cited as *HE*), vol. 2, p. 245, remark, "Possibly we should infer from a dedication to Urania that she would welcome a husband."

137. 6.25.

138. *Conjugal Precepts* 142D. In the fourteenth century A.D., the tortoise was still the exemplar of the good Christian wife, and in the seventeenth century the figure of the heavenly Aphrodite appears as a Christian nun embodying Pudicitia (Chastity). See W. S. Heckscher, "Aphrodite as a Nun."

139. Sarah B. Pomeroy, "Supplementary Notes on Erinna."

140. *Oneirocritica* 2.37.

141. See Fraser, *PA,* vol. 1, especially Chapters 3 and 10, for commentary and an extensive bibliography on Alexandrian literature.

142. See, e.g., Helmut Kyrieleis, *Bildnisse der Ptolemäer,* Plates 70–81.

143. I. U. Powell, *Collectanea Alexandrina,* pp. 82–89.

144. Pliny *HN* 34.148. According to Blanche R. Brown, "Novelty, Ingenuity, Self-aggrandizement, Ostentation, Extravagance, Gigantism, and Kitsch in the Art of Alexander the Great and His Successors," p. 8 n. 29, modern authority deems the project unfeasible. I am grateful to Professor Brown for this reference.

145. Posidipp. 12, 13; Call. 14 (= Gow and Page, *HE,* vol. I, 3110–25, 1109–20).

146. *Ant.* 26.1–3.

147. The bibliography on the Hellenistic Isis is enormous. In addition to the articles by Quaegebeur cited in note 67 above, see R. E. Witt, *Isis in the Graeco-Roman World,* and many publications in the series Etudes préliminaires aux religions orientales dans l'empire romain (EPRO), including Heyob, *Cult of Isis.*

148. See, e.g., Michel Malaise, *Les conditions de pénétration et de diffusion des cultes égyptiens en Italie,* pp. 94, 99; and Heyob, *Cult of Isis,* Chapter 4.

149. On the Hellenistic Dionysus, see, most recently, Albert Henrichs, "Greek and Roman Glimpses of Dionysos," pp. 8–10.

150. 1.27.2.

## CHAPTER 2

1. Homer *Od.* 2.211–78. On class structure and human relationships in Homeric society, see M. I. Finley, *The World of Odysseus.*

2. On the relationship of tragic and comic heroines to the status of real women in Athens, see Pomeroy, *GWWS*, pp. 93–97, and Helene P. Foley, "The Concept of Women in Athenian Drama."

3. The dedications discussed here have been published by T. B. Mitford, "The Hellenistic Inscriptions of Old Paphos," with references to earlier publications. In the notes below, they will be referred to as *I Hell Paphos*, followed by the number given in the Mitford article of 1961.

4. On the government of Cyprus, see Roger S. Bagnall, *The Administration of the Ptolemaic Possessions Outside Egypt*, especially Chapter 4 and Appendixes A and B.

5. For the Ptolemaic nobility in the second and first centuries B.C., see L. Mooren, "Ptolemaic Families."

6. Pliny *HN* 34.14. Some officials sometimes broke the rule and did take their wives.

7. On Cypriote portraiture, see Joan Bryton Connelly, "Votive Portraiture in Hellenistic Cyprus."

8. *I Hell Paphos*, number 40, n. In addition to their citations in the P.Pt. (see Chapter 1, note 80, above), three women of this family are listed in Ino Michaelidou Nicolaou, *Prosopography of Ptolemaic Cyprus:* Hermione: p. 59, 20; Zeuxo (daughter): p. 62, 2; Zeuxo (mother): p. 62, 3.

9. Polyb. 18.55.6–9.

10. Jeanne and Louis Robert, "Bulletin épigraphique," *REG* 61, number 202.

11. *Ibid.*

12. M. Ohnefalsch Richter, "Mittheilungen aus Cypern," p. 137, number 8.

13. For dedications by women in the Greek world, see David M. Schaps, *Economic Rights of Women in Ancient Greece*, pp. 71–73. See also p. 39 above.

14. *I Hell Paphos:* mother to son(s): numbers 19, 27, 31, 33; parents to daughter: numbers 23, 32, 66 (note misprint: "his parents" should be "her parents"), 108; mother to son and daughter number 61; parents to

son: number 49; daughter to father: number 47; wife and son to husband/father: number 60; grandchildren to maternal grandmother: number 48; and husband to wife: numbers 28, 30.

15. *I Hell Paphos*, number 41. Stratonice is P.Pt. VI 15939 and Nicolaou, *Prosopography*, p. 114, 42.

16. *Hermaphroditos* frag. 11 (Kock).

17. On sex ratios and female infanticide in Hellenistic Greece, see Pomeroy, *GWWS*, p. 140, and Sarah B. Pomeroy, "Infanticide in Hellenistic Greece."

18. J. K. Davies, *Athenian Propertied Families, 600–300 B.C.*, pp. xvii, xxv–xxvi.

19. *Ibid.*, pp. 256–57.

20. *Ibid.*, p. 217.

21. Plut. *Mor.* 871. I am grateful to R. Merkelbach for this suggestion.

22. P.Pt. III 5077.

23. See *I Hell Paphos*, number 72, for Mitford's conjecture about a fourth daughter, perhaps named Artemo.

24. See pp. 103–24 above.

25. See T. B. Mitford, "Ptolemy son of Pelops," p. 110, number 3.

26. T. B. Mitford, "Seleucus and Theodorus," p. 170.

27. For the legal code of Alexandria, see Fraser, *PA*, vol. 1, pp. 114–15, and R. Taubenschlag, "The Ancient Greek City-laws in Ptolemaic Egypt." I am grateful to F. D. Harvey and to Martin Ostwald for their comments on my work on women's citizenship.

28. *Pol.* 3.1.9 (1275b).

29. Pomeroy, *GWWS*, pp. 66–68; C. Hignett, *A History of the Athenian Constitution*, p. 346; W. K. Lacey, *The Family in Classical Greece*, p. 100; and A. W. Gomme, "The Law of Citizenship at Athens," in *Essays in Greek History and Literature*, p. 87 n. 1.

30. For the implications of this law, see Cynthia B. Patterson, *Pericles' Citizenship Law of 451–50 B.C.*

31. Lea Bringmann, *Die Frau im ptolemäisch-kaiserlichen Aegypten*, pp. 43–44, has little to say on the *aste* ("citizen") in the Ptolemaic period, but discusses the apposite provisions in the *Gnomon of the Idios Logos*.

32. Aristot. *Pol.* 3.2.10 (1277b)–3.3.2 (1278a).

33. The enrollment of women in tribes at Athens was apparently rare, but it did occur. See W. Wyse, *The Speeches of Isaeus*, pp. 357–59. For the declaration of women's births and marriages at the Apaturia, see L. Deubner, *Attische Feste*, pp. 232–34. The lack of such registration was never used as an argument to establish that a woman such as Neaera was not a citizen.

34. Fraser, *PA*, vol. 1, p. 42.

35. Fraser, *PA*, vol. 2, pp. 116–17 n. 24; Diana Delia, *Roman Alexandria: Studies in its Social History*, pp. 28–29, 138.

36. Fraser, *PA*, vol. 1, p. 76.

37. "The Alexandrian Citizenship," p. 113, adducing as evidence *P. Tebt.* II 316 (A.D. 99); *PSI* XII 1223 (A.D. 131), 1224 (A.D. 156/57), 1225 (A.D. 156) (improperly cited by El-Abbadi); and *P. Flor.* III 382 (A.D. 222/23). Vincenzo Arangio-Ruiz, "Intorno agli ΑΣΤΟΙ dell'Egitto greco-romano," p. 13, also notes that there are numerous *astai* in the ephebic lists.

38. J. E. G. Whitehorn accepts the interpretation of El-Abbadi and also points out that the *aparche* (a term that denotes both the fee paid out and the document issued when a parent registers a child as a citizen) has been used of female as well as male children. See "*C.P.Jud.* II 193 and *PSI* XII, 1225," p. 124. See also "The Functions of the Alexandrian Ephebeia Certificate and the Sequence of *PSI* XII 1223–1225," pp. 30, 32–33, for the identification of the mother at the time of a boy's admission to the ephebate; the relevant document (*Chrest. Wilck.* 143 [= *P. Flor.* I 57], 86, 89 A.D. 166]) is also from the Roman period.

39. M. Hombert and C. Préaux, *Recherches sur le recensement dans l'Egypte romaine*, p. 152, postulate that the requirement for metropolitan descent was an incentive for consanguineous marriages.

40. For the tomb, see Lidiano Bacchielli, "Le pitture dalla 'Tomba dell'Altalena di Cirene' nel Museo del Louvre." I am grateful to Natalie Kampen for this reference. I have used Bacchielli's sketches, but my interpretations of the scenes often differ from his.

41. *SLG* S 261A. According to M. Gronewald, "Fragmente aus einem Sapphokommentar: *Pap. Colon.* inv. 5860," the papyrus should be dated to the second century A.D. I am grateful to Judith P. Hallett for this reference. On the date of Callias, see A. Gudeman, s.v. "Kallias," P.W., *R.E.* 5.10.2, cols. 1629–30.

42. A female mummy from Memphis from the first century A.D. is inscribed "Hermione grammatike." It is now at Girton College, Cambridge. K. Parlasca, *Mumienporträts und verwandte Denkmäler*, pp. 81, 101–3; Plate 15.1; and *SB* I 5753. According to E. G. Turner, *Greek Papyri: An Introduction*, p. 77, she may have been a "literary lady" rather than a teacher. John of Ephesus, *Lives of the Eastern Saints, Patrologia Orientalis* 17.1, pp. 15–16, writes of a widow who taught art to girls for a fee.

43. Dionysus loved Erigone, daughter of Icarius. She hung herself. In her honor, swinging was practiced at the festival of the Aiora ("swing"). See *OCD*, 2d ed., s.v. "Icarius."

44. On the events surrounding the downfall of Agathocles and Agathoclea, see Polybius 15.29.1–15.36.10, and F. W. Walbank, *A Historical Commentary on Polybius*, vol. 2, *ad loc.*

45. Callimachus frag. 63 (Pfeiffer).

46. On Oenanthe, see A. Raubitschek, "Oenanthe (6)," P.W., *R.E.* 15.2.2, col. 2189. Agathoclea's sisters appear in Polybius 15.33.7. Oenanthe is P.Pt. VI 14731. For Agathoclea, see note 48 below.

47. Tentative identification by U. Wilcken, "Papyrus Urkunden," p. 74; P.Pt. IX 4986.

48. J. Ijsewijn, *De sacerdotibus sacerdotiisque Alexandri Magni et Lagidarum eponymis*, no. 74. P.Pt. IX 4984 = P.Pt. VI 14714(?).

49. Paul Maas, "Oenanthe's Husbands," argues that Oenanthe must have been "married at least twice," once to an Agathocles and once to a Theogenes [i.e., Diognetus], and that Agathocles and Agathoclea had different fathers. However, his account does not explain why the son and daughter bear virtually the same name.

50. Polyb. 15.31.9–10. An Agathoclea, daughter of Polycrates, occurs in an Alexandrian funerary epigram, but P. M. Fraser and W. Peek date the inscription to the third century B.C. See E. Bernand, *Inscriptions métriques de l'Egypte gréco-romaine, Recherches sur la poésie épigrammatique des Grecs en Egypte*, pp. 158–59, no. 30.

51. Scholia Aristophan. *Thesmoph.* 1059.

52. Polyb. 15.31.13.

53. Polyb. 15.27.2.

54. Thompson, "More Ptolemaic Queens," p. 182, points out that Berenice II and earlier queens are shown veiled in the visual arts, but Arsinoë III and later queens are portrayed unveiled. The wearing of the veil by some groups of women persisted into the Roman Empire. See Ramsay MacMullen, "Women in Public in the Roman Empire." Thompson, *Ptolemaic Oinochoai*, p. 160, also suggests that the pose of Arsinoë III with right arm lifted (see Plate 6) commemorates her role at the battle of Raphia (217 B.C.).

55. Polyb. 15.33.

56. Polyb. 15.33.11–12.

57. See E. R. Bevan, *The House of Seleucus*, vol. 2, p. 283, for uses of the word in relationship to Alexander and to the Seleucids.

58. 15.33.11.

59. Athen. 13.557c.

60. Athen. 13.578a *orchestrida* ("dancing girl"); Plut. *Alex.* 77.5 *adoxos kai koine* ("undistinguished and common"); Justin 9.8.2 *saltatrice* ("dancer"). On the status of Philinna, see Giallombardo, "Diritto Matrimoniale," p. 91.

61. Justin 15.2.7. On Thaïs, see W. W. Tarn, *Alexander,* pp. 47–48, 324. P.Pt. VI 14723.

62. Eirene is P.Pt. VI 14722; Ptolemy Apion is P.Pt. VI 14553.

63. On Bilistiche, see p. 20 above.

64. 13.576e–f.

65. *Amat.* 753f.

66. P.Pt. VI 14719.

67. P.Pt. VI 14733.

68. P.Pt. VI 14729.

69. P.Pt. VI 14728.

70. P.Pt. VI 14726.

71. P.Pt. VI 14713. For the suggestion that she is the same as the mistress of Ptolemy IV—hence a "ghost" in the earlier period—see Hans Hauben, "Agathokleia and her Boats," p. 290.

72. P.Pt. VI 16976.

73. P.Pt. VI 14718. See also Dorothy Burr Thompson, "Glauke and the Goose."

74. "Dames de la cour": P.Pt. VI 14714–37.

75. Jacques Tréheux, "Cleino à Délos," argues that the Cleino who sent a dedication to Delos as early as 279 B.C. cannot be Ptolemy's mistress, since, in that case, she would have been his mistress before the death of Arsinoë. I see no reason to assume that before Arsinoë's death Ptolemy did not have mistresses and did not pay them well enough for them to make dedications. However, Tréheux's argument that Cleino was a common name is more persuasive.

76. Paus. 5.8.11, *P. Oxy.* XVII 2082, Athen. 13.596e; see also p. 23 above.

77. *P. Hib.* II 261, 262.

78. See p. 20 above.

79. One other female shipowner, Archeboula, cannot be otherwise identified. See Hans Hauben, "A Jewish Shipowner in Third-century Ptolemaic Egypt," p. 168, and "Le transport fluvial" for references to earlier publications on women shipowners.

80. Athen. 10.425e–f (ψ *FHG* 161, frag. 3) ψ Polyb. 14.11.2; Athen. 13.576e–f (ψ *FHG* 234, frag. 4) ψ Polyb. 14.11.2.

81. Plut. *Amat.* 753f.

82. Tondriau, "Princesses ptolémaïques," p. 31. F. Lenormant, "La Vénus de l'Esquilin," pp. 142–43.

83. Athen. 13.595c.

84. *Amat.* 753f.

85. See references in P.Pt. VI 14717.

86. *P. Hib.* II, p. 160. Participation in pan-Greek festivals during the Hellenistic period is not incontrovertible evidence of Greek birth: see H. W. Pleket, *The Olympic Games: The First Thousand Years*, p. 62.

87. Athen. 13.576e–f calls her *epichoria gyne* ("a native woman").

88. *AP* 5.210 = Gow and Page, *HE*, vol. 1, 828–31.

89. For the eponymous priests, see Ijsewijn, *De sacerdotibus*, and P.Pt. III and IX *sub nomine*.

90. *OGIS* 90 (196 B.C.). Translation adapted from Roger S. Bagnall and Peter Derow, *Greek Historical Documents: The Hellenistic Period*, number 137.

91. S. R. K. Glanville and T. C. Skeat, "Eponymous Priesthoods of Alexandria from 211 B.C.," pp. 45–46. According to Ijsewijn, *De sacerdotibus*, p. 130, this rule was no longer followed in the last quarter of the second century B.C.

92. P.Pt. III 5148.

93. P.Pt. III 5158, 5159.

94. Ijsewijn, *De sacerdotibus*, no. 182; P.Pt. III 5139. Asclepiades uses the name Thaubarion (Gow and Page, *HE*, vol. 1, 936).

95. Ijsewijn, *De sacerdotibus*, nos. 107 and 108. P.Pt. III 5266. See Friedrich Zucker, "Simarist(ei)oi" and "Simaristos."

96. Jan Quaegebeur, "Contribution à la prosopographie des prêtres memphites à l'époque ptolémaïque," p. 106, notes that the names Berenice and Arsinoë appear among the purely Egyptian names in the sacred milieu at Memphis.

97. On the special background of the eponymous priests, see Ijsewijn, *De sacerdotibus*, pp. 149–57, as well as his comments on specific office-holders.

98. *Ibid.*, p. 145.

99. See Pomeroy, *GWWS*, pp. 76–77. For an insult to a potential canephore, see Thuc. 6.56–58; Arist. *Const. Athens* 18.2.

100. Willy Clarysse, "Harmachis, Agent of the Oikonomos: An Archive from the Time of Philopator."

101. Ijsewijn, *De sacerdotibus*, no. 88; P.Pt. III 5104. See T. B. Mitford, "Helenos, Governor of Cyprus," p. 126; "Seleucus and Theodorus," pp. 149–50; and "Ptolemy Macron," pp. 163–76. See also Bagnall, *Administration*, p. 255.

102. Ijsewijn, *De sacerdotibus*, nos. 146–71; P.Pt. IX 5039; and see Mitford, "Seleucus and Theodorus," p. 170.

103. According to scholia on Callimachus *Hymn* 6, Ptolemy II followed the Athenian model in creating the position of canephore. See O. Schneider, *Callimachea*, vol. 1, p. 133.

104. For the order of the procession, see *P. Oxy.* XXVII 2465 (Satyrus "On the Demes of Alexandria"), frag. 2, col. 1.8–11, 15.

105. For the other offices, see Ijsewijn, *De sacerdotibus,* pp. 137–39.

106. See Fraser, *PA,* vol. 1, p. 198.

107. The bibliography on Greek and indigenous religion in Ptolemaic Egypt is enormous. See Fraser, *PA,* vol. 1, Chapter 5, "Religious Life," and Orsolina Montevecchi, *La papirologia,* pp. 265–81.

108. Ijsewijn, *De sacerdotibus,* p. 97, points out that two sisters (Asteria, canephore in 181/180, and Timarion), members of the Ptolemaic nobility, made a dedication to the Egyptian Bubastis between 163 and 145 B.C.

109. For the education of women, see pp. 20 and 48 above and Pomeroy, "Technikai kai Mousikai." On women's literacy, see also F. D. Harvey, "Literacy in the Athenian Democracy," and Susan Guettel Cole, "Could Greek Women Read and Write?"

110. For the education of girls in Roman Egypt, see Sarah B. Pomeroy, "Women in Roman Egypt: A Preliminary Study Based on Papyri."

111. For attestations of the terracotta girl with diptych from Alexandria, see Philippe Bruneau, "Tombes d'Argos," p. 472.

112. *Pol.* 8.2 (1337b).

113. This stela is now in the Cairo museum, inventory no. 9259. J. G. Milne, *Cairo Cat. Gr. Inscrs.* 9259. For illustrations and a brief discussion, see Gunter Grimm and Dieter Johannes, *Kunst der Ptolemäer- und Römerzeit im Ägyptischen Museum Kairo,* Plate 6, and I. Noshy, *The Arts in Ptolemaic Egypt,* pp. 106–7, Plate 12.2. The lyre motif appears as well in Caranis on the funerary monument of a girl who died at twenty. See Bernand, *Inscr. métriques,* no. 83, p. 331 n. 10.

114. On women artists, see also Natalie Kampen, "Hellenistic Artists: Female."

115. P.Pt. VI 17084.

116. P.Pt. VI 17062. *EAA,* vol. 1, p. 351, s.v. "Anaxandra," notes that this painter is cited only in Clem. Al. *Strom.* 4.124, but suggests that "Anaxander" in Pliny *HN* 35.146 refers to the same person. Perhaps her name should be Alexandra; the name Anaxandra is unusual and not cited in F. Bechtel, *Die Attischen Frauennamen.*

117. Athen. 1.14d; Suda, s.v. "Anagallis." She is incorrectly named Dalis by Schol. *Il.* 18.483. For Agallias, see also Eustathius on Schol. *Il.* 18.491.

118. Str. 13.599; F. Susemihl, *Geschichte der griechischen Literatur in der Alexandrinerzeit,* vol. 2, pp. 148–49 and note 2. Eustathius, on B538.280.19, notes that the name is spelled Histiaia or Hestiaia. That

Hestiaea's work was a monograph is pointed out by Rudolf Pfeiffer, *History of Classical Scholarship: From the Beginnings to the End of the Hellenistic Age*, p. 250 n. 4. She is P.Pt. VI 16852.

119. Pfeiffer, *Callimachus*, vol. 1, pp. 118–19; vol. 2, pp. 115–16, citing the scholia on Callimachus frag. 10.

120. Holger Thesleff, *An Introduction to the Pythagorean Writings of the Hellenistic Period*, p. 7 n. 2. For the text, see Thesleff, *The Pythagorean Texts of the Hellenistic Period*, pp. 242–43. I am grateful to Flora R. Levin for discussing with me her unpublished work on Ptolemaïs.

121. For texts and commentary, see Thesleff, cited in note 120 above. See the remarks of Fraser on Thesleff in *PA*, vol. 2, pp. 714–15 n. 134–39. See also M. Meunier, *Femmes pythagoriennes. Fragments et lettres de Théano, Perictioné, Phintys, Mélissa et Myia*, for a discussion and translation of the fragments.

122. Fraser, *PA*, vol. 1, p. 493, suggests the possibility of a date earlier than the first century B.C. for the emergence of Neopythagoreanism in Alexandria. Among scholars who have written on the subject fairly recently, Thesleff proposed the earliest date, i.e., third or second century B.C. for the Doric pseudepigrapha. However, in "On the Problem of the Doric Pseudo-Pythagorica: An Alternative Theory of Date and Purpose," p. 72, influenced by W. Burkert's advocacy of a later date, Thesleff stated that although the third century might be too early, an early Imperial date was too late. Alfons Städele, *Die Briefe des Pythagoras und der Pythagoreer*, pp. 352–53, dates some of the letters by women as late as the second century A.D.

123. See Thesleff, *Introduction*, pp. 113–16 and *passim*.

124. See, for example, Cole, "Could Greek Women Read?" p. 229, and K. von Fritz, s.v. "Periktione (2)," P.W., *R.E.* 19, cols. 794–95.

125. Pomeroy, "Technikai kai Mousikai," pp. 57–58. See also Blaise Nagy, "The Naming of Athenian Girls: A Case in Point," for the tendency to give the name "Theano" to girls who might become priestesses, naming them after a literary model—the priestess in the *Iliad*. For the names of Christians as indications of faith, see Roger S. Bagnall, "Religious Conversion and Onomastic Change in Early Byzantine Egypt."

126. Diog. Laer. *Aristot.* 5.12–13; Marinus *Vita Procli* 29.

127. *VP* 267.

128. *FGrH* IIIB 328, frag. 91, nos. 25–26.

129. Iamblichus *VP* 267 and *passim;* Diog. Laer. 8.42–43; Porphyry *Vita Pythagorae* 4, 19.

130. 8.41, 43.

131. W. Burkert, *Lore and Science in Ancient Pythagoreanism,* pp. 156 and 200, has argued that since this tradition demands that Theano be literate, it is not credible. But for the literacy of women, see Pomeroy, "Technikai kai Mousikai."

132. *Dissertation upon the Epistles of Phalaris,* p. 304.

133. See Nancy Demand, "Plato, Aristophanes, and the *Speeches of Pythagoras.*" The tradition is accepted in the *Oxford Classical Dictionary,* 1st and 2d eds., s.v. "Pythagoras."

134. Aristophanes *Lys.* 1126–27.

135. Diog. Laer. 2.86.

136. Diog. Laer. 6.94, 96–98.

137. *IGR* IV 125. For other female philosophers named in inscriptions, see M. Tod, "Sidelights on Greek Philosophers," p. 140.

138. J. Charbonneaux, R. Martin, and F. Villard, *Hellenistic Art,* pp. 134–35. I am grateful to Arthur Eckstein for this reference. The precise identification of the characters cannot be secure, since the names are not written on the painting, but at any rate it is clear that a woman is listening to a philosopher.

139. Pomeroy, "Technikai kai Mousikai," pp. 57–58; Bernard Frischer, *The Sculpted Word,* pp. 54, 62, 206; and Catherine J. Castner, "Epicurean Hetairai as Dedicants to Healing Deities?"

140. E.g., for women in the circle of Jerome, see J. N. D. Kelly, *Jerome,* especially Chapters 10 and 23. The wife of Iamblichus was a pupil of Plotinus. Several other women are mentioned in Porphyry *Vita Plotini* 9, 11, and in later Neoplatonic circles (Marinus *Vita Procli* 28–29; Damascius *Vita Isidori* 2.1–13 [Zintzen]). Diogenes Laertius (3.47) dedicated part of his work to a woman Platonist. The priestess Clea discussed philosophy with Plutarch; see Plut. *Mulierum virtutes* 242F. She is mentioned also several times in Plut. *De Iside et Osiride.* On Clea, see also John G. Griffiths, *Plutarch's De Iside et Osiride,* pp. 95–98.

141. Stevan L. Davies, *The Revolt of the Widows,* Chapter 6 and *passim;* and Joanne McNamara, *The New Song: Celibate Women in the First Three Christian Centuries.* For some of the early Christian writings by women, see P. Wilson-Kastner et al., *A Lost Tradition: Women Writers of the Early Church.*

142. Cratinus *The Tarentines,* and *The Pythagorean Woman;* Alexis *The Pythagorean Woman.*

143. Meineke, *C.G.F.* 3.376 (*The Tarentines*).

144. See p. 190,, note 124 above.

145. On the manuals of Philaenis and Elephantis, see E. W. Thomson Vessey, "Philaenis," and p. 80 above.

146. M. L. West, "Erinna."

147. "Supplementary Notes on Erinna," pp. 19–21. Denys L. Page, *Further Greek Epigrams*, p. 344 n. 1, also disagrees with West, "Erinna."

148. Diog. Laer. 3.46, 4.2.

149. Thesleff, *Pythagorean Texts*, pp. 142–45 = Stob. 4.28.10, translated by Flora R. Levin.

150. See Helen North, *Sophrosyne: Self-Knowledge and Self-Restraint in Greek Literature*, index p. 388, s.v. "Feminine *arete*."

151. *Ibid.*, pp. 234–35.

152. Semonides frag. 7 (Diehl), trans. by Hugh Lloyd-Jones, *Females of the Species*, p. 52.

153. Thesleff, *Pythagorean Texts*, p. 152 (589.9).

154. See Pomeroy, "Technikai kai Mousikai," for references.

155. Laia or Lala in Pliny *HN* 35.147–48.

156. See R. Lattimore, *Themes in Greek and Latin Epitaphs*, passim.

157. W. Peek, *Griechische Versinschriften*, vol. 1, 866 = Fraser, *PA*, vol. 2, p. 866, n. 448.

158. Dioscurides *AP* 7.166 = Gow and Page, *HE*, vol. 1, 1707–12 = Fraser, *PA*, vol. 2, p. 855, n. 377; Dioscurides *AP* 7.167 = Gow and Page, *HE*, vol. 1, 1713–18 = Fraser, *PA*, vol. 2, p. 856, n. 383.

159. Herodes in Milne, *Cairo Cat. Gr. Inscrs.* 9206. See Fraser, *PA*, vol. 1, p. 615.

160. Dioscurides *AP* 7.484 = Gow and Page, *HE*, vol. 1, 1637–41.

161. G. Kaibel, *Epigrammata Graeca ex lapidus conlecta*, p. 40, no. 118.

162. *AP* 7.459 = Gow and Page, *HE*, vol. 1, 1215–18.

163. *AP* 5.181 = Gow and Page, *HE*, vol. 1, 920–31.

164. [Demos.] 59.122.

165. *AP* 12.153 = Gow and Page, *HE*, vol. 1, 898–901.

166. See, e.g., K. J. Dover, *Theocritus: Select Poems*, pp. 95–96 and 189 on the ambiguous status of Simaetha and Cynisca. Alan Cameron, "Asclepiades' Girl Friends," pp. 296–97, argues that the women may not be chaste but they are not prostitutes. Gow and Page, *HE*, vol. 2, p. 290, comment on a girl who makes a dedication to Aphrodite (following a symposium and a night spent with her lover) that she is not necessarily a *hetaira*.

167. *AP* 5.206 = Gow and Page, *HE*, vol. 1, 838–41 = Fraser, *PA*, vol. 2, p. 806 n. 103.

168. Walther Ludwig, "Plato's Love Epigrams."

169. For an analysis of the function of love and its relationship to marriage in modern societies, see William J. Goode, "The Theoretical Importance of Love."

170. Athen. 7.297a.

171. *AP* 6.292 = Gow and Page, *HE*, vol. 1, 1825–30.

172. See, e.g., Alcman *The Partheneion*, the description of Nausicaa in Homer *Od*. 6, and Sappho fragments 57 and 82a, in Edgar Lobel and Denys Page, *Poetarum Lesbiorum Fragmenta*.

173. Cic. *De inventione* 2.1.1.

174. For beauty contests at Lesbos, see Alcaeus G 2, frag. 1, col. 2.32–33, in Denys Page, *Sappho and Alcaeus*, pp. 168 and 199. For those at Tenedos as well as Lesbos, see Athen. 13.610a.

175. Athen. 13.565f–566a, 609e–f. Athenaeus also mentions the admiration enjoyed by the most beautiful woman and most handsome man in Sparta. See also M. P. Nilsson, "Kallisteia," P.W., *R.E.* 10.2, col. 1674.

176. Fraser, *PA*, vol. 1, p. 207.

177. See Frederick T. Griffiths, *Theocritus at Court*, pp. 116–20.

178. For intimacy and privacy in the visual arts of the Hellenistic period, see Otto J. Brendel, "The Scope and Temperament of Erotic Art in the Greco-Roman World."

179. 410–29.

180. G. Zanker, "Callimachus' Hecale: A New Kind of Epic Hero?" See also K. Ziegler, "Kallimachos und die Frauen."

181. Arch. frag. 196A (West).

182. *AP* 7.351 = Gow and Page, *HE*, vol. 1, 1555–64. A similar defense appears in *AP* 7.353 (Anon. or Meleager). See also Vessey, "Philaenis."

183. *AP* 7.450 = Gow and Page, *HE*, vol. 1, 1629–36. On the same theme, see Aeschrion's epigram (apparently the inspiration for Dioscurides) *AP* 7.345 = Gow and Page, *HE*, vol. 1, 1–9. See also Vessey, "Philaenis." For a fragment of the notorious handbook, see *P. Oxy*. XXXIX 2891 and a note on the text by M. Marcovich, "How to Flatter Women: *P. Oxy*. 2891."

184. I am grateful to Ann Ellis Hanson for information on Herophilus. For a general account of Herophilus, see Fraser, *PA*, vol. 1, pp. 348–58. For his place in the history of medicine, see G. E. R. Lloyd, *Science, Folklore, and Ideology: Studies in the Life Sciences in Ancient Greece, passim*.

185. E.g., his description of a two-chambered uterus with cornua and neck.

186. Soranus *Gynecology* (trans. by Owsei Temkin [Baltimore, 1956]) 1.32. The citations from Soranus are from this volume.

187. *Ibid.*, 1.27.

188. *Ibid.*, 3.2.

189. Gaye Tuchman, "Women and the Creation of Culture," p. 184.

CHAPTER 3

1. The material on marriage contracts was presented in my paper "The Married Woman: Honor and Shame in Ptolemaic Egypt."

2. Montevecchi, *La papirologia*, p. 203.

3. *Marriage and Matrimonial Property in Ancient Egypt: A Contribution to Establishing the Legal Position of the Woman;* see also E. Lüddeckens, *Ägyptische Eheverträge.*

4. The legal form of the marriage contract has been virtually the only aspect of marriage in Ptolemaic Egypt to be thoroughly studied, and, unfortunately, there has been much duplication of efforts by scholars. Iza Biezunska, "La condition juridique de la femme grecque d'après les papyri," and Lea Bringmann, *Die Frau im ptolemäisch-kaiserlichen Aegypten,* wrote major studies of women in Greco-Roman Egypt, apparently in ignorance of each other's efforts. Because these works appeared on the eve of World War II, they were not widely circulated. These studies, though useful, are seriously flawed insofar as they treat the material from approximately seven hundred years of Greco-Roman Egypt as one body of evidence, without attention to historical changes over time. A symptom of this lack of concern is that they often do not give the dates of documents cited. The extensive bibliography also includes H. J. Wolff, "Die Grundlagen des griechischen Eherechts" and *Das Recht der griechischen Papyri Ägyptens,* vol. 2: *Organisation und Kontrolle des privaten Rechtsverkehrs, passim;* Claude Vatin, *Recherches sur le mariage et la condition de la femme mariée à l'époque hellénistique* (hereafter cited as *FM*), pp. 163–80; Joseph Mélèze Modrzejewski, "La Structure juridique du mariage grec." Orsolina Montevecchi, "Ricerche di sociologia nei documenti dell'Egitto greco-romano, II: I contratti di matrimonio e gli atti di divorzio," does examine social as well as legal aspects. For documents published since 1936, see also Montevecchi, *La papirologia*, pp. 203–7.

5. For mixed marriages between Greeks, see Joseph Mélèze Modrzejewski, "Un aspect du 'couple interdit' dans l'antiquité: les mariages mixtes dans l'Egypte hellénistique," p. 57.

6. Diod. Sic. 1.27. See also p. 16 above.

7. See *Pap. Lugd. Bat.* XXIIA, pp. 56–63, for the evolution of these

status designations from true ethnics to pseudo-ethnics derived from military service. Toward the end of the second century B.C., "Persian of the Epigone" was used to signify the juridical status of debtor.

8. See G. E. M. de Sainte Croix, "Some Observations on the Property Rights of Athenian Women," on the minimum competence of Athenian women. The same principle was in force for women in Egypt acting under Greek law: see, inter alia, R. Taubenschlag, "La compétence du Kupios dans le droit gréco-égyptien"; Margaret Seymour Titchener, "Guardianship of Women in Egypt during the Ptolemaic and Roman Eras"; and p. 200, note 85 below.

9. On exchange of women, see Claude Lévi-Strauss, *The Elementary Structures of Kinship, passim.*

10. H. C. Youtie, " Ὑπογραφεύς: The Social Impact of Illiteracy in Greco-Roman Egypt," p. 213.

11. For the cult inscriptions, see Paton–Hicks, *Inscr. Cos* no. 367 ψ *SIG*³ 1023. This was republished by Giovanni Pugliese Carratelli, "Il damos Coo di Isthmos." Claire Préaux, "Le statut de la femme à l'époque hellénistique, principalement en Egypte," p. 148, suggested that *P. Eleph.* 1 is derived from Coan law of the fourth century B.C. Modrzejewski, "Structure juridique," p. 249 n. 71, points out that the law of Temnos, the bridegroom's polis, must also be involved. Whether Temnos had a restrictive citizenship law is not known. On the citizenship of Alexandrian women, see pp. 45–47 above.

12. For another illustration of women's increased legal capacity involving the appointment of a mother as her child's guardian, see Orsolina Montevecchi, "Una donna 'prostatis' del figlio minorenne in un papiro del II^a."

13. See Modrzejewski, "Structure juridique," pp. 252–55, for a discussion of the auto-ekdosis.

14. Jean Bingen, review of M. David and B. A. van Croningen, *Papyrological Primer.*

15. J. Lesquier, *Les institutions militaires de l'Egypte sous les Lagides,* addendum.

16. Plut. *Quaest. Rom.* 108 and Sarah B. Pomeroy, "The Relationship of the Married Woman to her Blood Relatives in Rome," p. 215.

17. For similar provisions, see S. D. Goitein, *A Mediterranean Society,* vol. 3: *The Family,* p. 129. I am indebted throughout this discussion to Goitein's analysis of the marriage contracts of the Cairo Geniza.

18. Specifically mentioned in *P. Giss.* I 2.17, 25; *P. Gen.* I 21.2; *P. Tebt.* I 104.16, 24 and IV 974.3, 8 (early second century B.C.).

19. *Ekballein: P. Tebt.* IV 974.17; *P. Gen.* I 21.6.

20. It is not possible to determine whether the contract was written in Elephantine, although it was found there.

21. Aischin. 1: *In Tim.* 183.

22. On marriage at Athens, see A. R. W. Harrison, *The Law of Athens: The Family and Property*, pp. 1–60; and Elaine Fantham, "Sex, Status and Survival in Hellenistic Athens: A Study of Women in New Comedy."

23. [Demos.] 59.122 ("Against Neaera").

24. See also *P. Gen.* I 21.10; *P. Giss.* I 2.24. Similar notions of behavior appropriate to each sex persist in Greek villages as described by Juliet Du Boulay, *Portrait of a Greek Mountain Village.* See also J. G. Peristiany, ed., *Honour and Shame: The Values of Mediterranean Society;* Julian Pitt-Rivers, *The Fate of Shechem or the Politics of Sex: Essays in the Anthropology of the Mediterranean;* J. K. Campbell, *Honour, Family and Patronage;* P. Bourdieu, *Outline of a Theory of Practice;* and Renée Hirschon, "Open Body/Closed Space: The Transformation of Female Sexuality."

25. For the sexual division of labor in traditional Greek societies today, see Du Boulay, *Portrait*, pp. 133–34, and Campbell, *Honour*, p. 274.

26. Eur. *Alc.* 946–47; Aristoph. *Lys.* 880–81.

27. On the connection between a woman's virtue and housekeeping, see Du Boulay, *Portrait*, p. 131.

28. Semonides frag. 7 (Diehl).

29. The material on soldiers' wives was presented in my paper "Wives of Hellenistic Soldiers."

30. Thuc. 7.19.27–8.

31. Aristoph. *Lys.* 538.

32. Xen. *Anabasis* 6.1.1–13; Plut. *Pel.* 27.4. I am grateful to J. Ober for the latter reference.

33. Athen. 557b.

34. For women accompanying Alexander's troops see Diod. Sic. 6.25.5 and 18.104.4, and Engels, *Alexander*, pp. 11–13.

35. Arr. *Anab.* 1.24.1.

36. Arr. *Anab.* 6.25.5.

37. Arr. *Anab.* 1.24.1.

38. Just. *Epit.* 12.3–4.

39. On the loyalty of the army to their "baggage," see H. W. Parke, *Greek Mercenary Soldiers*, pp. 207–8, and Rostovtzeff, *SEHHW*, p. 146 n. 17.

40. Diod. Sic. 20.47.4.

41. On the meaning of *aposkeue*, see E. Kiessling, *Wörterbuch der*

*griechischen Papyrusurkunden,* vol. 4, s.v., revising the interpretation in *WB* I. See also M. Holleaux, "Ceux qui sont dans le bagage," and U. Wilcken, "Papyrus-Urkunden," pp. 88–89, commenting on *P. Bad.* 48.

42. Richter, "Mittheilungen aus Cypern," p. 137, number 8.

43. *P. Bad.* IV 48; similarly *SB* V 8009 (= *P. Berl.* inv. 7415). By 126 B.C. the judgment as to whether a woman could claim the privileges of *aposkeuai* was not only in the hands of "designated courts," as stated in the Alexandrian civil code, but also could be made by a city magistrate, the chief of police. See E. Kiessling, "Die Aposkeuai und die prozessrechtliche Stellung der Ehefrauen im ptolemäischen Ägypten."

44. *P. Hal.* 1 = *Dikaiomata* consists of apparently a lawyer's notes on the code. Excerpts are translated in *Sel. Pap.* II 201–2.

45. *Philonis Mechanicae libri quartus et quintus,* ed. R. Schoene (Berlin, 1893), 5.94.21–22, 26–29. On the date of Philon, see Fraser, *PA,* vol. 1, pp. 428–29.

46. In *P. Col. Zen.* II 120.4 (229/228 B.C., possibly 187/186 B.C.)—the allocation of a new tax—the editors W.L. Westermann, C.W. Keyes, and H. Liebesny have proposed a restoration that would add wives to the list of relatives (parents, brothers, and sisters) responsible for registering the property of persons serving in the army. However, considering the state's tendency to exempt soldiers' wives from burdens, this restoration may not be correct.

47. Kiessling, "Die Aposkeuai," p. 249.

48. The material on Apollonia was presented in my paper "Apollonia (also called Senmonthis), Wife of Dryton: Woman of Two Cultures." Apollonia: P.Pt. IV 10642.

49. Dryton: P.Pt. II 2206. For a study of Dryton from the viewpoint of a soldier's life, see Jan K. Winnicki, "Ein ptolemäischer Offizier in Thebais." P. W. Pestman, *Pap. Lugd. Bat.* XIX, p. 32, points out that unfortunately the documents have been poorly edited and poorly published. The archive is distributed among at least ten West European and Russian collections. For a list, see Winnicki, p. 344. On the dates of *P. Giss.* II 36 and 37, see also *P. Mert.* I 5, p. 26. I have followed Winnicki's dates and sequence for all documents I discuss except *P. Bad.* II 5, which, because of its brevity, I believe to be the first will written by Dryton after he married Apollonia. That *P. Bad.* II 5 is not a copy of *P. Grenf.* I 12 + *SB* I 4637, as Pestman suggests (*Pap. Lugd. Bat.* XIX, p. 33), is indicated by the fact that the provisions for Esthladas and Apollonia appear in a different sequence in each document. It may, however, be a draft. Dryton also refers to a will, no longer extant, written at Diospolis Magna in 176/175 B.C. (*P. Grenf.* I 21.4–5). For a suggestion that Dryton wrote his first will on

the occasion of a marriage of which nothing else is known, see N. Lewis, "Dryton's Wives: Two or Three?" *P. Stras.* W. G. *dem.* 16 (135 B.C.) and *Pap. Lugd. Bat.* XIX 4 should now be added to Winnicki's list of documents (p. 344), and Πανοβχύνιος, another son of Callimedes, should be added to Winnicki's genealogical chart, p. 353. Thomas S. Pattie has kindly examined some of the papyri in the British Library and has written (in a personal communication) that he is unable to establish Dryton's autograph.

50. Pestman, *Pap. Lugd. Bat.* XIX, p. 33.

51. F. Uebel, *Die Kleruchen Ägyptens unter den ersten sechs Ptolemäern,* p. 27, dates Dryton's birth to around 200 B.C. Winnicki, "Offizier," p. 345, places it before 192 B.C.

52. Orsolina Montevecchi, "Contributi per una storia sociale ed economica della famiglia nell'Egitto greco-romano," p. 302; *Pap. Lugd. Bat.* V, p. 160.

53. U. Kaplony-Heckel, *Forschungen und Berichte* (1967), pp. 80–82, no. 7.

54. *P. Grenf.* I 1 = *P. Lond. Litt.* 50; see *Coll. Alex.* pp. 177ff.

55. See Chapter II. *P. Eleph.* 1 and 2 are good examples of marriage between immigrants from the same or neighboring cities. Perhaps this tendency was especially pronounced in the earlier period of Ptolemaic rule.

56. Esthladas: P.Pt. II 2895. He is thirty-five years old in 123 B.C. (*P. Cairo* inv. 10388) = *Archiv* I [1901], pp. 63–65.

57. Apollonia the elder daughter: P.Pt. IV 11223; Apollonia the younger: P.Pt. IV 11224; Aristo: P.Pt. IV 11254; Aphrodisia: P.Pt. IV 11291; Nicarion: P.Pt. IV 11537. According to P.Pt., Apollonia the younger is the Apollonia named in *P. Grenf.* I 44. P. W. Pestman, "A proposito dei documenti di Pathyris I," p. 12, has dated this document to 163–124 B.C. Apollonia the younger is the least likely of all the Apollonias in this family to be mentioned, since she would have been a child in 124 B.C. This document must be attributed to the elder sister Apollonia, or to the mother Apollonia-Senmonthis. On the double names of Apollonia and her sisters and daughters, see R. Calderini, "I due elementi del doppio nome nei loro rapporti reciproci di significato," p. 25.

58. On the sources of slaves, see Iza Biezunska-Malowist, *L'esclavage dans l'Egypte gréco-romaine,* vol. 1: *Période ptolémaïque* (hereafter cited as *EP*), Chapter 1. See also Chapter 4 above.

59. H. Ranke, *Die ägyptischen Personennamen,* vol. 1, p. 368; vol. 2, pp. 243–44. L. Youtie, *P. Coll. Youtie* II, p. 630, points out that there is an abundance of names in Sen- in the Thebaid.

60. I am grateful to Erika Feucht and Wolfgang Brunsch for their comments on the Egyptian names.

61. *The Family*, pp. 314–19.

62. Dryton's final will refers to a Petras, son of Esthladas, as the owner of neighboring property (*P. Grenf.* I 21.10). When his father wrote the will, Esthladas was about thirty-two. It is not clear whether he ever married or had a son, and any son he may have had would have been extremely young to own property. It is far more likely that the Petras who owned the property was the son of the first known Esthladas, and thus the brother of Dryton's first wife.

63. Uebel, *Die Kleruchen*, p. 27, and W. Peremans, "Sur l'identification des Egyptiens et des étrangers dans l'Egypte des Lagides," p. 32. J. Lesquier, *Les institutions militaires*, p. 108.

64. Orsolina Montevecchi, "Ricerche di sociologia nei documenti dell'Egitto greco-romano, I: I testamenti," pp. 100–102. For a new edition of some of the soldiers' wills in *P. Petrie* III, see W. Clarysse, "Three Soldiers' Wills in the Petrie Collection: A Reedition." Pestman points out (*Pap. Lugd. Bat.* XIX, p. 32 n. 1) that although *Pap. Lugd. Bat* XIX 4 gives the impression that Esthladas is the sole heir, the daughters do possess property after their father's death.

65. Montevecchi, "I testamenti," pp. 101, 109.

66. *Ibid.*, p. 119.

67. *P. Giss.* II 36 and the Demotic version of the same text, *P. Stras. dem.* W.G. 16.

68. *P. Grenf.* I 15 and 16 are dated by the editor to "no later than 146 or 135." In view of the sequence of events in Apollonia's life, the later date is preferable.

69. Préaux, *MH*, p. 364.

70. This loan was interest-free (*atoka*). Since Apollonia was exacting such a heavy penalty for nonrepayment, the original loan was probably not truly without interest. Such loans may have existed between members of a family or friends. Apollonia's loan, however, could have included the interest in the sum loaned, i.e., no interest had to be added. See P. M. Pestman, "Loans Bearing No Interest."

71. Biezunska-Malowist, *EP*, p. 78, and see p. 132 above.

72. Pomeroy, "Women in Roman Egypt."

73. *Pap. Lugd. Bat.* XIX 4, p. 33.

74. Claire Préaux, *L'économie royale des Lagides* (hereafter cited as *ER*), pp. 239–40, suggests that these ostraca record payment of πηλιχισμὸς περιστερεωνων. For dovecotes, see Maria Cobianchi, "Ricerche di ornitologia nei papiri dell'Egitto greco-romano."

75. P. W. Pestman, *Pap. Lugd. Bat.* XIV, p. 57.

76. Geneviève Husson, "La maison privée à Oxyrhynchos aux trois premiers siècles de notre ère," p. 18.

77. *Ant.* 27.3.

78. W. Spiegelberg, "Papyrus Erbach," *ZAS* 42 (1905): 51.

79. For a discussion of bilingual mummy labels that illuminates the subject of bilingualism in Hellenistic Egypt, see Jan Quaegebeur, "Mummy Labels: An Orientation," pp. 244–47.

80. See H. C. Youtie, "Ὑπογραφεύς," p. 213, and "'ΑΓΡΑΜΜ-ΑΤΟΣ: An Aspect of Greek Society in Egypt," especially pp. 165–70 (or *Scriptiunculae* pp. 615–20), on the detection of women's ability to write, or at least sign a document, in Greek.

81. On the dual legal system, see, most recently, H. J. Wolff, "The Political Background of the Plurality of Laws in Ptolemaic Egypt."

82. Pestman, *Pap. Lugd. Bat.* XIV, p. 102; and see Quaegebeur, "Mummy Labels," pp. 244–47.

83. *Pap. Lugd. Bat.* XIV, p. 59 n. 91 and p. 102.

84. Pestman, *Marriage and Matrimonial Property*, pp. 54, 156.

85. P. W. Pestman, *Over Vrouwen en Voogden in het Oude Egypte*, pp. 17–19. Pestman also draws attention to the numerous cases in which women acted under Greek law without using a *kyrios* and notes that no scholar has been able to determine whether the use of the *kyrios* changed over time, or whether such assistance was required only in certain kinds of cases.

86. V. Tcherikover, *Hellenistic Civilization and the Jews*, p. 350. Philo *De specialibus legibus* 3.67 confirms the evidence of the papyri. Similarly in Babylonia, beginning with the reign of Antiochus I Soter, women lost an aspect of legal competence they had previously enjoyed and were represented by husbands or sons in certain types of judicial matters. Whether the women relinquished their competence voluntarily is not clear. See Gilbert J. P. McEwan, *Texts from Hellenistic Babylonia in the Ashmolean Museum*, p. 8.

87. *Marriage and Matrimonial Property*, p. 184.

88. *Panegyricus* 50.

89. Hdt. 4.153, 186 (Cyrene) and 4.110–17 (Amazons). See also p. 6 above. See Vatin, *FM*, pp. 133–34, for a few examples of families in which Egyptian and Greek names are transmitted to successive generations along gender lines.

90. J. Herrmann, *Studien zur Bodenpacht im Recht der graeco-aegyptischen Papyri*, p. 58.

91. *Pap. Lugd. Bat.* XIX, p. 36 n. 16.

92. On mixed marriages in Egypt, see, most recently, W. Peremans, "Les mariages mixtes dans l'Egypte des Lagides," and Modrzejewski, "Couple interdit," pp. 53–73.

93. Pomeroy, "Infanticide in Hellenistic Greece." See also C. Bradford Welles, "The Population of Roman Dura," p. 263.

94. H. Liebesny, "Ein Erlass des Königs Ptolemaios II Philadelphos über die Deklaration von Vieh und Sklaven in Syrien und Phönikien (*PER* inv. Nr. 24.552 gr.)," p. 258, no. 11.12–15.

95. *The Greeks in Bactria and India*, p. 36.

96. *P. Petr.* II, pp. 19–20.

97. *A History of Egypt under the Ptolemaic Dynasty*, p. 87.

98. "La société indigène en Egypte au III^e siècle avant notre ère d'après les archives de Zénon," p. 259.

99. See in particular the work of W. Peremans, "Ethnies et classes dans l'Egypte ptolémaïque," and a series of articles in *AncSoc*, vols. 1–9.

### Chapter 4

1. For a survey of scholarly views on slavery in Ptolemaic Egypt, see Biezunska-Malowist, *EP,* pp. 5–8; and William Linn Westermann, *Upon Slavery in Ptolemaic Egypt,* "Sklaverei," and *The Slave Systems of Greek and Roman Antiquity.*

2. For criticism of Westermann, see, most recently, M. I. Finley, *Ancient Slavery and Modern Ideology,* p. 54.

3. A. Momigliano, "M. I. Rostovtzeff," p. 98, discusses Rostovtzeff's contributions, but also mentions the "vulgar mistakes in detail" that appear in Rostovtzeff's important work of 1918–26. Westermann's personal copy of Rostovtzeff's *A Large Estate in Egypt in the Third Century B.C.* is in the library of Columbia University. In the margins of his copy, Westermann noted, in ink, Rostovtzeff's errors and omissions. I myself have observed that some of the minor errors in the earlier work, especially wrong citations, appear—again uncorrected—in *SEHHW.*

4. *A Large Estate,* pp. 135, 180.

5. *PA,* vol. 1, pp. 90–91; vol. 2, pp. 171–72.

6. Pp. 54–55.

7. *SEHHW,* pp. 322, 1229.

8. *Ibid.,* p. 1393.

9. See works cited under the name of the author in the bibliography of *EP.*

10. *EP,* p. 17; similarly Préaux, *ER,* pp. 306–12. Heinz Heinen, "Zur

Terminologie der Sklaverei im ptolemäischen Ägypten," is also in agreement with Biezunska-Malowist.

11. Pomeroy, *GWWS*, pp. 71–73; P. Herfst, *Le travail de la femme dans la Grèce ancienne, passim.*

12. Biezunska-Malowist, *EP*, p. 141, and "L'esclavage à Alexandrie dans la période gréco-romaine," p. 298, is more conservative than Fraser in estimating the number of slaves.

13. "L'esclavage à Alexandrie," p. 299, and *EP*, p. 136.

14. *Politics* 6.5.13(1323a). Hopkins, "Brother–Sister Marriage," p. 331, found that in Roman Egypt small families or those with young children were more likely to own slaves than larger families who could perform their work for themselves.

15. Sidonian, rather than Babylonian, based on V. Tcherikover's restoration in *C.P. Jud.* I 1.5.

16. P.Pt. V 12816.

17. According to Louise A. Tilly and Joan W. Scott, *Women, Work, and Family*, p. 113, in 1840, in Amiens, children as young as six or seven were employed in textile production in factories.

18. Biezunska-Malowist, *EP*, p. 68, thinks there are two women. *Pap. Lugd. Bat.* XXI, p. 422, s.v. "Sphragis," lists Sphragis twice, but suggests that the *paidiskē* may be the same as the worker in the wool factory.

19. Despite the "large fluctuations" in prices noted by Tcherikover, "Palestine under the Ptolemies," p. 75 n. 15, those of female slaves in the Zenon papyri are steady.

20. Biezunska-Malowist, *L'esclavage dans l'Egypte gréco-romaine*, vol. 2: *Période romaine*, p. 165, lists the *pais* as "*un enfant.*" However, the word may indicate status and not necessarily age.

21. Isidora (P.Pt. V 14383) and her mother A..ol....m.. (P.Pt. V 14324), other slaves mentioned in the Zenon papyri, may also have been Jewish. However, it is difficult to determine ethnicity in Egypt on the basis of names alone; see p. 124.

22. P. Ducrey, *Le traitement des prisonniers de guerre dans la Grèce antique des origines à la conquête romaine*, pp. 84–87. Ducrey's suggestion is rejected by Biezunska-Malowist, *EP*, pp. 23–27.

23. Ludwig Koenen, "Royal Decree of November 12, 198 B.C.(?) on Sale of Egyptians Enslaved in Unrest (*P. Mich.* inv. 6947)."

24. See *P. Hamb.* I 91 (167 B.C.) and the discussion by Biezunska-Malowist, *EP*, p. 26.

25. For a definition of breeding, see Herbert Gutman and Richard Sutch, "Victorians All? The Sexual Mores and Conduct of Slaves and Their Masters," pp. 154–55.

26. *The Black Family in Slavery and Freedom*, pp. 75–76.

27. *Agr.* 1.8.19; cf. Varro *Rust.* 21.1.26.

28. On this document, see Préaux, *ER*, p. 311, and Biezunska-Malowist, *EP*, p. 97.

29. She is P.Pt. V 14403. According to Frank M. Snowden, Jr., *Blacks in Antiquity*, p. 15, the name Melaenis (or Melainis) indicates a "Negroid type."

30. Iza Biezunska-Malowist and Marian Malowist, "La procréation des esclaves comme source de l'esclavage"; *EP*, pp. 50–51.

31. Finley, *Ancient Slavery*, p. 91, alleges that the Greeks and Romans were incompetent in the field of accounting and in calculations concerning slaves.

32. *Oec.* 9.5.

33. Maria Nowicka, *La maison privée dans l'Egypte ptolémaïque*, pp. 155–56.

34. *Ibid.*, pp. 132–35.

35. Aristoph. *Thes.* 502–9.

36. 1.80; similarly Aristot. *HA* 7.4 (584b) and Strabo 17.2.5.

37. 15.3.

38. A. Cameron, "The Exposure of Children and Greek Ethics," pp. 112–13.

39. M. A. Manca Masciadri and Orsolina Montevecchi, "Contratti di baliatico e vendite fiduciarie a Tebtynis," p. 157.

40. For examples and detailed discussion see Pomeroy, *GWWS*, pp. 36, 40, 46, 69–70, 127, 140, 164–65, 228; "Infanticide in Hellenistic Greece"; and "Copronyms and the Exposure of Infants in Egypt." See also Vatin, *FM*, pp. 228–40.

41. *Hermaphroditus* frag. 11 (Kock).

42. 36.17.

43. G. Plaumann, *Ptolemais in Oberägypten*, pp. 54–58; also published by J. Zingerle, *Strena Buliciana*, pp. 176–82, number 2. I am grateful to Georg Petzl for this reference.

44. Plaumann, *Ptolemais*, pp. 55–56.

45. *LSAM* 84.3–4 = *SEG* XIV 752. I am grateful to George Petzl for sending me his version of this inscription before its publication.

46. Contra Zingerle, *Strena*, p. 179, who finds in this provision "*ethische Forderungen und Verbote.*"

47. Pomeroy, "Infanticide in Hellenistic Greece."

48. *Recherches sur le recensement*, pp. 155–56.

49. For the attractions of Egypt for enterprising Greeks, see Roger S. Bagnall, "Egypt, the Ptolemies, and the Greek World," pp. 10–11.

50. Masciadri and Montevecchi, "Contratti," p. 150, point out that

almost all the documentation for child exposure in Egypt derives from Alexandria and other Greek cities.

51. For nursing contracts from the Roman period, see Masciadri and Montevecchi, "Contratti"; J. Herrmann, "Die Ammenverträge in den gräko-ägyptischen Papyri"; and Keith R. Bradley, "Sexual Regulations in Wet-Nursing Contracts from Roman Egypt."

52. For the prices of slaves in both Ptolemaic and Roman Egypt, see Biezunska-Malowist, *L'esclavage dans l'Egypte gréco-romaine*, vol. 2: *Période romaine*, pp. 165–67.

53. Masciadri and Montevecchi, "Contratti," p. 156; Pomeroy, "Copronyms."

54. *ER*, p. 473. Vatin, *FM*, p. 233, in turn cites Préaux in support of his statement that child exposure was practiced in Ptolemaic Egypt.

55. *EP*, p. 52.

56. For the *opsonion* ("allowance"), see T. Reekmans, *La sitométrie dans les Archives de Zénon*, p. 65.

57. *Ibid.*, pp. 22, 61.

58. *Ibid.*, p. 32.

59. *Agr.* 56.

60. See, e.g., Plut. *Cato Major*, 3.1, 4.4, 5.1–2, 21.2.

61. Reekmans, *La sitométrie*, pp. 52–53.

62. *Encyclopaedia Britannica*, 15th ed., vol. 13, p. 419, Table 2.

63. Dorothy Crawford, *Kerkeosiris: An Egyptian Village in the Ptolemaic Period*, p. 130, used 3,150 calories as the yield from a kilogram of unmilled wheat. She found an average caloric intake of 2,175 at Cerceosiris. Since Reekmans, *La sitométrie*, p. 32, used 3,300 calories as the yield from a kilogram of wheat, I have altered Crawford's figures by Reekmans' standard to obtain comparable figures. In any event, as Crawford cautions (p. 129), these calculations can only be approximate.

64. Robert William Fogel and Stanley L. Engerman, *Time on the Cross*, vol. 2, p. 97.

65. See Richard Sutch, "The Care and Feeding of Slaves," pp. 265–82, for a critical review of Fogel's and Engerman's estimates of caloric intake.

66. Reekmans, *La sitométrie*, pp. 27–28. Three of the four are P.Pt. V 12832, 14383, and 14454.

67. *Encyclopaedia Britannica*, 15th ed., vol. 13, p. 420, Table 3.

68. Richard T. Hallock, *Persepolis Fortification Tablets*, pp. 344–53 (Ionian women in number 1224).

69. For slaves and free working side by side and earning the same salary among the Greeks, see Finley, *Ancient Slavery*, p. 100.

70. Biezunska-Malowist, *EP*, pp. 77, 79.

71. *Ibid.*, pp. 135, 138.

72. Nowicka, *La maison privée*, p. 114.

73. See S. M. Treggiari, "Jobs for Women."

74. P.Pt. 14436.

75. E. Piekniewski, "Die Rätsel um *P. Eleph.* 3 und 4," p. 291.

76. Biezunska-Malowist, *EP*, p. 129, reviving the earlier interpretations of J. Partsch and U. Wilcken.

77. [Demos.] 59.26,29–32.

78. On prostitutes and *hetairai* in Greece, see Pomeroy, *GWWS*, pp. 88–92, 114–17, and 139–41; and Hans Herter, "Die Soziologie der antiken Prostitution im Lichte des heidnischen und christlichen Schrifttums." On homosexuality, often as an attribute of the upper class, see K. J. Dover, *Greek Homosexuality.*

79. The Artemidorus who wrote *PSI* IV 352 is identified as an *enkautes* in *Pap. Lugd. Bat.* XXI, "Prosopography."

80. *LSJ*, s.v. "Προσχράομαι." "Abuse" is a dubious sense.

81. Tcherikover, "Palestine under the Ptolemies," pp. 16–17, discusses this document and suggests that the border guard ran an inn.

82. 2.16.

83. Tcherikover, "Palestine under the Ptolemies," p. 16.

84. Aunchis in *P. Lond.* VII 1976; P.Pt. V 12470.

## CHAPTER 5

1. I have discussed some of the issues pertaining to women and land ownership in Egypt in "Women in Egypt under Roman Domination" and "Women in Roman Egypt."

2. Préaux, *MH*, p. 540.

3. See, most recently, Joseph Mélèze Modrzejewski, "Régime foncier et status social dans l'Egypte ptolémaïque." Crawford, *Kerkeosiris*, p. 103, gives an illuminating and detailed study of how the land-tenure system functioned in one village.

4. Diod. Sic. 1.21.7, 73.2; Crawford, *Kerkeosiris*, p. 93.

5. I have not added any people who have appeared in documents published since P.Pt. IV, for I could not achieve the thoroughness of the P.Pt. To add haphazardly would be to invalidate the sample.

6. Préaux, *ER*, p. 470.

7. Her. 2.168; Diod. Sic. 173.7–9; Préaux, *ER*, p. 465.

8. See Schaps, *Economic Rights*, pp. 6–7.

9. See Uebel, *Die Kleruchen*, for the difference between cleruchs and salaried soldiers.

10. Préaux, *ER*, p. 464.

11. P.Pt. I 9726, 9727.

12. P.Pt. I 9764.

13. *CAH* 11, p. 653.

14. Women constitute the majority of owners in *P. Lond.* II 193 (Fayum [?], first century A.D.), a register of catoecic land. They are numerous as well in other registers, including *P. Vindob. Tandem* 13–15 and *P. Upps.* 14 (Theadelphia, second century A.D.), a document recording the inspection of catoecic land.

15. Préaux, *ER,* p. 467.

16. *Ibid.,* p. 475.

17. Uebel, *Die Kleruchen,* p. 41 note 2, and Clarysse, "Three Soldiers' Wills," p. 19.

18. *BGU* VIII 1734 (Heracleopolis) = *SB* VIII 9790, edited by Wolfgang Müller in "Bemerkungen zu den spätptolemäischen Papyri der Berliner Sammlung," p. 190.

19. P.Pt. III 8028; IV 8404, 8405, 8406, 8407, 8409.

20. P.Pt. IV 8147. See pp. 158–60 ff. above.

21. P.Pt. IV 8404, 8405, 8407, 10717, 10741, 10743, 10744, 10745, 10776, 10777, 11004, 11008, 11009, 11010, 11011, 11032, 11033, 11035, 11037, 11040, 11041, 11043, 11044, 11045, 11046a, 11047, 11049a, 11050, 11052, 11053, 11054, 11055, 11057, 11080, 11080a, 11111.

22. P.Pt. IV 10655, 10703, 10712, 10732a, 10769, 10808, 11029, 11070, 11364.

23. P.Pt. IV 10628, 10642, 20731, 20732.

24. P.Pt. IV 11191 vineyard, 11268 vineyard, 11269, 11270 vineyard, 11296, 11297, 11298 *gē politikē,* 11299 vineyard, 11314 vineyard, 11315, 11364, 11377, 11380 vineyard, 11387, 11391, 11393, 11397 vineyard?, 11398, 11399, 11428 vineyard, 11486, 11534, 11541 vineyard, 11542 vineyard, 11691, 11755 vineyard, 11759, 11784 vineyard, 11788.

25. P.Pt. IV 11287 vineyard, 11370, 11389, 11416, 11430, 11433 vineyard, 11532, 11722, 11727 vineyard, 11764, 11765 vineyard, 11766 vineyards, 11767, 11768, 11769, 11770, 11779, 11796.

26. P.Pt. IV 11223, 11224, 11254, 11291, 11537 share a vineyard; P.Pt. IV 11418 is not related to the five preceding women.

27. For the history of the Fayum, including its geology and geography, see *P. Fay.,* pp. 1–17, and *I. Fayum* I, introduction.

28. J. G. Keenan and J. C. Shelton, *P. Tebt.,* IV pp. 2, 6; Crawford, *Kerkeosiris,* pp. 43–44, 93.

29. M.-T. Lenger, *Corpus des Ordonnances des Ptolémées* 17.12–15 = *P. Revenue Laws* col. 36.12–15.

30. Rostovtzeff, *SEHHW,* p. 1188, notes that grain was more profitable than wine or oil.

31. P.Pt. IV 12055, 12065, 12094, 12106, 12177, 12188, 12195, 12212.

32. Herrmann, *Bodenpacht*, p. 58. Most of the leases studied by Herrmann are from the Roman period. In a study of land leases published in 1967, women appear as active participants in only two Ptolemaic documents. In 224/223 B.C., in the Oxyrhynchite nome, Cleopatra leased land to Eupolis for a rent of 30 artabs of wheat (*P. Hib.* I 91). In 109 B.C., in Pestenemenophis, Pathyris, Tachratis leased $7\frac{1}{2}$ arouras of land planted with arax (a legume) to a man (*PSI* IX 1021). See D. Hennig, *Untersuchungen zur Bodenpacht im ptolemäisch-römischen Ägypten*, p. 179, lease no. 31; p. 190, lease no. 68.

33. *Women's Role in Economic Development*, pp. 32–33.

34. P.Pt. IV, third century B.C.: 8404, 8405, 8407, 10703, 10741, 10744, 10808, 11004, 11010, 11033, 11037, 11043, 11044, 11052, 11053, 11054, 11057; second century B.C.: 10628, 10642, 10655, 10712, 10717, 10731, 10732, 10743, 10745, 10769, 10776, 10777, 11008, 11009, 11029, 11032, 11035, 11040, 11041, 11045, 11046a, 11049a, 11055, 11070, 11080, 11080a, 11111: first century B.C.: 10732a, 11047, 11050.

35. P.Pt. IV, third century B.C.: 11268, 11270, 11296, 11297, 11314, 11428, 11433, 11541, 11542, 11691, 11722, 11779, 11784; second century B.C.: 11191, 11223, 11224, 11254, 11269, 11287, 11291, 11298, 11315, 11364, 11377, 11380, 11387, 11391, 11393, 11397, 11398, 11399, 11416, 11430, 11486, 11534, 11727, 11755, 11759, 11764, 11765, 11767, 11768, 11770, 11788, 11796; second–first century B.C.: 11766; first century B.C.: 11299, 11370, 11289, 11532, 11769.

36. For the surveys of men, I studied the first 150 men listed in P.Pt. in the categories of sacred and private land.

37. See Schaps, *Economic Rights*, pp. 4–7, and p. 91 above.

38. Land is not part of matrimonial property in Pestman, *Marriage and Matrimonial Property*.

39. According to Deborah H. Samuel, "Women as Property Owners in Roman Egypt," women at Socnopaiou Nesos as well most frequently came into possession of land by means of inheritance; they are rarely found as purchasers of land.

40. "I testamenti," p. 116.

41. Eirene is P.Pt. IV 8147. Her archive is distributed between Columbia University and the University of Michigan. To these documents, the editors of P.Pt. add *P. Petr.* II 30e and *P. Petr.* III 69b, a bilingual text (one text is not a translation of the other, for they differ in such details as the measures of wine stipulated). Eirene was a common name and, as V. B. Schuman pointed out (*P. Mich.* III 182, n. 8), the location

of the property in the Petrie documents is not the same as the location in the rest of the archive. The editors of the Columbia papyri also do not include the Petrie documents. The information on the Petrie documents is not incompatible with the picture of the activities of Eirene, wife of Agamemnon. Thus the Petrie papyri may be included in this archive; however, they are too short and fragmentary to contribute much to our knowledge of Eirene's activities.

42. The editors of *P. Col. Zen.* II suggest (p. 201) that Eirene's husband acted as her manager. There is no justification for this notion in the sources, nor is there any indication that she hired a manager.

43. W. Peremans, "Egyptiens et étrangers dans l'agriculture et l'élevage en Egypte ptolémaïque," p. 129.

44. *P. Col. Zen.* II, p. 188.

45. Nicander is P.Pt. II 2806, IV 8241, and IV 8816. Listed in Uebel, *Die Kleruchen,* no. 281, p. 105.

46. See, e.g., A. F. Shore, "The Sale of the House of Senkhonsis, Daughter of Phibis," for a husband who sold a house that had belonged to his wife in order to pay for the funeral expenses of his wife, father-in-law, and mother-in-law.

47. P.Pt. V 12954 (second century B.C.).

48. *P. Tebt.* III 814 col. ii.47.

49. *SB* I 1080 (second century B.C.); *BGU* VII 1528, Philopator.

50. Praxinoa is in the same circumstances as the housewife described in Lysias 1.12 who has one slave and who nurses her baby herself.

51. See Sister Mary Rosaria, *The Nurse in Greek Life,* pp. 7–15, and pp. 138–39 above.

52. S. Mollard-Besques, *Catalogue raisonné des figurines et reliefs en terre-cuite grecs et romains,* vol. 2: *Myrina.* P. 113, MYR 266: an old female slave holds a little girl by the hand; p. 137, MYR 258: an old nurse holds infant on her lap. Berlin, Staatliche Museum, terracotta 7946: a woman dressed well enough to be the mother holds a baby.

53. P.Pt. V 14213. Thasis (P.Pt. V 14201), a nurse, is named in a list of recipients of grain (*P. Cair. Zen.* II 59292.157 [250 B.C.]).

54. Breccia *Iscriz.* 40b.

55. Sponnesis is P.Pt. V 14255.

56. See Masciadri and Montevecchi, "Contratti," for the stipulations in wet-nursing contracts.

57. Bradley, "Sexual Regulations."

58. P.Pt. V 12606, 12607, 12612, 12613, 12614, 12616, 12649.

59. T. Reil, *Beiträge zur Kenntnis des Gewerbes im hellenistischen Ägypten,* p. 164. Unfortunately this excellent book devotes only two short paragraphs specifically to women's work.

60. *Ibid.*, p. 166.

61. P.Pt. V 12470, 12477, 12512, 12516.

62. *P. Lond.* VII 1976 (253 B.C.).

63. Préaux, *ER*, p. 156.

64. Pomeroy, *GWWS*, pp. 9, 30, 40, 149, 199–200; Jane McIntosh Snyder, "The Web of Song: Weaving Imagery in Homer and the Lyric Poets."

65. Sutton, *Interaction Between Men and Women*, pp. 49, 355–56.

66. Pomeroy, "Supplementary Notes on Erinna," pp. 17–22; Marylin B. Arthur, "The Tortoise and the Mirror: Erinna *PSI* 1909."

67. Wesley Thompson, "Weaving: A Man's Work," gives the citations but does not draw attention to the chronological framework.

68. Pomeroy, "Technikai kai Mousikai."

69. Theocritus, *Idyll* 15.18–37, adapted from the translation by A. S. F. Gow (Cambridge, 1952).

70. P. 115.

71. P. 1227.

72. See *P. Cair. Zen.* II 59241 (253 B.C.), introduction, for a mattress to be manufactured in a "wool factory."

73. Pomeroy, "Technikai kai Mousikai," p. 54.

74. Milne, *Cairo Cat. Gk. Inscrs.* p. 46, number 9259. See p. 189 n.113 above.

75. In *P. Mich. Zen.* 58.22–23 (248 B.C.), a cloak is being woven for Zenon under the supervision of one of his farmers. Whether the weaver is a man or a woman is not stated.

76. Préaux, *ER*, p. 105; and see Françoise Dunand, "L'artisanat du textile dans l'Egypte lagide."

77. Hdt. 2.35 and *Dissoi Logoi* 2.17 exaggerate the difference between Greece and Egypt by pointing to men's weaving in Egypt and ignoring women's.

78. Roger S. Bagnall, "Notes on Greek and Egyptian Ostraka," pp. 145–46.

79. "Sklaven in der Textilindustrie des ptolemäischen Ägypten."

80. Dunand, "L'artisanat," p. 63.

81. See, e.g., Tilly and Scott, *Women, Work, and Family*, especially pp. 1–8.

82. "Sklaven in der Textilindustrie," p. 31.

83. P.Pt. V 12734, 12740 (an epithet of Berenice, wife of Euergetes: "weaver of linen"), 12742, 12754, 12755, 12756, 12758, 12768, 12772, 12805, 12806, 12815, 12816, 12820, 12832, 12853.

# Works Cited

With a few obvious exceptions, journal titles are abbreviated according to the form in *L'Année philologique*. Editions of Greek papyri and ostraca usually follow the forms in J. F. Oates, Roger S. Bagnall, and William H. Willis, *Checklist of Editions of Greek Papyri and Ostraca*, 2d ed. (*BASP* Supplement 1 [1978]). Accepted abbreviations will be used for standard works. Lists of such abbreviations may be found in reference books such as the *Oxford Classical Dictionary* and in the major Greek and Latin dictionaries.

El-Abbadi, M. A. H. "The Alexandrian Citizenship." *JEA* 48 (1962): 106–23.
Anderson, J. K. *Ancient Greek Horsemanship*. Berkeley and Los Angeles, 1961.
Arangio-Ruiz, Vincenzo. "Intorno agli ΑΣΤΟΙ dell'Egitto greco-romano." *RIDA* 4 (1950): 7–20.
Archaeological Museum of Thessaloniki. *Treasures of Ancient Macedonia*, edited by K. Ninou. Athens, 1979.
Ardener, Edwin. "Belief and the Problem of Women." In *The Interpretation of Ritual*, edited by J. S. La Fontaine, pp. 133–58. London, 1972. Also in *Perceiving Women*, edited by S. Ardener, pp. 1–17. London, 1975.
Arthur, Marylin B. "The Tortoise and the Mirror: Erinna *PSI* 1909." *CW* 74 (1980): 53–65.
Bacchielli, Lidiano. "Le pitture dalla 'Tomba dell'Altalena di Cirene' nel Museo del Louvre." *QAL* 8 (1976): 355–83.
Badian, Ernst. "The Deification of Alexander the Great." In *Ancient Macedonian Studies in Honor of Charles F. Edson*, pp. 27–71. Thessaloniki, 1981.

———. "Eurydice." In *Philip II, Alexander the Great, and the Macedonian Heritage*, edited by W. Lindsay Adams and Eugene N. Borza, pp. 99–110. Washington, D.C., 1982.

Bagnall, Roger S. *The Administration of the Ptolemaic Possessions Outside Egypt*. Leiden, 1976.

———. "Egypt, the Ptolemies, and the Greek World." *Bulletin of the Egyptological Seminar* 3 (1981): 5–21.

———. "Notes on Greek and Egyptian Ostraka." *Enchoria* 8 (1978): 143–50.

———. "Religious Conversion and Onomastic Change in Early Byzantine Egypt." *BASP* 14 (1982): 105–24.

Bagnall, Roger S., and Derow, Peter. *Greek Historical Documents: The Hellenistic Period* (Chico, Calif., 1981).

Balsdon, J. P. V. D. Review of H. Volkmann, *Cleopatra*. *CR* 74 (1960): 68–71.

Bechtel, F. *Die attischen Frauennamen*. Göttingen, 1902.

Bengtson, Hermann. *Herrschergestalten des Hellenismus*. Munich, 1975.

Bentley, Richard. *Dissertation upon the Epistles of Phalaris*. 1699; London, 1816.

Bernand, E. *Inscriptions métriques de l'Egypte gréco-romaine, Recherches sur la poésie épigrammatique des Grecs en Egypte*. Annales littéraires de l'Université de Besançon, vol. 98. Paris, 1969.

Berve, H. *Das Alexanderreich*. 2 vols. Munich, 1926.

Bevan, E. R. *A History of Egypt under the Ptolemaic Dynasty*. London, 1927.

———. *The House of Seleucus*. 2 vols. London, 1902; reprint, New York, 1966.

Biezunska, Iza. "La condition juridique de la femme grecque d'après les papyri." *Hermaion*, fasc. 4 (1939).

Biezunska-Malowist, Iza. "L'esclavage à Alexandrie dans la période gréco-romaine." *Actes du Colloque 1973 sur l'esclavage*. Annales littéraires de l'Université de Besançon, vol. 182, pp. 293–312. Paris, 1976.

———. *L'esclavage dans l'Egypte gréco-romaine*. Vol. 1: *Période ptolémaïque* (cited as *EP*). Warsaw, 1974. Vol. 2: *Période romaine*. Warsaw, 1977.

Biezunska-Malowist, Iza, and Malowist, Marian. "La procréation des esclaves comme source de l'esclavage." In *Mélanges Michalowski*, pp. 275–80. Warsaw, 1966.

Bingen, Jean. Review of M. David and B. A. van Groningen, *Papyrological Primer*. *CE* 41 (1966): 403.

Borza, Eugene N. "The Macedonian Royal Tombs at Vergina: Some Cautionary Notes." *Arch N* 10 (1981): 73–87.

Boserup, Ester. *Women's Role in Economic Development*. New York, 1970.

212     WORKS CITED

Bourdieu, P. *Outline of a Theory of Practice.* Translated by R. Nice. Cambridge, 1977.
Bradley, Keith R. "Sexual Regulations in Wet-Nursing Contracts from Roman Egypt." *Klio* 62 (1980): 321–25.
Brendel, Otto J. "The Scope and Temperament of Erotic Art in the Greco-Roman World." In *Studies in Erotic Art,* edited by T. Bowie and C. Christenson, pp. 41–54. New York, 1970.
Bringmann, Lea. *Die Frau im ptolemäisch-kaiserlichen Aegypten.* Ph.D. dissertation, University of Bonn, 1939.
Brown, Blanche R. "Novelty, Ingenuity, Self-aggrandizement, Ostentation, Extravagance, Gigantism, and Kitsch in the Art of Alexander the Great and His Successors." In *Art, the Ape of Nature: Studies in Honor of H. W. Janson,* edited by M. Barasch and L. Friedman, pp. 1–13. New York, 1981.
Bruneau, Philippe. "Tombes d'Argos." *BCH* 94 (1970): 437–531.
Burkert, W. *Lore and Science in Ancient Pythagoreanism.* Cambridge, 1972.
Burstein, Stanley Mayer. "Arsinoë II Philadelphos: A Revisionist View." In *Philip II, Alexander the Great, and the Macedonian Heritage,* edited by W. Lindsay Adams and Eugene N. Borza, pp. 197–212. Washington, D.C., 1982.
Calder, William M., III. "Diadem and Barrel Vault: A Note." *AJA* 85 (1981): 334–35.
Calderini, R. "I due elementi del doppio nome nei loro rapporti reciproci di significato." *Aegyptus* 22 (1942): p. 281.
Cameron, A. "The Exposure of Children and Greek Ethics." *CR* 46 (1932): 112–13.
Cameron, Alan. "Asclepiades' Girl Friends." In *Reflections of Women in Antiquity,* edited by Heler.e P. Foley, pp. 275–302. London, 1981.
———. "Two Mistresses of Ptolemy Philadelphos." Unpublished essay.
Campbell, J. K. *Honour, Family and Patronage.* Oxford, 1964.
Castner, Catherine J. "Epicurean Hetairai as Dedicants to Healing Deities?" *GRBS* 23 (1982): 51–57.
Cawkwell, George. *Philip of Macedon.* London, 1978.
Cerfaux, L., and Tondriau, J. L. *Un concurrent de christianisme: Le culte des souverains dans la civilisation gréco-romaine.* Paris, New York, and Rome, 1957.
Černy, Jaroslav. "Consanguineous Marriages in Pharaonic Egypt." *JEA* 40 (1954): 23–29.
Charbonneaux, J.; Martin, R.; and Villard, F. *Hellenistic Art.* Translated by Peter Green. New York, 1973.

Clarysse, Willy. "Harmachis, Agent of the Oikonomos: An Archive from the Time of Philopator." *AncSoc* 7 (1976): 185–90.

———. "Three Soldiers' Wills in the Petrie Collection: A Reedition." *AncSoc* 2 (1971): 7–20.

Cobianchi, Maria. "Ricerche di ornitologia nei papiri dell'Egitto greco-romano." *Aegyptus* 16 (1936): 94–121.

Cole, Susan Guettel. "Could Greek Women Read and Write?" *Women's Studies* 8 (1981): 129–55. Reprinted in *Reflections of Women in Antiquity*, edited by Helene P. Foley, pp. 219–45. London, 1981.

Connelly, Joan Bryton. "Votive Portraiture in Hellenistic Cyprus." Paper delivered at the annual meeting of the Archaeological Institute of America, December 30, 1982. Abstract in *AJA* 87 (1983): 230.

Coppola, G. "Callimachus Senex." *RFC* 58 (1930): 273–91.

Crawford, Dorothy. *Kerkeosiris: An Egyptian Village in the Ptolemaic Period.* Cambridge, 1971.

David, T. "La position de la femme en Asie centrale." *Dialogues d'histoire ancienne* 2 (1976): 129–62.

Davies, J. K. *Athenian Propertied Families, 600–300 B.C.* Oxford, 1971.

Davies, Stevan L. *The Revolt of the Widows.* Carbondale, Ill., 1980.

Delia, Diana. *Roman Alexandria: Studies in its Social History.* Ph.D. dissertation, Columbia University, 1982.

Demand, Nancy. "Plato, Aristophanes, and the *Speeches of Pythagoras.*" *GRBS* 23 (1982): 179–84.

Deubner, L. *Attische Feste.* Berlin, 1932.

Dover, K. J. *Greek Homosexuality.* Cambridge, Mass., 1978.

———. *Theocritus: Select Poems.* London, 1971.

Du Boulay, Juliet. *Portrait of a Greek Mountain Village.* Oxford, 1974.

Ducrey, P. *Le traitement des prisonniers de guerre dans la Grèce antique des origines à la conquête romaine.* Paris, 1968.

Dunand, Françoise. "L'artisanat du textile dans l'Egypte lagide." *Ktema* 4 (1979): 47–69.

*Encyclopaedia Britannica.* 15th ed. 1974.

Engels, Donald W. *Alexander the Great and the Logistics of the Macedonian Army.* Berkeley, 1978.

Eyben, E. "Family Planning in Graeco-Roman Antiquity." *AncSoc* 11–12 (1980–81): 5–82.

Fantham, Elaine. "Sex, Status and Survival in Hellenistic Athens: A Study of Women in New Comedy." *Phoenix* 29 (1975): 44–74.

Farnell, Lewis. *Cults of the Greek States.* 5 vols. Oxford, 1896–1909.

Finley, M. I. *Ancient Slavery and Modern Ideology.* London, 1980.

————. *The World of Odysseus.* 2d ed. New York, 1978.

Fogel, Robert William, and Engerman, Stanley L. *Time on the Cross.* 2 vols. Boston, 1974.

Foley, Helene P. "The Concept of Women in Athenian Drama." In *Reflections of Women in Antiquity,* edited by Helene P. Foley, pp. 127–68. London, 1981.

Fraser, P. M. "Bibliography. Graeco-Roman Egypt. Greek Inscriptions 1960." *JEA* 47 (1961): 139–49.

————. *Ptolemaic Alexandria* (cited as *PA*). 3 vols. Oxford, 1972.

Fredericksmeyer, E. A. "Again the So-Called Tomb of Philip II." *AJA* 85 (1981): 330–34.

Friedrich, Paul. *The Meaning of Aphrodite.* Chicago and London, 1978.

Frischer, Bernard. *The Sculpted Word.* Berkeley, Los Angeles, and London, 1982.

Fuchs, W. *Die Skulptur des Griechen.* 2d ed. Munich, 1979.

Gagé, Nicholas, and Gagé, Jean. "Treasures from a Golden Tomb." *The New York Times Magazine,* December 25, 1977.

Giallombardo, Anna Maria Prestianni. "Diritto matrimoniale, ereditario e dinastico nella Macedonia di Filippo II." *RSA* 6–7 (1976–77): 81–110.

————. "Eurydike-Kleopatra. Nota ad Arr., Anab., 3, 6, 5." *ASNP,* 3d ser., 2 (1981): 295–306.

Giallombardo, Anna Maria Prestianni, and Tripodi, Bruno. "Le Tombe Regali di Vergina: Quale Filippo?" *ASNP,* 3d ser., 10 (1980): 989–1001.

Glanville, S. R. K., and Skeat, T. C. "Eponymous Priesthoods of Alexandria from 211 B.C." *JEA* 40 (1954): 45–58.

Goitein, S. D. *A Mediterranean Society.* Vol. 3: *The Family.* Berkeley and Los Angeles, 1978.

Gomme, A. W. *Essays in Greek History and Literature.* Oxford, 1937.

Goode, William J. "The Theoretical Importance of Love." *American Sociological Review* 24 (1959): 33–47.

Goodenough, E. R. "The Political Philosophy of Hellenistic Kingship." *YCS* 1 (1928): 55–102.

Gow, A. S. F., and Page, D. L. *The Greek Anthology: Hellenistic Epigrams* (cited as *HE*). 2 vols. Cambridge, 1965.

Green, Peter. "The Royal Tombs of Vergina: A Historical Analysis." In *Philip II, Alexander the Great, and the Macedonian Heritage,* edited by W. Lindsay Adams and Eugene N. Borza, pp. 129–51. Washington, D.C., 1982.

Griffiths, Frederick T. *Theocritus at Court.* Leiden, 1979.

Griffiths, John Gwyn. "The Death of Cleopatra VII." *JEA* 47 (1961): 113–18.

———. *Plutarch's De Iside et Osiride*. Cambridge, 1970.

Grimm, Gunter, and Johannes, Dieter. *Kunst der Ptolemäer- und Römerzeit im Ägyptischen Museum Kairo*. Mainz, 1975.

Gronewald, M. "Fragmente aus einem Sapphokommentar: *Pap. Colon.* inv. 5860." *ZPE* 14 (1974): 114–18.

Gutman, Herbert. *The Black Family in Slavery and Freedom*. New York, 1976.

Gutman, Herbert, and Sutch, Richard. "Victorians All? The Sexual Mores and Conduct of Slaves and Their Masters." In *Reckoning with Slavery*, edited by P. David et al., pp. 134–62. New York, 1976.

Hallock, Richard T. *Persepolis Fortification Tablets*. Chicago, 1969.

Hammond, N. G. L. "Philip's Tomb in Historical Context." *GRBS* 19 (1978): 331–50.

Hammond, N. G. L., and Griffith, G. T. *A History of Macedonia*. 2 vols. Oxford, 1972–79.

Harrison, A. R. W. *The Law of Athens: The Family and Property*. Oxford, 1968.

Harvey, F. D. "Literacy in the Athenian Democracy." *REG* 79 (1966): 585–635.

Hauben, Hans. "Agathokleia and her Boats." *ZPE* 16 (1975): 289–91.

———. "A Jewish Shipowner in Third-century Ptolemaic Egypt." *AncSoc* 10 (1979): 167–70.

———. "Le transport fluvial en Egypte ptolémaïque: Les bateaux du roi et de la reine." *Actes du XV<sup>e</sup> Congrès international de papyrologie*. Vol. 4: *Papyrologie documentaire*, pp. 68–77. Brussels, 1979.

Havelock, Christine M. "The Portrayal and Significance of the Goddess Aphrodite in the Hellenistic Period." Paper delivered at the annual meeting of the Archaeological Institute of America, December 30, 1982. Abstract in *AJA* 87 (1983): 238–39.

Headlam, Walter. *Herodas: The Mimes and Fragments*. Cambridge, 1922.

Heckel, Waldemar. "Kleopatra or Eurydike?" *Phoenix* 32 (1978):155–58.

———. "Polyxena, the Mother of Alexander the Great." *Chiron* 11 (1981): 79–86.

Heckel, Waldemar, and Yardley, John C. "Roman Writers and the Indian Practice of Suttee." *Philologus* 125 (1981): 305–11.

Heckscher, W. S. "Aphrodite as a Nun." *Phoenix* 7 (1953): 107–17.

Heinen, Heinz. "Zur Terminologie der Sklaverei im ptolemäischen

Ägypten." Paper delivered at the XVII Congresso Internazionale di papirologia, Naples, 1983.

Hennig, D. *Untersuchungen zur Bodenpacht im ptolemäisch-römischen Ägypten.* Munich, 1967.

Henrichs, Albert. "Greek and Roman Glimpses of Dionysos." In *Dionysos and His Circle: Ancient through Modern*, edited by C. Houser, pp. 1–11. Cambridge, Mass., 1979.

———. "Greek Maenadism from Olympias to Messalina." *HSPh* 82 (1978): 121–60.

Herfst, P. *Le travail de la femme dans la Grèce ancienne.* Utrecht, 1922.

Herrmann, J. "Die Ammenverträge in den gräko-ägyptischen Papyri." *ZRG* 76 (1957): 490–99.

———. *Studien zur Bodenpacht im Recht der graeco-aegyptischen Papyri.* Münchener Beiträge zur Papyrusforschung und antiken Rechtsgeschichte, vol. 41. Munich, 1958.

Herter, Hans. "Die Soziologie der antiken Prostitution im Lichte des heidnischen und christlichen Schrifttums." *JbAC* 3 (1960): 70–111.

Heyob, Sharon Kelly. *The Cult of Isis Among Women in the Graeco-Roman World.* Etudes préliminaires aux religions orientales dans l'empire romain, vol. 51. Leiden, 1975.

Hignett, C. *A History of the Athenian Constitution.* Oxford, 1953.

Hirschon, Renée. "Open Body/ Closed Space: The Transformation of Female Sexuality." In *Defining Females*, edited by Shirley Ardener, pp. 66–88. New York, 1978.

Holleaux, M. "Ceux qui sont dans le bagage." *REG* 39 (1926): 355–66. Reprinted in *Etudes d'épigraphie et d'histoire grecques*, vol. 3, pp. 15–26. 6 vols. Paris, 1938–69.

Hombert. M., and Préaux, C. *Recherches sur le recensement dans l'Egypte romaine. Pap. Lugd. Bat.* V. Brussels, 1952.

Hopkins, M. Keith. "Brother–Sister Marriage in Roman Egypt." *CSSH* 22 (1980): 303–54.

———. "Contraception in the Roman Empire." *CSSH* 8 (1965): 124–51.

Husson, Geneviève. "La maison privée à Oxyrhynchos aux trois premiers siècles de notre ère." *Ktema* 1 (1976): 5–27.

Huzar, Eleanor Goltz. *Mark Antony: A Biography.* Minneapolis, 1978.

Ijsewijn, J. *De sacerdotibus sacerdotiisque Alexandri Magni et Lagidarum.* Brussels, 1961.

Kahrstedt, U. "Frauen auf antiken Münzen." *Klio* 10 (1910): 261—314.

Kaibel, G. *Epigrammata Graeca ex lapidus conlecta.* Berlin, 1878.

Kampen, Natalie. "Hellenistic Artists: Female." *ArchClass* 27 (1975): 9–17.

Kelly, J. N. D. *Jerome*. New York, 1975.

Kiessling, E. "Die Aposkeuai und die prozessrechtliche Stellung der Ehefrauen im ptolemäischen Ägypten. *APF* 8 (1927): 240–49.

————. *Wörterbuch der griechischen Papyrusurkunden*. 4 vols. Berlin and Amsterdam, 1944–71.

Koenen, Ludwig. "Royal Decree of November 12, 198 B.C.(?) on Sale of Egyptians Enslaved in Unrest (*P. Mich.* inv. 6947)." Paper delivered at the XVII Congresso internazionale di papirologia, Naples, 1983.

Kornemann, E. *Grosse Frauen des Altertums im Rahmen zweitausendjährigen Weltgeschehens*. 2d ed. Bremen, 1958.

Kyrieleis, Helmut. *Bildnisse der Ptolemäer*. Berlin, 1975.

Lacey, W. K. *The Family in Classical Greece*. London, 1968.

Lattimore, R. *Themes in Greek and Latin Epitaphs*. Illinois Studies in Language and Literature, vol. 28. Urbana, 1942.

Lehmann, Karl. *Samothrace: A Guide to the Excavations and the Museum*. Locust Valley, N.Y., 1975.

Lenormant, F. "La Vénus de l'Esquilin et le Diadumène de Polyclète." *Gazette archéologique* 3 (1877): 138–52.

Lesquier, J. *Les institutions militaires de l'Egypte sous les Lagides*. Paris, 1911.

Lévi-Strauss, Claude. *Les Structures élémentaires de la Parenté*. Paris, 1949. 2nd edition, Paris, 1967. Translated as *The Elementary Structures of Kinship*. Boston, 1969.

Lewis, N. "Dryton's Wives: Two or Three?" *CE* 57 (1982): 317–21.

Liebesny, H. "Ein Erlass des Königs Ptolemaios II. Philadelphos über die Deklaration von Vieh und Sklaven in Syrien und Phönikien (*PER* inv. Nr. 24.552 gr.)." *Aegyptus* 16 (1936): 255–88.

Lloyd, G. E. R. *Science, Folklore, and Ideology: Studies in the Life Sciences in Ancient Greece*. Cambridge, 1983.

Lloyd-Jones, Hugh. *Females of the Species*. London, 1975.

Lobel, Edgar, and Page, Denys. *Poetarum Lesbiorum Fragmenta*. Oxford, 1955.

Longega, Gabriella. *Arsinoë II*. Università degli Studi di Padova Pubblicazioni dell'Istituto di Storia Antica, vol. 6. Rome, 1968.

Ludwig, Walther. "Plato's Love Epigrams." *GRBS* 4 (1963): 59–82.

Lüddeckens, E. *Ägyptische Eheverträge*. Wiesbaden, 1960.

Maas, Paul. "Oenanthe's Husbands." *JEA* 31 (1954): 74. Reprinted in *Kleine Schriften*, pp. 107–8. Munich, 1973.

McEwan, Gilbert J. P. *Texts from Hellenistic Babylonia in the Ashmolean Museum*. Oxford, 1982.

MacMullen, Ramsay. "Women in Public in the Roman Empire." *Historia* 29 (1980): 208–18.

McNamara, Joanne. *The New Song: Celibate Women in the First Three Christian Centuries.* Women and History, vols. 6 and 7. New York, 1983.

Macurdy, Grace. *Hellenistic Queens* (cited as *HQ*). Baltimore, 1932.

Malaise, Michel. *Les conditions de pénétration et de diffusion des cultes égyptiens en Italie.* Etudes préliminaires aux religions orientales dans l'empire romain, vol. 22. Leiden, 1972.

Marcovich, M. "How to Flatter Women: *P. Oxy.* 2891." *CP* 70 (1975): 123–24.

Masciadri, M. A. Manca, and Montevecchi, Orsolina. "Contratti di baliatico e vendite fiduciarie a Tebtynis." *Aegyptus* 62 (1982): 148–61.

Meillier, C. "Callimaque (P.L. 76d, 78abc, 79, 82, 84, 111c), Stésichore (?) (P.L. 76abc)." *CRIPEL* 4 (1976): 257–360.

Meunier, M. *Femmes pythagoriennes. Fragments et lettres de Théano, Périctioné, Phintys, Mélissa et Myia.* Paris, 1932.

Mitford, T. B. "Helenos, Governor of Cyprus." *JHS* 79 (1959): 94–131.

———. "The Hellenistic Inscriptions of Old Paphos." *BSA* 56 (1961): 1–41.

———. "Ptolemy Macron." In *Studi in onore di Aristide Calderini e Roberto Paribeni*, vol. 2, pp. 163–87. Milan, 1956–57.

———. "Ptolemy son of Pelops." *JEA* 46 (1960): 109–11.

———. "Seleucus and Theodorus." *Op. Ath.* 1 (1953): 130–71.

Modrzejewski, Joseph Mélèze. "Un aspect du 'couple interdit' dans l'antiquité: les mariages mixtes dans l'Egypte hellénistique." In *Le couple interdit: Entretiens sur le racisme, Actes du colloque tenu en mai 1977 au Centre culturel international de Cerisy-la-Salle*, edited by Léon Poliakov, pp. 53–73. Paris, 1980.

———. "Régime foncier et status social dans l'Egypte ptolémaïque." In *Terre et paysans dépendants dans les sociétés antiques (Colloque Besançon, 1974)*, pp. 163–88. Paris, 1979.

———. "La structure juridique du mariage grec." In *Scritti in onore di Orsolina Montevecchi*, pp. 231–68. Bologna, 1981.

Mollard-Besques, S. *Catalogue raisonné des figurines et reliefs en terre-cuite grecs et romains.* Vol. 2: *Myrina.* Paris, 1963.

Momigliano, A. "M. I. Rostovtzeff." *The Cambridge Journal* 7 (1945): 334–46. Reprinted in *Studies in Historiography*, pp. 91–104. London, 1966.

Montevecchi, Orsolina. "Contributi per una storia sociale ed economica della famiglia nell'Egitto greco-romano." In *Actes du Congrès internationale du papyrologie*, pp. 300–313. Brussels, 1938.

———. "Una donna 'prostatis' del figlio minorenne in un papiro del IIᵃ." *Aegyptus* 61 (1981): 103–15.

———. *La papirologia.* Turin, 1973.

———. "Ricerche di sociologia nei documenti dell'Egitto greco-romano, II: I contratti di matrimonio e gli atti di divorzio." *Aegyptus* 16 (1936): 3–83.

———. "Ricerche di sociologia nei documenti dell'Egitto greco-romano, I: I testamenti." *Aegyptus* 15 (1935): 67–121.

Mooren, L. "Ptolemaic Families." *Proceedings of the XVI International Congress of Papyrology*, edited by Roger S. Bagnall, pp. 289–301. Chico, Calif., 1981.

Müller, Wolfgang. "Bemerkungen zu den spätptolemäischen Papyri der Berliner Sammlung." *Proceedings of the IX International Congress of Papyrology, Oslo, 1958*, pp. 183–93. Oslo, 1961.

———. "Sklaven in der Textilindustrie des ptolemäischen Ägypten." *Acta antiqua Philippopolitana*, 1963, 27–32.

Nachtergael, G. "Bérénice II, Arsinoé III et l'offrande de la boucle." *CE* 55 (1980): 240–53.

Nagy, Blaise. "The Naming of Athenian Girls: A Case in Point." *CJ* 74 (1979): 360–64.

Neumer-Pfau, Wiltrud. *Studien zur Ikonographie und gesellschaftlichen Funktion hellenistischer Aphrodite-Statuen.* Bonn, 1982.

Nicolaou, Ino Michaelidou. *Prosopography of Ptolemaic Cyprus.* Göteborg, 1976.

North, Helen. *Sophrosyne: Self-Knowledge and Self-Restraint in Greek Literature.* Ithaca, N.Y., 1966.

Noshy, I. *The Arts in Ptolemaic Egypt.* London, 1937.

Nowicka, Maria. *La maison privée dans l'Egypte ptolémaïque.* Inst. d'hist. de la culture matérielle, Bibl. antiqua, vol. 9. Warsaw, 1969.

Otto, W., and Bengtson, H. *Zur Geschichte des Niederganges des Ptolemäerreiches. Bayer Abh.*, n.s. vol. 17. Munich, 1938.

Page, Denys L. *Further Greek Epigrams.* Cambridge, 1981.

———. *Sappho and Alcaeus.* Oxford, 1955.

Parke, H. W. *Greek Mercenary Soldiers.* 1933; Oxford, 1970.

Parlasca, K. *Mumienporträts und verwandte Denkmäler.* Wiesbaden, 1966.

Parsons, P. J. "Callimachus. Victoria Berenicis." *ZPE* 25 (1977): 1–50.

Patterson, Cynthia B. *Pericles' Citizenship Law of 451–50 B.C.* Salem, N.H., 1981.

Peek, W. *Griechische Versinschriften.* Vol. 1. Berlin, 1955.

Peremans, W. "Egyptiens et étrangers dans l'administration civile et financière de l'Egypte ptolémaïque." *AncSoc* 2 (1971): 33–45.

———. "Egyptiens et étrangers dans l'agriculture et l'élevage en Egypte ptolémaïque." *AncSoc* 5 (1974): 127–35.

———. "Egyptiens et étrangers dans l'armée de terre et dans la police de l'Egypte ptolémaïque." *AncSoc* 3 (1972): 67–76.

———. "Egyptiens et étrangers dans le clergé, le notariat et les tribunaux de l'Egypte ptolémaïque." *AncSoc* 4 (1973): 59–69.

———. "Egyptiens et étrangers dans le commerce et l'industrie, le transport sur terre et la flotte, la domesticité." *AncSoc* 6 (1975): 61–69.

———. "Egyptiens et étrangers dans le milieu d'Alexandrie au temps des Lagides." *AncSoc* 7 (1976): 167–76.

———. "Ethnies et classes dans l'Egypte ptolémaïque." In *Recherches sur les structures sociales dans l'antiquité classique*. Colloque de Caen, avril, 1969, pp. 213–23. Paris, 1970.

———. "Un groupe d'officiers dans l'armée des Lagides." *AncSoc* 8 (1977): 175–85.

———. "Les indigènes égyptiens dans l'armée de terre des Lagides. Recherches anthroponymique." *AncSoc* 9 (1978): 83–100.

———. "Les mariages mixtes dans l'Egypte des Lagides." In *Scritti in onore di Orsolina Montevecchi*, pp. 273–81. Bologna, 1981.

———. "Sur l'identification des Egyptiens et des étrangers dans l'Egypte des Lagides." *AncSoc* 1 (1970): 25–38.

Peremans, W.; van't Dack, E.; et al. *Prosopographia Ptolemaica*. Studia Hellenistica, vols. 6– (1950– ). (Cited as P.Pt.)

Peristiany, J. G., ed. *Honour and Shame: The Values of Mediterranean Society*. Chicago, 1966.

Pestman, P. W. "A proposito dei documenti di Pathyris I." *Aegyptus* 43 (1963): 5–14.

———. *Chronologie égyptienne d'après les textes démotiques. Pap. Lugd. Bat. XV* (cited as *Pap. Lugd. Bat.* XV). Leiden, 1967.

———. "Loans Bearing No Interest." *JJP* 16–17 (1971): 7–29.

———. *Marriage and Matrimonial Property in Ancient Egypt: A Contribution to Establishing the Legal Position of the Woman. Pap. Lugd. Bat.* IX. Leiden, 1961.

———. *Over Vrouwen en Voogden in het Oude Egypte*. Leiden, 1969. Pfeiffer, Rudolf. *Callimachus*. 2 vols. Oxford, 1949–53.

———. *History of Classical Scholarship: From the Beginnings to the End of the Hellenistic Age*. Oxford, 1968.

Piekniewski, E. "Die Rätsel um *P. Eleph.* 3 und 4." *Eos* 52 (1962): 287–93.

Pitt-Rivers, Julian. *The Fate of Shechem or the Politics of Sex: Essays in the Anthropology of the Mediterranean.* Cambridge, 1977.

Plaumann, G. *Ptolemais in Oberägypten.* Leipzig, 1910.

Pleket, H. W. *The Olympic Games: The First Thousand Years.* New York, 1976.

Pomeroy, Sarah B. "Apollonia (also called Senmonthis), Wife of Dryton: Woman of Two Cultures." Paper delivered at the colloquium on "Social History and the Papyri," Columbia University, April 9, 1983.

———. "Charities for Greek Women." *Mnemosyne* 35 (1982): 115–35.

———. "Copronyms and the Exposure of Infants in Egypt." Paper delivered at the XVII Congresso internazionale di papirologia, Naples, 1983. To be published in *Studies in Honor of A. Arthur Schiller,* edited by Roger S. Bagnall and William V. Harris.

———. *Goddesses, Whores, Wives, and Slaves: Women in Classical Antiquity.* New York, 1975.

———. "Infanticide in Hellenistic Greece." In *Images of Women in Antiquity,* edited by Averil Cameron and Amélie Kuhrt, pp. 207–22. London, 1983.

———. "Macedonian Queens and the Feminization of Greek Culture." The George Rudé Inaugural Lecture, Concordia University, Montreal, September 25, 1980.

———. "The Married Woman: Honor and Shame in Ptolemaic Egypt." Paper presented before the Society for the Study of Egyptian Antiquities at the University of Toronto, November 22, 1980, and the Classical Association of the Atlantic States, Newark, Del., May 2, 1981.

———. "The Relationship of the Married Woman to her Blood Relatives in Rome." *AncSoc* 7 (1976): 215–27.

———. "Selected Bibliography on Women in Antiquity." *Arethusa* 8 (1973): 127–55. Reprinted with additions in *Women in the Ancient World: The Arethusa Papers,* edited by John Peradotto and John P. Sullivan, pp. 315–72. Albany, N.Y., 1984.

———. "Supplementary Notes on Erinna." *ZPE* 32 (1978): 17–22.

———. "Technikai kai Mousikai: The Education of Women in the Fourth Century and in the Hellenistic Period." *AJAH* 2 (1977): 51–68.

———. "Where Are the Classical Women?" *Humanities* 7.3 (June, 1981): 1, 4–5.

———. "Wives of Hellenistic Soldiers." Paper delivered at the annual meeting of the Association of Ancient Historians, University Park, Pa., May 7, 1982.

———. "Women in Egypt under Roman Domination." Paper delivered at the annual meeting of the American Historical Association, Washington, D.C., December 28, 1980.

———. "Women in Roman Egypt: A Preliminary Study Based on Papyri." In *ANRW* 2.10.1, forthcoming. Published in a longer version in *Reflections of Women in Antiquity*, edited by Helene P. Foley, pp. 303–22. London, 1981.

Porter, B., and Moss, R. *Topographical Bibliography*. Vol. 1: *The Theban Necropolis*. Part 2: "Royal Tombs and Smaller Cemeteries." 2d ed. Oxford, 1964.

Powell, I. U. *Collectanea Alexandrina*. Oxford, 1925.

Préaux, Claire. *L'économie royale des Lagides* (cited as *ER*). Brussels, 1939.

———. *Le monde hellénistique: La Grèce et L'Orient (323–146 av. J.-C.)* (cited as *MH*). 2 vols. Paris, 1978.

———. "Le statut de la femme à l'époque hellénistique, principalement en Egypte." *Recueils de la Société J. Bodin*. Vol. 11: *La Femme*, vol. 1, pp. 127–75. Brussels, 1959.

Pugliese Carratelli, Giovanni. "Il damos Coo di Isthmos." *ASAA*, 41–42, n.s., 25–26 (1963–64): 147–202.

———. "Supplemento epigrafico di Iasos." *ASAA*, 45–46, n.s., 29–30 (1969): 437–86.

Quaegebeur, Jan. "Contribution à la prosopographie des prêtres memphites à l'époque ptolémaïque." *AncSoc* 3 (1972): 77–109.

———. "Documents Concerning a Cult of Arsinoë Philadelphos at Memphis." *JNES* 30 (1971): 239–70.

———. "Mummy Labels: An Orientation." *Pap. Lugd. Bat.* XIX, pp. 232–59. Leiden, 1978.

———. "Ptolémée II en adoration devant Arsinoé II divinisée." *BIAO* 69 (1970): 191–217.

———. "Reines ptolémaïques et traditions égyptiennes." In *Das ptolemäische Ägypten*, edited by H. Maehler and V. M. Strocka, pp. 245–62. Mainz, 1978.

Ranke, H. *Die ägyptischen Personennamen*. 2 vols. Glückstadt, 1935–52.

Reekmans, T. *La sitométrie dans les Archives de Zénon*. Pap. Brux., vol. 3. Brussels, 1966.

Reil, T. *Beiträge zur Kenntnis des Gewerbes im hellenistischen Ägypten*. Leipzig, 1913.

Reinhold, Meyer. "The Declaration of War Against Cleopatra." *CJ* 77 (1981–82): 97–103.

Richter, M. Ohnefalsch. "Mittheilungen aus Cypern." *MDAI(A)* 9 (1884): 133–40.

Ricketts, Linda M. "A Chronological Problem in the Reign of Cleopatra VII." *BASP* 16 (1979): 213–17.

Robert, Jeanne, and Robert, Louis. "Bulletin épigraphique." *REG* 61 (1948): 137–212; 84 (1971): 397–540; and 86 (1973): 48–211.

Robert, Louis. "Sur un décret d'Ilion et sur un papyrus concernant des cultes royaux." In *Essays in Honor of C. Bradford Welles.* American Studies in Papyrology, vol. 1, pp. 175–211. New Haven, 1966.

Rosaldo, Michelle Zimbalist. "A Theoretical Overview." In *Woman, Culture, and Society,* edited by Michelle Zimbalist Rosaldo and Louise Lamphere, pp. 17–42. Stanford, 1974.

Rosaria, Sister Mary. *The Nurse in Greek Life.* Boston, 1917.

Rostovtzeff, M. I. *A Large Estate in Egypt in the Third Century B.C.* Madison, Wisc., 1922.

———. *The Social and Economic History of the Hellenistic World* (cited as *SEHHW*). 3 vols. Oxford, 1941.

Sainte Croix, G. E. M. de. "Some Observations on the Property Rights of Athenian Women." *CR* 20 (1970): 273–78.

Samuel, A. E. *Ptolemaic Chronology.* Münchener Beiträge zur Papyrusforschung und antiken Rechtsgeschichte, vol. 43. Munich, 1962.

Samuel, Deborah H. "Women as Property Owners in Roman Egypt." Paper delivered at the annual meeting of the American Philological Association, New Orleans, December 28, 1980.

Schaps, David M. *Economic Rights of Women in Ancient Greece.* Edinburgh, 1979.

Schneider, O. *Callimachea.* 2 vols. Leipzig, 1870–73.

Shore, A. F. "The Sale of the House of Senkhonsis, Daughter of Phibis." *JEA* 54 (1968): 193–98.

Skeat, T. C. *The Reigns of the Ptolemies.* Münchener Beiträge zur Papyrusforschung und antiken Rechtsgeschichte, vol. 29. Munich, 1954.

Snowden, Frank M., Jr. *Blacks in Antiquity.* Cambridge, Mass., 1970.

Snyder, Jane McIntosh. "The Web of Song: Weaving Imagery in Homer and the Lyric Poets." *CJ* 76 (1981): 193–96.

Spiegelberg, W. "Papyrus Erbach." *ZÄS* 42 (1905): 43–60.

Städele, Alfons. *Die Briefe des Pythagoras und der Pythagoreer.* Beiträge zur Klassischen Philologie, vol. 115. Meisenheim am Glan, 1980.

Sulimirski, T. *The Sarmatians.* New York, 1970.

Susemihl, F. *Geschichte der griechischen Literatur in der Alexandrinerzeit,* 2 vols. Leipzig, 1891–92.

Sutch, Richard. "The Care and Feeding of Slaves." In *Reckoning With Slavery,* edited by P. David et al., pp. 231–301. New York, 1976.

Sutton, Robert F. *The Interaction Between Men and Women Portrayed on*

*Attic Red-Figure Pottery.* Ph.D. dissertation, The University of North Carolina at Chapel Hill, 1981.

Swiderek, A. "La société indigène en Egypte au III<sup>e</sup> siècle avant notre ère d'après les archives de Zénon." *JJP* 7–8 (1953–54): 231–84.

Taeger, F. *Charisma: Studien zur Geschichte des antiken Herrscherkultes.* Stuttgart, 1957.

Tarn, W. W. *Alexander.* 2d ed. Cambridge, 1948.

———. *The Greeks in Bactria and India.* 2d ed. Cambridge, 1951.

Taubenschlag, R. "The Ancient Greek City-laws in Ptolemaic Egypt." *Actes du V<sup>me</sup> Congrès international de papyrologie, Oxford, 1937,* pp. 471–89. Brussels, 1938.

———. "La compétence du Kupios dans le droit gréco-égyptien." *AHDO* 2 (1938): 293–314. Reprinted in *Opera minora* 2 (Warsaw, 1959): 353–77.

Tcherikover, V. *Hellenistic Civilization and the Jews.* Translated by S. Applebaum. New York, 1950.

———. "Palestine under the Ptolemies." *Mizraim* 4–5 (1937): 9–69.

Thesleff, Holger. *An Introduction to the Pythagorean Writings of the Hellenistic Period.* Åbo, 1961.

———. "On the Problem of the Doric Pseudo-Pythagorica: An Alternative Theory of Date and Purpose." In *Pseudepigrapha I: Entretiens sur l'antiquité classique,* vol. 18, edited by K. von Fritz, pp. 57–102. Geneva, 1972.

———. *The Pythagorean Texts of the Hellenistic Period.* Åbo, 1965.

Thompson, Dorothy Burr. "Glauke and the Goose." In *Essays in Memory of Karl Lehmann,* edited by Lucy Freeman Sandler, pp. 314–22. New York, 1964.

———. "More Ptolemaic Queens." *AK* 12 (1980): 181–84.

———. *Ptolemaic Oinochoai and Portraits in Faience: Aspects of the Ruler Cult.* Oxford, 1973.

Thompson, Wesley. "Weaving; A Man's Work." *CW* 75 (1982): 217–22.

Tilly, Louise A., and Scott, Joan W. *Women, Work, and Family.* New York, 1978.

Titchener, Margaret Seymour. "Guardianship of Women in Egypt during the Ptolemaic and Roman Eras." In University of Wisconsin Studies in Language and Literature, vol. 15, pp. 20–28. Madison, 1922.

Tod, M. "Sidelights on Greek Philosophers." *JHS* 77 (1957): 132–41.

Tondriau, L. "Princesses ptolémaïques comparées ou identifiées à des déesses." *BSAA* 37 (1948): 12–33.

Treggiari, S. M. "Jobs for Women." *AJAH* 1 (1976): 76–104.

Tréheux, Jacques. "Cleino à Délos." *CE* 32 (1957): 147–51.

Tritsch, Walther. *Olympias: Die Mutter Alexanders des Grossen.* Frankfurt, 1936.

Tuchman, Gaye. "Women and the Creation of Culture." In *Another Voice: Feminist Perspectives on Social Life and Social Science,* edited by Marcia Millman and Rosabeth Moss Kanter, pp. 171–201. Garden City, N.Y., 1975.

Turner, E. G. *Greek Papyri: An Introduction.* Princeton, 1968.

Uebel, F. *Die Kleruchen Ägyptens unter den ersten sechs Ptolemäern.* ADAW, vol. 3. Berlin, 1968.

Vatin, Claude. *Recherches sur le mariage et la condition de la femme mariée à l'époque hellénistique* (cited as *FM*). Paris, 1970.

Vessey, E. W. Thomson. "Philaenis." *RBPh* 54 (1976): 78–83.

Volkmann, Hans. *Kleopatra: Politik und Propaganda.* Munich, 1953. Translated as *Cleopatra: A Study in Politics and Propaganda.* Translated by T. J. Cadoux. London, 1978.

Walbank, F. W. *A Historical Commentary on Polybius,* vol. 2. Oxford, 1967.

Wehrli, C. "Phila, fille d'Antipater et épouse de Démétrius, roi des Macédoniens." *Historia* 13 (1964): 140–47.

Welles, C. Bradford. "The Population of Roman Dura." In *Studies in Roman Economic and Social History in Honor of Allen Chester Johnson,* edited by P. R. Coleman-Norton, pp. 251–74. Princeton, 1951.

West, M. L. "Erinna." *ZPE* 25 (1977): 116–19.

Westermann, William Linn. *Upon Slavery in Ptolemaic Egypt.* New York, 1929.

———. "Sklaverei." In P.W., *R.E.,* 1935, Supp. 5, cols. 894–1068.

———. *The Slave Systems of Greek and Roman Antiquity.* Philadelphia, 1955.

Whitehorn. J. E. G. "*C.P.Jud.* II 193 and *PSI* XII 1225." *BASP* 12 (1975): 121–26.

———. "The Functions of the Alexandrian Ephebeia Certificate and the Sequence of *PSI* XII 1223–1225."*BASP* 14 (1977): 29–38.

Wilcken, U. "Papyrus-Urkunden."*APF* 7 (1927): 63–104.

Will, E. "Histoire grecque." *RH* 246 (1971): 129–31.

Wilson-Kastner, P., et al. *A Lost Tradition: Women Writers of the Early Church.* Lanham, Md., 1981.

Winnicki, Jan K. "Ein ptolemäischer Offizier in Thebais."*Eos* 60 (1972): 343–53.

Witt, R. E. *Isis in the Graeco-Roman World.* London, 1971.

Wörrle, Michael. "Epigraphische Forschungen zur Geschichte Lykiens, II: Ptolemaios II und Telmessos." *Chiron* 8 (1978): 201–46.

Wolff, H. J. "Die Grundlagen des griechischen Eherechts." *Tijdschrift voor Rechtsgeschiedenis* 20 (1952): 157–81.

———. "The Political Background of the Plurality of Laws in Ptolemaic Egypt." *Proceedings of the XVI International Congress of Papyrology,* edited by Roger S. Bagnall, pp. 313–18. Chico, Calif., 1981.

———. *Das Recht der griechischen Papyri Ägyptens.* Vol. 2: *Organisation und Kontrolle des privaten Rechtsverkehrs.* Handbuch der Altertumswissenschaft, 10.5.2. Munich, 1978.

Wyse, W. *The Speeches of Isaeus.* Cambridge, 1904.

Youtie, H. C. "ʼΑΓΡΑΜΜΑΤΟΣ: An Aspect of Greek Society in Egypt." *HSPh* 75 (1971): 161–76. Reprinted in *Scriptiunculae,* vol. 2, pp. 611–27. Amsterdam, 1973.

———. "Ὑπογραφεύς: The Social Impact of Illiteracy in Greco-Roman Egypt." *ZPE* 17 (1975): 201–21.

Zanker, G. "Callimachus' Hecale: A New Kind of Epic Hero?"*Antichthon* 11 (1977): 68–77.

Ziegler, K. "Kallimachos und die Frauen." *Die Antike* 13 (1937): 24–25.

Zingerle, J. *Strena Buliciana.* Zagreb, 1924.

Zucker, Friedrich. "Simarist(ei)oi." *Philologus* 101 (1951): 164–66.

———. "Simaristos." *RhM* 95 (1952): 338–42.

# Index of Greek Papyri and Ostraca

# General Index